Labour, Mobility and Temporary Migration

LABOUR, MOBILITY AND TEMPORARY MIGRATION

A Comparitive Study of Polish Migration to Wales

JULIE KNIGHT, JOHN LEVER
and ANDREW THOMPSON

UNIVERSITY OF WALES PRESS

2017

© Julie Knight, John Lever and Andrew Thompson, 2017
All rights reserved. No part of this book may be reproduced in any material form
(including photocopying or storing it in any medium by electronic means and whether
or not transiently or incidentally to some other use of this publication) without the
written permission of the copyright owner. Applications for the copyright owner's
written permission to reproduce any part of this publication should be addressed to the
University of Wales Press, 10 Columbus Walk, Brigantine Place, Cardiff CF10 4UP.

www.uwp.co.uk
British Library CIP Data
A catalogue record for this book is available from the British Library

ISBN 978-1-78683-0807
eISBN 978-1-78683-0814

The right of Julie Knight, John Lever and Andrew Thompson to be
identified as authors of this work has been asserted in accordance with
sections 77 and 79 of the Copyright, Designs and Patents Act 1988.

Typeset by Biblichor Ltd, Edinburgh
Printed by CPI Antony Rowe, Melksham

Contents

List of Abbreviations   vii

PART I

CHAPTER 1: EU Enlargement, Migration and the UK   3

CHAPTER 2: Theorising Migration – Understanding Motivations, Networks and Mobility   20

CHAPTER 3: Locations and Research Methodology   39

PART II

CHAPTER 4: Why Migrate? Motivations and Migrant Decision-Making   63

CHAPTER 5: Polish Migrants in Cardiff: Changing Motivations in a Diverse City Environment   88

CHAPTER 6: Polish Workers in Merthyr Tydfil: Happily Resigned to Life in the Valleys?   107

CHAPTER 7: Polish Migrants in Llanelli: What Happens after the Initial Migration Period?   121

PART III

CHAPTER 8: 'Migratory Drift' (or Why Migrants Nearly Always Stay Longer than Planned)   139

CONTENTS

CHAPTER 9: Polish Migrant Integration 164

CHAPTER 10: Policy Implications 180

Notes 201
References 231
Index 249

List of Abbreviations

3D	Dirty, dangerous and dull
A2	Accession 2 Countries – Bulgaria and Romania
A8	Accession 8 Countries – Poland, Estonia, Latvia, Lithuania, Czech Republic, Slovakia, Slovenia, Hungary
BBC	British Broadcasting Corporation
CAB	Citizens Advice Bureau
CEE	Central and Eastern Europe
CV	Curriculum Vitae
EAL	English as an Additional Language
EU	European Union
EU-15	European Union Original Member States
GBP	Great British Pound
GDP	Gross Domestic Product
GNP	Gross National Product
GP	General Practitioner
GVA	Gross Value Added
IOM	International Organization for Migration
IT	Information Technology
LA	Local Authority
MAC	Migration Advisory Committee
MADF	Multi Agency Diversity Forum
MEAG	Minority Ethnic Achievement Grant
MPI	Migration Policy Institute
MWF	Migrant Workers Forum
NATO	North Atlantic Treaty Organization
NHS	National Health Service
NINo	National Insurance Number

LIST OF ABBREVIATIONS

NUTS	Nomenclature of Territorial Units for Statistics
OECD	Organization of Economic Cooperation and Development
ONS	Office of National Statistics
PCVA	Polish Community of the Valleys Association
PLASC	Pupil Level Annual School Census
PLZ	Polish Zloty
PWMA	Polish Welsh Mutual Association
SWC	South Wales Coalfied
UK	United Kingdom
UKBA	UK Border Agency
USA	United State of America
WAG	Welsh Assembly Government
WAL	Welsh as an Additional Language
WIMD	Welsh Index of Multiple Deprivation
WRS	Worker Registration Scheme
WW2	World War Two

PART I

I

EU Enlargement, Migration and the UK

Introduction

In 2004, the European Union (EU) expanded to include ten new member states from Central and Eastern Europe (CEE). The new member states to join at this time were: Cyprus, the Czech Republic, Estonia, Hungary, Latvia, Lithuania, Malta, Poland, Slovakia and Slovenia.[1] While Bulgaria and Romania joined the EU in 2007 and Croatia in 2013, the 2004 EU enlargement was one of the most contentious, not least because the strengths of the economies of the existing fifteen member states were juxtaposed with the weaknesses of the economies of the ten new members.[2] As a result, the 2004 enlargement was met with a variety of responses within the national governments in Europe. Many of the old member states used restrictive policies to curb or completely stop the flow of migrants from CEE countries on a temporary basis. Interestingly, not all of the CEE countries were viewed as a threat to the old member states' labour markets. Eight of the ten countries posed a concern for old member states. These eight countries became known as the 'Accession 8', or 'A8', and included all of the aforementioned CEE countries with the exception of Malta and Cyprus.

In the period immediately following accession, thousands of CEE migrants entered the UK, the majority coming from Poland. Academics, policy-makers and the media classified these Polish migrants as young, well-educated and economically motivated individuals who were planning to migrate to the UK for the short term and return home. However, it is only in hindsight, a decade after this enlargement, that academics are beginning to understand how these Polish migrants have influenced the labour market of Britain and how their motivations and characteristics have evolved over time. This is where the book begins: looking back over the past ten years to understand how the Polish migrants have changed in the UK, including their changing labour market mobility, their social network formation and their plans to stay in the UK. The last point is of particular importance as the vast majority of these migrants originally intended to stay in the UK for less than a year. However, ten years after enlargement, many have remained in the UK with no immediate plan to remigrate making their migration marked by temporariness and migratory drift.

Labour, Mobility and Temporary Migration draws on a substantial body of qualitative data derived from interviews with Polish migrants living and working in three localities across the South Wales region – in Cardiff, Llanelli and Merthyr Tydfil – to explore the forces and stories behind one of the largest population movements in recent European history. It will fill a significant gap in the literature on labour migration in the EU in three distinct ways.

First, it is unique in reviewing the topic of Polish migration to the UK over time to understand the continuing evolution of migrants' motivations and characteristics. This is of particular importance for policy-makers, who have only recently begun to understand the major impact that these migrants have on the British labour market. Migrants almost always plan to come only for a relatively short stay abroad, but the majority stay considerably longer, often years after they had expected to return. Understanding why this 'migratory drift' occurs is critical for policy knowledge, especially in learning more about how migrants' analyses of comparative economic conditions in their home and destination countries influence how far they stretch their stay abroad. This book will contribute to this knowledge because the early studies on which it is based were undertaken as the financial crisis and subsequent recession in the UK were breaking, while the later research was undertaken when the recession was peaking. Our research enables us to show that for as long as migrants are able to secure work, the quality of life in the UK, especially for those with children, has an important bearing on the decision of many to ride out the economic downturn.

Second, the book will fill a gap in the literature on migration to Wales. Historians of Wales have skilfully dissected previous migrations from Ireland and, later, from Italy. However, more contemporary migration patterns to Wales, particularly those from further afield, such as Poland, have not received a significant amount of attention. This book brings together the single largest body of data on Polish migration to Wales which, significantly, was undertaken as it was unfolding after EU enlargement in 2004. It thus provides a unique snapshot of social change in Wales at an important moment when the UK was experiencing and adjusting to an unexpectedly large wave of migration from CEE countries. The experience of Wales, and the lessons of the book, will nevertheless be of wider significance. A striking feature of A8 migration was the movement of migrants to all parts of the UK, and across urban and rural localities alike. Staffing agencies played a key role in shuttling workers to all four corners of the UK, and in the cases of Llanelli and Merthyr Tydfil we are able to report on just how important these commercial middlemen are for labour migration.

Third, the book is unique in its ability to capture the migrants' story across different localities. As mentioned, many of the studies completed on post-2004 Polish migrants in England and other parts of the UK are largely city-based. It has only been in the recent past that a handful of journal articles have begun to approach the subject of Polish migration from a more spatial dimension focusing on non-city regions; however, these articles focus on specific areas outside of Wales and are not comparable. This comparative study aims to highlight the evolution of post-2004 Poles throughout three distinct regions in the South Wales area, making the implications for its use considerably more widespread.

This last point regarding the comparative spatial considerations is a major theme of this book, which was born out of three independently conducted studies coming together in this monograph. Despite the methodological commonalities across these studies, their findings were considerably different. These variations in the findings make this book essential reading for those interested in understanding the evolution of post-2004 Polish migrants' characteristics and motivations in the South Wales region. The findings from each study will contribute to three locality chapters – urban, semi-urban and rural – using specific cross-cutting themes to shape each chapter. These cross-cutting themes include, but are not limited to, the following: labour market experiences, human capital development, social network construction and usage, and future plans.

This Introduction will set the stage for the rest of the book by outlining three distinct points. First, the role of history in shaping both EU and UK government policy in relation to migration will be explored to understand why migrants chose to migrate to the UK. Second, the number of CEE migrants, particularly Poles, that have entered the UK since 2004 will be reviewed. Owing to the number of sources that collect information on migrant numbers, as well as the limitations of each of these sources, the number of Poles that actually entered and stayed in the UK is highly contentious. Third, this chapter will review the economic, social and political landscape of Wales to provide the reader with a better understanding of the attractiveness of this country to a new migrant group.

By arranging this chapter in this way, the government hierarchy is subtly presented, highlighting how the EU policy on migration informs UK policy, and how UK policy, with the exception of certain social issues like housing and education, informs Wales policy. This was an intentional effort by the authors to explain how individual countries such as Wales are engaged in a complex political system in regard to migration. The authors also acknowledge that there are significant political, social and economic changes occurring across the EU and the UK at the time of writing. These changes can have an impact on both UK and EU migration policy and the role of devolved governments like the Welsh Assembly Government in future.

The EU referendum on 23 June 2016, with a vote in favour of the UK leaving the EU, has sparked the resignation of a Prime Minister, the appointment of a new Prime Minister with a new Cabinet, and the strong possibility of the UK starting the process to leave the EU.[3, 4] These changes have all occurred in the course of the last three months, making the topic of migration, particularly from the EU member states into the UK, both a pivotal point of discussion and also an option that may not exist in the near future. As the large-scale migration of EU migrants to Britain formed a significant argument in the Leave campaign in these times of uncertainty, it is of the utmost importance to understand the impact of migration to the UK, and more specifically, Wales.[5]

EU History and the 2004 Enlargement

Over the last fifty years, since the signing of the Treaty of Rome in 1957 which established the EU, the number of EU member states has grown from the six founding members to twenty- eight.[6] The original aim of the

EU was to prevent future conflict among the member states. To meet this aim, the principles of free movement of goods, finance and labour within the EU area were the core tenets to increase cohesion among the member states.[7, 8] The free movement of finance and goods was widely accepted from the outset, particularly with the creation of the Eurozone in 1999; however, the free movement of labour has traditionally been less accepted. For new member states, the right to free movement of labour is traditionally received last, on the date of accession, with the barriers to trade and capital flows being lifted in advance.[9] The rationale for the free movement of labour is that it would allow supplies of labour to move where a demand for labour exists as well as creating social cohesion among the EU member states.[10] In addition, there are economic benefits associated with the free movement of labour such as a boost in economic productivity and migrants are less likely to claim benefits.[11]

While the free movement of labour was intended to support both cultural and economic development between the new and the old member states, initially limitations existed for those interested in migrating within the EU for labour purposes. For example, from 1990 to 1993 the EU migrant was expected to be at least in part-time employment in the settlement location, which then allowed a five-year right of abode that was renewable.[12] In 1993 with the Treaty of Maastricht, this limitation was removed, which allowed a truly free movement of labour within the EU member states. This also included European Free Trade Association (EFTA) immigrants, as they were no longer required to register for a visa. In 1997 the Schengen Agreement (1985) which allowed completely free movement, with no passport checks, between thirteen of the fifteen EU member states (excluding Ireland and the UK) was adopted in the Amsterdam Treaty. This treaty made the Schengen Agreement a part of EU law which new EU members would have to adopt. More recently, in 2004, the Free Movement Directive, the core legislation on free movement of labour in the EU, was constructed. This allows the free movement of labour, but, if the 'EU citizen' in question does not have a job or a means of financial support in the destination country, then the migrant must return home after three months. If migrants intend to stay beyond the three months, they could be required to register with the host member state. Under this scheme, it is difficult to track intra-EU migrants and for the destination country to have them removed after the three-month period.

This brief review of EU doctrine relating to the free movement of labour highlights two points. First, there is a changing emphasis on labour movement among the member states. Second, with the Free Movement Directive, 'free movement' is still not actually possible in the EU among existing members. However, the most severe limitations to labour movement within the EU are established for new member states through transition arrangements which the fifth enlargement of the EU, starting in 2004, clearly demonstrates. The transition arrangements allow a buffer between EU accession and labour movement to reduce the impact of mass migration on the labour markets of the existing EU countries. These arrangements are on a country-to-country basis, subject to a periodic review, and can vary from one accession to another. These restrictions do not traditionally apply to students or self-employed migrants. The transition arrangements for the 2004 accession were set out in the Accession Treaty of 2003.[13] In the 2004 enlargement of the EU, 'the provisional arrangements for the transition policy combine a two-phase transition period of five years with a review after two years. There is the possibility of a prolongation for individual member states, if requested, of a period of two years.'[14] In total, with the prolongation of the transition policy by the member state, the transition period is potentially seven years.

For the 2004 enlargement, the individual member states' transition arrangements were carried out in phases starting on the day of accession on 1 May 2004 and ending, at the latest, on 30 April 2011. To protect their labour markets from the anticipated mass migration of A8 migrants, the existing EU member countries invoked their right to a transition arrangement requiring visas, and visa-like access or a complete delay to access their labour markets. The majority of existing EU members imposed a two- to four-year transition policy to protect their labour markets, while the A8 countries' economies had time to adjust and potentially provide employment for the would-be labour migrants. However, other countries went to extremes with their policies, either enforcing the maximum transition time of seven years, as was the case with Austria and Germany, or allowing immediate access to the labour markets, as was done by the UK, Ireland and Sweden.

For the maximum-transition policy enforcers, the reason for the extreme limitation had to do with their proximity to the A8 countries, the strength of their economies in comparison, and the historic migration from the A8 countries across their borders. Alternatively, those countries that did not impose a transition policy on the A8 countries refrained because they estimated a low number of inward migrants from the A8 countries owing to the lack of the similar language, the distance between the sending and receiving countries (which influences social networks) and the potential devaluation of qualifications.[15] These reasons for predicting small numbers of migrants were reinforced by EU labour migration history. In 2002, it was found that only 1.5 per cent of EU workers lived in different member states, which was a statistic that had not changed in thirty years.[16] When creating the transition arrangements, the UK government expected to receive inflows of 5,000–13,000 A8 migrants.[17]

Although the UK constructed an open transition arrangement, the A8 migrants who were entering the UK were expected to register with the Worker Registration Scheme (WRS). The WRS was similar to the Free Movement Directive. Registration for A8 migrants on the WRS ended in April 2011, but during the course of the 2004–11 period, when the scheme was active, it was used for: gathering statistics on the inflows of A8 migrants and understanding the location within the UK of major migration inflows, the economic impact of these migrant inflows and the type of work the migrants were doing.[18] While there was little incentive for the migrants in signing up for the WRS, they were able to claim certain benefits, if working, only when signed up to the WRS. Claiming benefits, such as job seeker's allowance, could only occur after the migrant had worked in the UK for twelve consecutive months, with no more than a thirty-day break.[19]

The exact number of migrants entering the UK from the date of enlargement onwards varies by data source, and the data on CEE migrants leaving the UK are even more varied.

There are several limitations to WRS data which highlight that, while it is a well-cited source, the WRS may not have accurately captured the number of CEE migrants entering the UK from 2004 to 2011 for the following reasons:

- The registration fee was high for migrants, making them unwilling to register.
- The migrants who were self-employed or students were not counted through the WRS.

- The statistics did not take into account return migration.
- The statistics were cumulative, which made the accurate counting of migrants who re-enter and reapply problematic.
- The regional count did not reflect the actual number of migrants in the area owing to intra-UK migration.
- The scheme was not easily enforced for migrants, or for employers, who were supposed to have the WRS registration before employing the migrant.[20]

Despite these limitations, the authors will use the data where possible when discussing the number of Poles in their regions from 2004 to 2011 as this is one of the few data sources that can be narrowed down to local authority level. During this period of time, from 2004 to 2011, the number of Poles entering the UK changed, and the perception of Poles in the UK also changed. With many Poles staying in the UK longer than they and others, expected, the original set of characteristics outlined in the first section of this chapter were no longer relevant. While we can only understand this in hindsight, the implications of a large group of migrants residing in the long term has a significant impact on the social, political and economic environment in the UK.

Polish Migration in the UK: Ten Years after Enlargement

Over ten years since enlargement, Polish migrants continue to arrive in the UK, and many of those who migrated since 2004 continue to thrive in the UK. According to the WRS, from May 2004 to April 2011, over 1 million A8 migrants (1,133, 950) entered the UK.[21, 22] Throughout this period, 62 per cent, or 703,049, of the A8 migrants entering the UK were from Poland, producing the largest single inflow of migrants to the UK in its history.[23, 24] Comparing National Insurance Number (NINo) with WRS data, Harris, Moran and Bryson highlight the conservative nature of the WRS-produced figures.[25] The study found that the NINo allocations for Poles from 2004 to 2009 were 27 per cent higher (with 821,000) than the WRS registrations (597,000) during the same period.[26] In view of limitations of the WRS figures, it is interesting that they could be conservative, given their cumulative nature as well as the inability to subtract the number of Poles who left the UK.[27] Nonetheless, the 2011 census has 579,000 Poles living in the

UK, making this migrant group the second largest (after migrants from India) in the UK at that time.[28, 29] The demographic change resulting from this migrant flow is the largest in Europe since the end of WW2.[30] With a larger number of Poles entering the UK than originally planned, did any of the other original conceptions of Poles change over time as well?

An array of reports characterised the Polish migrants entering the UK post-enlargement as being young, highly educated, willing to take low-skilled jobs, highly mobile and planning to stay in the UK for the short term.[31, 32, 33] Some authors noted the 'migrant paradox' with high-skilled workers taking low-skilled jobs, others noted that the Polish migrants were starting to set up ethnic businesses, and yet others focused on the 'dangers' of having a supply of labour during a recession and 'job-taking'.[34, 35, 36] Regardless of the positive or negative connotation that research on Polish migrants has taken, academics agree that the aforementioned characterisation of this migrant group has changed over time.[37]

Many of these once considered 'short-term' migrants have remained in the UK and are thriving.[38] It is expected that anywhere from 50 to 70 per cent of the migrants that entered the UK from Poland since 2004 have stayed in the UK.[39, 40] This range is supported by the aforementioned NINo figures in 2009, in contrast to the 2011 census figures. Research suggests that, like nomadic tribes in the Sudan or flocks of birds blown off course, these migrants are 'drifting' and have no definite plans to return to Poland or to settle in the UK.[41] More recent research highlights that some Poles return-migrate to Poland only to return to the UK to settle.[42]

These long-term migrants are making an impact in the UK – spatially, politically and culturally. The Poles' geographic spread within the UK is of interest.[43, 44] Unlike other historic migrant groups to enter the UK, through the use of their social networks and recruitment agencies, the Poles are spatially dispersed in rural, urban and semi-urban spaces.[45] In addition, owing to the academic, media and government interest in this migrant group, the inflow of Poles since 2004 has had an impact on British migration policy. The UK changed its policies towards EU migrants, enacting transition policies for the 2007 (Bulgaria and Romania) and 2013 (Croatia) enlargements.[46] The UK opened its doors to Bulgarian and Romanian labour migrants in January 2014 and the

Croatian labour migrants will be able to enter the UK in 2020, depending on the EU migration policy post-Brexit.[47] More recently, in the run-up to the referendum, the Leave campaign used the free flow of EU migration as one of the reasons that UK should leave the EU.[48] In regard to the cultural impact, the British Future survey conducted in December 2013 highlighted that British workers perceive Polish migrants as 'hard-working' and 'making a contribution to Britain'; however, the same survey also reported that British workers perceived Polish migrants as 'not making an effort to integrate'.[49] In addition, Amnesty International reported (2016) that hate crimes in the UK against immigrants of all nationalities increased by over 60 per cent in the post-referendum period, highlighting some of the tensions experienced between migrants and the local population.[50]

The fate of the EU migrants currently in the UK or planning to migrate to the UK is in flux. With the referendum results, as well as other events with the new Prime Minister and Cabinet, it is unclear what the situation at the present time is for EU citizens currently living in the UK or planning to enter the UK in the future.

Migrants in Wales 2004–2015

Given the overarching aim of this book in focusing on migration to Wales, the foregoing text sets the stage for the remainder of this chapter and this book. Specifically focusing on Wales, this section will explain the historic migrations to the country, as well as the social and economic attributes of Wales, to provide the reader with a better understanding of what attracted Polish migrants to come there in the post-2004 period.

According to the 2011 UK census, Wales is a country with a population of 3,063,000 people, including migrants and migrant communities.[51] The Annual Population Survey noted that the number of migrants in Wales has increased over time with approximately 25,000 migrants in the Welsh labour force in 1993, and over 83,000 in 2013.[52] Throughout history, Wales has been a prominent country for incoming migration. With its long coastline and good transport connections, Wales has an established history of migration, welcoming migrants from Eastern Europe, Somalia, Germany, Ireland, India and other parts of Asia. Interestingly, these migrants are not all centred in specific cities in Wales but are geographically dispersed throughout the country.

The desire for migrants to live outside major cities is unusual. Cities provide public transport, jobs within walking distance, nightlife, employment and housing opportunities that can support a new migrant. For example, according to the 2011 census, migrants from India are clustered in major cities in England and Wales such as London, Leicester and Cardiff.[53] Migrants from Pakistan are clustered in major centres in England and Wales such as London, Slough and Bradford.[54] This clustering has not changed dramatically for decades. Yet apart from these two major migrant groups, Wales has been the recipient of incoming migrants that choose to live in both urban and rural settings.

In Cardiff, the urban case study in this book, the once prominent docklands area in Tiger Bay brought inflows of migrants from popular port countries such as Somalia, Ireland, Spain and Portugal.[55] Through generations of settlement, the Somali population in Cardiff is thriving. It is now the second largest Somali settlement outside London. In addition to the impact of the former docklands, with major universities and business hubs in the Cardiff region, there is a diversity of population represented in 111 different nationalities.[56] While this inflow of migrants to port cities is common in other UK cities such as Liverpool, Bristol and London, the wave of migrants to Wales is not confined to the urban example.[57]

Other regions in rural and semi-urban areas of Wales have also been historic magnets for migrants. For example, the rural West Wales region, with its ferry connections to Ireland, has long been a destination for Irish migrants. Northern Wales, a rural and semi-urban location has also been a destination for migrants, including many intra-UK migrants who can reside comfortably in Wales while working in England. The semi-urban and rural areas of Wales are primary the sites of intra-UK migration; however, they are also considered an area for settlement. For example, a migrant who originally entered Wales via the Cardiff docklands may live in the Cardiff area for a time and then settle in the rural or semi-urban Wales area because of its proximity to major cities and affordability.

Interestingly, the spatial distribution of migrants, even those that may have originally been perceived as being economic, can be in economically underdeveloped regions. According to the EU Cohesion Policy guidelines, there are three regional classifications, which are also general objectives within the regions: (1) convergence; (2) regional competitiveness and employment; and (3) European territorial cooperation. The convergence regions have access to the most funds from the EU as their per capita GDP is lower that 75 per cent of the EU average.[58] At this level, the aim of the policy is simply to reduce regional disparities with the help of structural funds that are allocated to the member state and can also be applied for on a project basis. The projects range from providing high-speed Internet connections to job creation and training and to more location-specific issues such as stimulating return migration. Wales is a country of two halves, with the west side of the country, including Llanelli and Merthyr Tydfil, largely considered a Convergence region, and the east side, including Cardiff, in the Regional Competitiveness and Employment region. While many regions that started in the Convergence area have successfully emerged as regions for Competitiveness and Employment, others have not, as the transition can be the beginning of a long journey. Like the historic migration flows to Wales, the Polish migrants who came to Wales were not discouraged by the perception of a weak economy in comparison to other EU regions. As a result, starting in 2004, a large number of Poles came to Wales, and many stayed for the long term.

The information on A8 migrants in Wales illustrated in Table 1 highlights where Polish migrants are working and living in Wales.

Table 1: WRS Data for A8 Migrants in Wales at the Local Authority level May 2004-April 2011

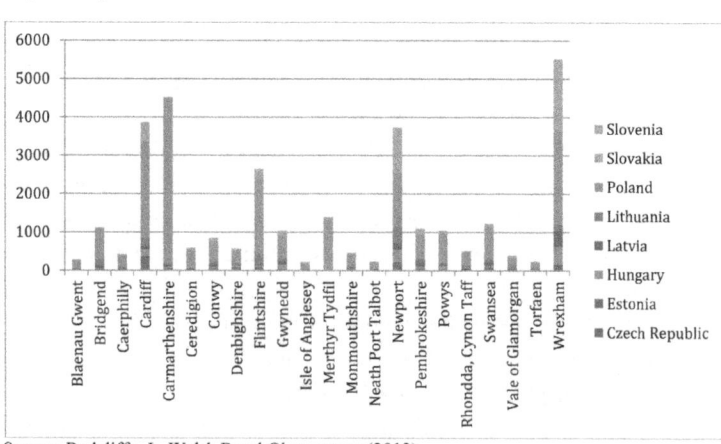

Source: Radcliffe, J., Welsh Rural Observatory (2013)

Using the WRS data, the local authority of Wrexham has received the highest number of A8 migrants during the WRS intake period (2004–11). While Wrexham did receive a large number of Polish migrants during this period, the third highest in Wales, the high number of A8 migrants is attributed to the influx of non-Polish migrants, namely Slovakians, who are underrepresented in other local authorities in Wales. Specifically focusing on Polish migrants, the Carmarthenshire local authority, where Llanelli is located, received the highest number of Poles within the WRS intake period. The local authority of Cardiff received the second highest number, and Merthyr Tydfil received significantly fewer Poles during this period, and many that were in this study went to other parts of Wales before going to Merthyr. As a result, the number of Poles in Merthyr from the WRS data is considered to be conservative as a result of intra-UK migration. The Poles in Wales, particularly Cardiff, Llanelli and Merthyr Tydfil, will be the focus of the remainder of this book.

Signposting for the Rest of the Book

This book is divided into three distinct parts, each building on what precedes to provide the reader with an in-depth understanding of the key topics surrounding why Poles migrated to Wales and what their experience has been over the last ten years since enlargement. As a high-level overview, Chapters 1, 2 and 3 compose Part I. This part provides background information on the book's topics, introduces the reader to relevant theory, and reviews both the methods used in the studies as well as the case-study locations. Part II includes Chapters 4, 5, 6 and 7. This part focuses on explaining the findings from the three studies in relation to the topics presented in Part I. There is a time dimension to this section as well. For example, Chapter 4 reviews the findings from all three case studies in regard to the migrants' initial arrival in Wales. The succeeding chapters follow the migrants in each study beyond this initial phase, when their paths begin to branch in a variety of directions. Part III includes Chapters 8, 9 and 10. These final chapters provide an overview of the findings in relation to future themes, including why migrants are staying in the UK longer than expected, their potential to integrate with British society and the implications for policy.

This book will continue as follows. Chapter 2 will be a review of migration and migration-related theory. As there is a significant amount of migration theory to cover in this chapter, it will be divided into two sections: (1) theories relating to economic migration; and (2) theories relating to non-economic migration. Also, because of the volume of literature on this topic, where possible, theory focusing on post-2004 Polish migration to the UK as well as authorised systems of migration will be referenced. The major themes that will be discussed in this theory chapter, both in terms of economic migration and non-economic migration, will include: typologies and trajectories of migration patterns; social network use over time; the experience of migrants in the labour market of the destination country; the creation and contributions to an ethnic economy; human capital development; and migrants' decision to stay in the destination country or return-migrate. While these themes will be introduced and discussed in Chapter 2, they will also be features of the remaining chapters.

Chapter 3 will provide a methodological and locational overview of the three studies that were combined to create this book. The methodologies for each study will be reviewed in depth to provide the reader with an understanding of the questions asked in the interviews, the way the samples were created and the unique characteristics of each of the three samples. The limitations, both to using these methodologies and to combining the three studies, will also be presented. In regard to the location discussion, through Chapter 1 the uncommon spatial distribution of the Poles in Wales is known, but more information on the social and economic aspects of each region will be presented in this chapter.

Chapter 4 introduces the findings from the three case studies focusing on the migrants' initial arrival in Wales. All of the case-study data were reviewed in this chapter, as the findings had significant commonalities in regard to how migrants acted when they first arrived in Wales. This period was marked by uncertainty for all of the migrants in terms of their employment, their accommodation and determining if they made the right choice when migrating. Chapter 4 is the transition chapter, introducing the reader to the findings from the studies. The following three chapters, written by each author that studied the respective region being discussed, review the study findings in relation to the period of migration after the initial arrival.

In Chapter 5, Knight begins by discussing the motivations and labour market mobility of post-2004 Poles in the Cardiff area of Wales, using a number of studies which she carried out in the city. The Cardiff area will be the basis for the urban-locality chapter. These spatial characteristics will be reviewed throughout the chapter in relation to the evolving motivations and actions of the Polish migrants living in an urban setting. The migration-related aspects include (but are not limited to) social network formation, labour market mobility, employment options, human capital development and social capital formation. For example, on the social side, the diversity of the city as the catalyst for migrants to form local social networks will be discussed. On the economic side, the vast service sector in the city will be reviewed, connecting the migrants' first job in this sector to the availability of these employment positions in the labour market. These are two examples, out of many, where the social, economic and geographic aspects of the study are integrated and reviewed.

In Chapter 6, Lever draws on studies which he undertook on Polish migrants living in Merthyr Tydfil, the basis for the semi-urban locality chapter. Poles have been migrating to the South Wales Valleys (SWV) for much of the last decade. After EU expansion in 2004 there was a significant influx of migrant workers from CEE countries, most notably from Poland. During this period, employment agencies servicing the region switched their focus from Portuguese migrants, who had hitherto filled most vacancies in food and meat-processing factories, to Polish workers, in order to challenge the established organisation of the Portuguese community and to achieve lower costs. While the number of Portuguese migrants has declined, the number of Poles has continued to increase, with competition between the two groups for jobs in local factories, and local consumers for new migrant businesses remaining strong to this day. The vast majority of Poles in Merthyr generally are recruited for and seek low-skilled employment in local factories, irrespective of their human capital. Some Poles have tried and failed to find work matching their qualifications, but most remain dependent on this low-skill sector for their livelihood.

Chapter 7 concludes Part III with Thompson focusing on the studies for which he was responsible in Llanelli in South-West Wales. This town is the basis for the rural-locality chapter. In the wake of EU expansion in 2004, the Carmarthenshire area, in which Llanelli is located, became one of the unanticipated hotspots in Wales for labour migration from CEE. One of the principal aims of the chapter is to ask how this came about. In answering this question, we show that, as in Cardiff and Merthyr Tydfil, migrant social networks feed international mobility. They act as circuits for the flow of information about migration opportunities both from contacts living in Poland and from those working abroad. Llanelli, however, arguably more than Merthyr Tydfil, also highlights the powerful role of employment agencies in sourcing migrants for labour and making full use of Europe's enlarged single market. The Llanelli case study also allows us to show how for some migrants, with comparatively low levels of education and competency in English, their migratory career is largely contingent on a supply of work within a relatively small local economy. All of those interviewed in Llanelli had stayed long past the point at which they had envisaged they would return, with most planning to stay for as long as possible.

Chapter 8 picks up on the theme that the previous three chapters left undiscussed: what happens, the chapter asks, to transform migrants' attitudes to life abroad, making them stay longer than they originally expected? Our answer is that, while money and work are what motivate most to move, when we look at why migrants stay, these factors are only part of what persuades them to remain away from their country of origin. In the majority of cases, it is the change in migrants' broader outlook and lifestyle in the South Wales region which makes them want to stay. None of this diminishes the significant challenges all face in adapting to life in Wales, but the longer individuals are abroad the more they come to see migration as a positive change in their circumstances. It is a finding which is likely to be replicated elsewhere across the UK.

Building on the understanding that Poles are staying in the UK in the long term, in some cases settling, in others 'waiting and seeing', Chapter 9 focuses on the integration of Polish migrants. This is an increasingly important issue in the UK, particularly given the spatial distribution of Poles in urban, rural and semi-urban settings and the unique challenges to integration that each locale can bring. The integration of the migrant is viewed as a multi-stage process that builds upon itself, starting with legal migration and ending with political integration. Both this chapter and Chapter 10 assume that EU citizens living in the UK will be able to remain in the UK if they wish to do so, even if the UK leaves the EU.

The final chapter of the book discusses the EU, UK and Welsh government migration policy implications of having a young, relatively well-educated, highly motivated migrant group that is staying in Wales for the longer term. This chapter outlines the complex political system that was alluded to in Chapter 1, explaining the policies that can be enacted at

Welsh government level, with its devolved status, versus the policies enacted at the other government levels. The chapter concludes with policy recommendations, taking into account the referendum decision.

Overall, using data from across South Wales, *Labour, Mobility and Temporary Migration* examines what drove this migration, why 'temporary' migration is stretched, in part because of migrants' transformative experiences in-country but also because of the unique qualities of the European single market, and what the lessons are for policy-makers in Wales, London and Brussels. The book is informed by a rich body of data which the authors will weave together to present a case which will stand out as one of the key texts in this field.

2

Theorising Migration – Understanding Motivations, Networks and Mobility

Introduction

One of the fundamental questions which informed our research – indeed, perhaps the principal trigger for this work – was 'Why Wales?' How had this part of the EU, on the margins geographically of the usual migratory pathway, become a destination for migrants from the new EU member states in the years following 2004? The opening chapter provided a brief political, economic, and spatial analysis of Wales as a receiving country for Polish migration from 2004 to 2015. It introduced our case-study locations in South Wales, where the empirical studies at the core of the book were conducted, and the methods used to carry out this research. Indirectly, the chapter also highlighted how Polish migrants in these locations transitioned from migrants with short-term intentions to ones with indefinite plans to remain in Wales. Although they were young, well educated, economically motivated and highly mobile, most of these migrants originally took low-skilled jobs when they arrived in the UK[1,2] and most were found in employment classed by Favell as '3D' – dirty, dangerous and dull.[3,4] Over ten years after enlargement, this situation has changed fundamentally and many migrants are still in Wales many years after they intended to return.

As the book unfolds, to understand what has happened in Wales we need to set it against a backdrop of similar experiences in other regions of the UK with similar migration from Poland post-2004. We also need to frame this migratory process using general theoretical models, and this chapter therefore reviews some key themes emerging from the social science literature on the motivations of migrants. The first section considers the literature on how to classify migrant groups, using migratory patterns and characteristics as a guide. The next reviews migrant motivation theories, starting with neo-classical economic theories before turning to approaches that put greater emphasis on cultural factors. These different theoretical approaches highlight the complexity of migrant motivations as well as the potential for them to change and evolve over time.

To assess the various motivations evident throughout the migratory period, we begin by reviewing a variety of core themes, including:

- labour market mobility;
- social networks;
- ethnic economy;
- ethnic entrepreneurship;
- return migration.

While these themes are drawn from a substantial corpus of social scientific research, each motive or combination of motives can be a significant spur for migrants, as is evident in our review of the body of work on Polish migration to the UK that has emerged over the last decade. The structure of the theoretical analysis will be guided by the migratory journey, from the initial motivation to migrate through to the decision to stay in the destination country.

Framing Migration Patterns

There are many ways to differentiate between migrant groups — i.e. economic migrants, chain migrants, circular migrants, 'settlers' and 'storks'. This brief list alludes to the possible migration patterns that can be used by migrants, as well as the typologies created to explain migrant characteristics. The term 'circular migrant' refers to individuals who exhibit short-term, repetitive migration patterns and are often in a destination country for specific seasonal demand. These migrants fill the demand for low-wage positions that are not taken up by the native labour force.[5] Alternatively, the transient migrant is highly mobile and will migrate from one country after another. While 'country-hopping' can occur within an open-border region such as the Schengen area of the EU, in reality many such migrants will often be crossing borders illegally.[6] Increasingly, these two migration patterns are supported by the hypermobile global landscape, with low-cost airlines shuttling migrants quickly and inexpensively from one location to another.[7]

Another option for migrants is 'chain migration', which often occurs in one of two principal ways. First, chain migration can unite a family with the first family member to migrate and thereby starting a 'chain', with the additional family members trickling into the destination country thereafter;[8] according to White, this approach is used extensively by Poles in the UK.[9] Second, chain migration can involve migrants from one community settling in another country and starting a chain to the destination country. Both types of chain migration can reunite family members in the destination country, and both can be facilitated by recruitment agencies.[10] In the period immediately following enlargement in 2004, when the average Polish migrant was considered young, single and highly mobile, the majority of Polish migrants in the UK exhibited circular migration patterns. Family members may have been involved in this type of migration, but owing to their circular migration patterns they would be considered circular migrants instead of chain migrants. However, as time has passed, the migration patterns of the average Polish migrant in the UK changed and they began staying in the UK for longer periods.[11]

Beyond migration patterns, the literature provides novel ways to categorise migrant groups as well as migrant subgroups through various typologies. Typologies represent categories that migrants can move through over time. In contrast, the increasingly popular notion of trajectories illustrates dynamic categories that focus on the evolution of migrants over time with some form of predictive capacity for future plans. The classic migration typology, derived from research on Chinese immigrants to the US, considers migrants to be either 'sojourners', temporary migrants, or 'settlers', long-term migrants who share a 'myth of return'.[12, 13] Focusing particularly on Polish migrants in the UK, Eade et al. created specific typologies from subgroups in their sample of Polish migrants in London, including: 'storks', 'hamsters', 'searchers' and 'stayers'.[14] 'Storks' are synonymous with circular migrants who rely on economic motivations to migrate and use the ethnic economy significantly, before return-migrating to start the cycle again. 'Hamsters' are likewise economically motivated but focus more on human capital development that can be exploited upon return to their country of origin. 'Searchers' are the most fluid migrants, open both to return migration or living abroad. As a result, this group is most likely to exhibit a transient identity – living in several different countries to capitalise on accession through legal mobility in the EU. The 'stayers' are those migrants who stay in the UK for good – what has classically been referred to as 'settlers'. These typologies take into account the migration pattern, social class and employment potential of the migrants.

Realising that the Polish migrants in the UK have, over time, transitioned from storks to stayers, there is an increased emphasis on creating trajectories to account for their changing characteristics during the period from initial migration to possible settlement. It should be noted that trajectories are not new and that there is an extensive literature focused on migrant-related trajectories in different capacities such as labour market mobility[15, 16] and changing roles in the high-skilled visa system.[17] Thus, focusing on Polish migrants in the UK, the findings from a pilot study of four Polish migrant entrepreneurs in Glasgow were used to construct trajectories.[18] Helinksa-Hughes et al explained their findings using a trajectory approach that reviewed major themes over time, including why migrants decided to start a business, and the role of social networks as a source of finance and demand for the business.[19] Another study of post-2004 Polish migrants in Belfast is based on narrative interviews with three respondents, and explores the different trajectories migrants take over time.[20] While this study provides an in-depth account of the sample's complex motivations during the migration period, these studies are limited by their exploratory nature and small sample size.

Research conducted on Polish entrepreneurs in Munich used trajectories to examine the shifting cultural capital of Poles with ties to both their country of origin and destination country.[21] The sample of seven Poles living in Munich, interviewed in 2006/7, have similar characteristics to Poles living in the UK in the post-2004 period, as both groups are characterised as exhibiting circular migration patterns, which may occur over years. Nowicka's construction of trajectories over time for migrants embedded in the ethnic economy as well as the non-ethnic economy, sometimes in high-skilled professions, is a significant contribution to the literature.[22] Knight, Thompson and Lever also used trajectories to compare the labour market mobility of Poles in the UK focusing on three different spatial areas in Wales.[23] The construction of the trajectories highlighted the migrants' need for language skills if wanting to have upward mobility in the local labour market. In discussing the possible migration patterns and terms to describe Polish migration to the UK post-2004, this section highlights the changing characterisations of Polish migrants over time. We next consider theories relating to time in destination countries, including a review of the literature on why migrants stay in the destination country longer than they initially planned. By approaching the literature in this manner, we aim to provide an account of the lives of migrants and the evolution of their views in the UK over time.

Understanding Motivations for Migration

The motivations of migrants can be complex, not least because the forces that act as the trigger for migration may not be the same as those which keep individuals abroad. More particularly, there are a variety of other, more particular scenarios to gauge, from the motivations for moving to a particular region to motivations for taking up low-paid employment with demanding physical conditions. In later chapters, most notably the three locality studies, we ask how it was that our participants ended up moving to Wales, which, compared to some other regions of the UK, has not been a traditional migration hotspot, and specifically how they came to live in places which, by most measures, are not the most obvious destinations for Polish migrants. In broad terms, the 'stimulus' for migration can be the result of economic or non-economic factors, or a combination thereof. To begin with, we want to look at some of the differing perspectives on economic motives on the one hand and, on the other, at what a number of key studies have identified as cultural or social influences on the decision not only to move, but also to draw out the migratory period and extend it over time.

Economic motivations to migrate

The role of economic forces in motivating migrants is generally regarded as significant. According to Becker, who also argues that there are many seemingly non-economic human behaviours that are intrinsically economic, migrants are rational actors whose motivations are utilitarian and economically based.[24] This conceptualisation posits migrants as being committed to the economic aspects of migration, the implication being that they make every decision based on the perceived economic benefits for maximum utility. Both characterisations imply that migrants are motivated by economic means. It should, however, be noted that the economics-based theories reviewed do not hold economics as the sole motivating factor for migrants. Rather, they hold economics as the paramount motivatory factor.

Neo-classical economic approaches to migration rely on the migrant embodying the *homo economicus* persona, with the economic motivations trickling down from the initial decision to migrate. This theory considers the sending and receiving countries as systems that, ideally, are in equilibrium. This equilibrium is contingent on the flows of real wages in two phases. The first flow is low-skilled labour from low-wage regions migrating to high-wage regions.[25] The result of this flow is that the capital gained from it transfers back to the low-wage region in the form of remittances, putting the system in economic equilibrium.[26] Once real-wage equilibrium is set within the system, the high-skilled labourers can begin their migration to the high-wage region, thereby allowing the migrants to occupy all parts of the division of labour in the destination country. This model holds economic motivations as the sole incentive for migration, with a supply of workers migrating to fill the demand for jobs.[27]

This theoretical approach has been subject to important critiques over time.[28, 29] In relation to Polish migration to the UK, it has also been challenged in three ways. First, Poles migrating to the UK were high-skilled migrants taking low-skilled jobs, which upsets the equilibrium-based approach of this theory, where low-skilled migration should lead to high-skilled migration. Second, by inaccurately assessing the characteristics of the Polish migrant group, as noted in the first point, the theory does not take into account the globalised world in which migration is occurring. Third, the theory hinges on the remittances that put the system in equilibrium; however, studies of recent Polish migration have found mixed evidence for the importance of remittance payments as a migrant practice.

Massey et al. consider the more historic, household-based migration theories in which it was the decision of the family in the home country to encourage their children to migrate for economic purposes in order to send home remittance payments.[30] However, more in line with the 2004 Polish migrant characteristics, Dustmann and Weiss argue that migrants are attracted to earning wages abroad and spending them in their home country, thus reaping the benefits of favourable currency exchange rates.[31] When considering remittance payments in this way, this is why migrants do not migrate as a single household. Nelson's previous work supports this claim by noting that, even in relation to developing countries, most migrants come from middle-class families, making remittances less likely.[32] In this case, those Poles that were able to migrate in the post-2004 period came from more affluent homes, as opposed to the traditional migrations during the post-WWII period. This change of affluence therefore ends the need for remittance payments and allows migrants to migrate to enhance their human capital and use it in the labour market when they return-migrate.

This argument is disputed by Fihel et al., their study of migrants from new member states (A8) to the EU-15 in the post-2004 period pointing to significant remittance payments.[33] In relation to the neo-classical model, the income of the A8 countries would therefore rise as a result of remittance payments that would in turn impact Gross National Product (GNP). The effects on the EU-15 countries' GNP would be minimal, given the higher wages found in those countries in contrast to the wages in the A8 countries. Even if we accept remittance payments, the cyclical nature of the theory implies that real-wage equilibrium as a catalyst for high-skilled migration will not be reached. This point ties in with the second point regarding the role of globalisation and migration. In the globalised world, high-skilled labour can be recruited from a worldwide labour market regardless of previous migrations, thereby making the neo-classical theory, where high-skilled labour migrates as a result of previous successful low-skilled migration, obsolete.

The neo-liberal framework provides an update to neo-classical economic theory in that it takes into account global markets, thus making it more contemporary by conceptualising migrant actions in the globalised world. This framework is also discussed in relation to the role of the government in constructing immigration policy for the nation-state as well as from the perspective of the EU citizen who is free to move throughout the EU.[34] Through globalisation, the role of the nation-state in regions such as the EU with supranational governance has become blurred. While the flow of capital and goods across borders falls in line with the traditional neo-liberal rhetoric, according to this framework the flow of people across borders should be more closely governed at the national level.[35,36] Economically, this would make aspects of migration that reduce the 'cost' of migration increasingly important for migrants.

Borjas's global migration market theory focuses on the costs and benefits that migrants consider when deciding to migrate.[37] This theory is an extension of Sjaastad's human capital theory that was the first attempt at describing migration in a cost/benefit analysis format where the most influential motivation is the expected wage prospects in the destination country.[38] Global migration market theory says that migrants will weigh the costs of moving against the commensurate level of wages and chances of finding employment in the destination country.[39] In this scenario, if the latter is more than the former then migration will occur.

Similarly, Drinkwater and Clark's 'push/pull' theory takes the basic cost/benefit analysis that Borjas used but assigns labels such as 'push' and 'pull' to specific aspects of migrant life to determine what motivates migrants.[40] Taking into account a multitude of motivating factors, this approach highlights the unachievable aspect of the cost/benefit theory, as a migrant would not necessarily be able to consider all of the future costs and benefits associated with migration.[41] Using push/pull theory, there is still an economic focus but it is considerably less than in the work of Borjas. This theory assigns labels to both economic motivations such as unemployment in country of origin and real wages in the destination country. To distinguish the motivations, the push factors are those driving migrants away from their country of origin and the pull factors are those factors drawing them to their destination country. As a purely economic example, a push factor could be high unemployment in the migrant's country of origin and a pull factor could be the existing ethnic economy in the destination country that provides employment opportunities. As demonstrated in other forms of migration, such as refugees escaping genocide or conflict, there are other, non-economic aspects that can push and pull migrants to leave their country of origin.

Non-economic motivations to migrate

There is also a substantial weight of work that presses for an understanding of the significance of cultural and social factors. Regardless of their migration pattern, migrants' actions and decisions will be responses to a multitude of motivations throughout their migratory trajectory that can be both economic and non-economic in nature. Verwiebe's study of intra-EU migration to Berlin from the early 1980s provides a nice illustration of the interplay of these factors.[42] Given the focus of this book, it is important to mention that Verwiebe's sample did not include Polish migrants who migrated to Berlin in the post-accession period.[43] Regardless, the findings from this quantitative study demonstrate that intra-EU migrants can have a complex range of motivations. Verwiebe's research on intra-EU migration, using migrants from several EU countries, has been updated for post-2004 Polish migrants focusing on their integration plans in Ireland.[44] The findings from the study were organised into pathways focused on integration but had similar findings to Verwiebe's work. The majority of the qualitative sample originally migrated for social and/or cultural reasons and, through the pathways, the authors considered the migrants' ability to integrate over time.[45] The findings also introduce social reasons for migration for post-2004 Poles and more classic migration patterns for post-2004 Poles migrating because of family ties.[46] With respect to Poles and family ties, this finding could be seen as an extension of Kofman's work on the prevalence of family ties in the traditionally perceived economic motivations of EU migrants.[47] If 'the perception of migration as temporary is linked to an understanding of migration as economic', then the economic rationality of the migration is questioned if the migration is not temporary.[48] The temporary nature of the migrants journey is discussed extensively throughout this book. In addition, a smaller study of three post-2004 Polish migrants in Belfast described their non-economic motivations to initially migrate, including the aim of increasing their cultural capital.[49]

Polish migrants' interest in migrating to the UK post-2004 for the short term may have been economically motivated, but as we observe throughout this book, migrant motivations can change over time. Given the amount of time that has passed since 2004, and the continued interest in Polish migrants staying in the UK, the remainder of the chapter considers alternative economic and non-economic motivations.

Social Networks

Social capital has been defined in several ways ranging from Fukuyama's 'shared norms or values that promote social cooperation, instantiated in actual social relationships' to Putnam's 'social networks and the associated norms of reciprocity and trustworthiness'.[50, 51] Despite the apparent applicability of these definitions to migrants, both of them heavily rely on the exchange of social capital occurring locally, such as in exchanges between neighbours.[52] At first glance, this assertion greatly hinders the use of social capital accrued transnationally through migrant groups that utilise circular migration patterns to live two lives. This is where the uses of social capital need to be specified. Social capital for migrants can revolve around the aforementioned transnational exchange; however, it can also be used, as described by Putnam, as a form of social currency among migrants in a destination country, which we will discuss in further detail when we discuss the 'commitment' to a migratory career.[53] This section focuses on the use of a migrant's social capital to gain entry into social networks and kinship networks.

Once migrants arrive in their destination country, they tend to group into networks based on trust, reciprocity and similarities (bonding contacts).[54] In this context, social networks are not motivating migrants but facilitating migrants to migrate to a specific area. For Massey et al., social network theory states that migrants are more likely to move to another country where there is a social network as it 'lowers the costs and risks of movement while increasing the expected net return of migration'.[55] It thus favours increased migration as the expanding network lowers the risk for new migrants. Accordingly, migrant networks, composed predominantly of bonding contacts that have similar characteristics to the migrant's, have many roles during this initial phase, mainly as pull factors encouraging new migration through providing short-term accommodation in the destination country and assistance in finding a job.[56] As a result of their migration facilitation role, scholars of migration have shown how these social networks serve to direct new migrants to particular localities in destination countries. Patterns observed in other contexts, such as in North America, are evident in post-2004 Polish migration to the UK. Garip and Asad show how, in nearly all their studied cases of Mexican migration to the United States, individuals spoke of how network contacts reduced the risk of migration through the assistance they provided in-country.[57] Similarly Ryan et al. report that among new Polish migrants in London many had, at least initially, relied extensively on social support from close contacts on arrival in London.[58]

The use of recruitment agencies as facilitators of Polish migration, and A8 migration more widely to the UK has received a significant amount of attention from social scientists.[59, 60, 61] Jones found that the use of recruitment agencies to facilitate migration to the UK has led to unlikely migrant destinations arising within the UK outside of large cities.[62, 63] Interestingly, through the recruitment agency facilitation, these migrants are seen to be exhibiting 'herd behaviour' with the population of many small towns in Poland being transported to work in non-urban locations in the UK.[64] It should be noted that 'herd behaviour' within migrant groups does not require recruitment agency facilitation but *is* greatly supported by it. In addition, the literature notes that recruitment agencies recruit migrants for lower-level positions in the service sector or for agricultural work, which often becomes available at short notice.[65] As a result, migrants are expected to migrate quickly once receiving the call from an agency, leaving in days instead of weeks or months. Furthermore, in considering the recruitment agency as a facilitator of migration, which lowers the risk of migrating – the trip and accommodation being repaid through migrant earnings – it could be argued that these agencies are similar to the illegitimate coyotes aiding illegal immigration from South America to the US.[66] In this way, the recruitment agency is a manufactured social network for migrants, facilitating their initial migration and potentially influencing the migration of the rest of the 'herd'.[67]

The argument that social networks are facilitators of employment and wealth for migrants has its critics. According to White and Ryan, the social networks that are supposed to be available to new Polish migrants (post-2004) are not what they seem.[68] White and Ryan found that the Poles in their study had little support from the 'social network' in their region as their fellow Polish migrants were focused on making money through work instead of making connections.[69] This lack of support for fellow migrants could be aligned with Piore's work on labour shortages where, as migrant supply increases, competition ensues and wages decrease.[70] Nonetheless, these findings support Putnam's constrict theory that when 'in more diverse settings, Americans distrust not merely people who do not look like them, but also people who do.'[71] Both White and Ryan, as well as Putnam's work, highlight the dynamic between new migrants and the existing social network in the destination country.

Over time, social networks can evolve to include a combination of bonding and bridging contacts, which can be used throughout the migrant's time in the destination country. For the long-term migrant, the composition of the social network can change over time with an increase in bridging contacts or an increase in bonding contacts or both.[72] Migrants that were interested in bonding contacts to have a sense of home when initially migrating, may find that through their own personal human capital development, or through the lack of trust from fellow migrants, they outgrow these networks, searching for new contacts.[73] Interestingly, these new contacts may be 'bonded' to them through different ways. For example, a Polish migrant may have initially had bonded contacts through fellow Polish family and friends when initially migrating, but later acquire bonded contacts in non-Polish migrant friends. Through being fellow migrants, the homogeneity of the bond is maintained yet the diversity of the network has increased. This scenario highlights that migrants' social networks are dynamic and may change positively over time.[74]

The evolution of the migrants' social network can be a unique experience that, unbeknownst to the migrants, is having an impact on the their social and economic progression in the destination country. For example, a network that is solely composed of bonding contacts may not necessarily be positive, as it can cut off its members from information about the wider community in which they are living in.[75] According to Hickman et al., these types of networks have lead to negative social capital with the wider community, thereby threatening social cohesion.[76]

Labour Market Mobility

The importance of finding work when initially migrating is of significant importance to migrants. This point was demonstrated in the push/pull motivations of the migrants as well as the social networks that they use to facilitate employment when they initially migrate. These economic motivations can lead migrants to take low-skilled positions when initially entering the country of origin to start accruing capital, both financial and human, while deciding their next steps. The 'next steps' in this timeline are a major turning point for the migrants in regard to their work experience in the labour market of the destination country in the long-term.

In her study of Polish and Lithuanian migrants in the UK, Parutis focuses on the labour market mobility of migrants and the entry point of migrants at the bottom of the labour market.[77] This acceptance of low-wage, low-skilled jobs by migrants can be attributed to their need to earn. Parutis describes them using the term 'middling transnationalism', which alludes to the paradoxical nature of the migrants as high-skilled individuals taking low-skilled jobs.[78, 79, 80] In terms of migrant motivations this 'middling transnationalism' will seek any position when reaching the destination country to earn enough to live.[81] Once savings are accrued, the migrant can then move on to a better job. Through the migrant starting at the bottom of the labour market in the destination country when initially migrating and then moving up the division of labour, Parutis' theory is based on Chiswick et al.'s U-shaped pattern of migrant progression in the division of labour of the destination country.[82]

Chiswick et al.'s findings relate to the migrants' changing position in the division of labour of the destination country.[83] This strand of work argues that the 'U-shaped' pattern depicts the high level of occupational achievement the migrants had in their home country, the low level position they took when initially migrating and the migrants' ascent up the division of labour in the destination country.[84] To achieve this occupational attainment in the destination country, the migrants will have had a high-level occupation prior to migrating, have developed their human capital prior to migrating, and will acquire additional 'location-specific' human capital in the destination country.[85] The more non-transferable the skills of the migrant are between the country of origin and the destination country, the more likely the migrant is to immediately have low employment options but, over time, to have significant upward occupational mobility in the destination country because location-specific human capital is acquired.[86] In contrast, Parutis discusses the migrant's ascent up the division of labour from when the migrant enters the country, and only mentions the migrants' high-skilled nature prior to migrating through the migrant paradox.[87] Through this comparison, the studies show similar findings of labour market mobility once migrants are in the destination country, but the pre-migration characteristics highlight the multiple interpretations of 'high-skilled'. Parutis considers 'high-skilled' to mean a higher education level and higher language levels where the U-shaped pattern research focuses on 'high-skilled' as employment experience.[88, 89]

Through these theories and more recent research, the mobility of Polish migrants in the labour market of the destination country is largely reliant on the human capital that they continue to develop over time.[90] This is particularly the case when considering the development of migrants' language skills. However, the role of 'location' cannot be overlooked. A notable feature of post-2004 Polish migration has been its geographical spread across all parts of the UK. London and the surrounding areas have been the principal magnets for migrants coming to the UK, but research has shown how places with no previous history of international migration, such as south-west England and Northern Ireland, have attracted significant numbers of post-2004 migrants from Poland and other CEE countries.[91] Rural areas, too, saw sizeable immigration, such as in the Highlands of Scotland, the east of England, and west and south Wales. Trevena was one of the first scholars to note that rural localities can create unique challenges for migrants, particularly owing to the nature of local labour markets, which can be seasonal and limited in scope.[92] For example, the food production industry has been one important source of employment for post-2004 Polish migrants and a determinant of their movement to rural parts of the UK.[93] Trevena, McGhee and Heath highlighted how the internal mobility of international migrants is not driven by location per se but rather by the availability of work and accommodation.[94] In rural areas the staffing agencies provide leverage, particularly in localities with little local experience of migration. Jentsch et al. show how recruitment agencies have made the far north of Scotland one of the premier locations for CEE migrants in recent years.[95] Moreover, these agencies demonstrate how direct recruitment can replace local social networks, at least with respect to their role in securing employment in specific localities where previous knowledge of employment opportunities would have spread by word of mouth.[96]

Taking into account the role of human capital development in labour market mobility in the destination country, the next section will focus on the ethnic economy and employment in the ethnic economy.

The Ethnic Economy

The ethnic economy can be another 'pull' factor in motivating a migrant to migrate internationally; but, after reviewing social network theory, it is difficult to determine where the social network ends and where the ethnic economy begins. The most popular and most encompassing type of economy for migrants in the new country is the ethnic economy. It takes into account all ethnic businesses (of the same ethnicity) in an area and, as defined by Bonacich and Modell the 'group's self-employed, employers, and co-ethnic employees'.[97] While other ethnic group members may be employed in the local community they do not count towards the ethnic economy.[98] The ethnic economy is solely set up for the benefit of the ethnic community it serves. In some cases, where there is a labour shortage within the ethnic economy, people may migrate specifically for an employment opportunity. However, for the most part, this economy is used solely by those migrants already in the area.[99]

The ethnic economy, with its ethnic businesses, can provide more than employment opportunities.[100] As Metykova states, it is a way for migrants in a foreign country to construct familiarity.[101, 102] Burrell's research found that the ethnic economy was used by Poles in Britain to recreate the feeling of home through the shared use of use of language and food, and a place to catch up on events with co-ethnics.[103] Through these factors, the ethnic economy is a relevant pull factor for migrants, particularly those that are temporary or involved in a circular migration pattern. Furthermore, in addressing the relationship between social networks and the ethnic economy, it becomes more apparent that they rely on one another to exist. However, the relationship is not mutually exclusive. To have an ethnic economy there must be a social network composed of bonding contacts, but an ethnic economy is not needed to have a social network.

The ethnic economy concept falls between two other ethnic-based economy concepts, which differ in terms of the geographic proximity of the businesses and the interconnectedness of the group actors. The 'ethnic enclave economy' is the most integrated of the three economies through 'locational clustering of firms, economic interdependency and ethnic employees'.[104] A defined location is needed with examples ranging from Little Havana in Miami[105] to Little Italy in New York.[106] On the other side, the informal economy is based on ethnic groups who have businesses where there are no social or legal restrictions.[107] In this economy there are no taxes.[108] Unlike the other types of economy where proximity and social cohesion are central, this informal economy is more loosely defined and less regulated.

Using the ethnic economy definition, the role of ethnic businesses is clearly outlined as it further embeds the ethnic community in the surrounding region. Many of these businesses are owned and operated by ethnic entrepreneurs who are embedded in and rely heavily upon a number of social networks.[109] There are many theories that focus on entrepreneurship as a last resort or necessity, and entrepreneurship as a goal, or opportunity.[110] For example, the disadvantage theory describes this scenario when noting that a[111] lack of desirable job opportunities can be a driving force for ethnic entrepreneurs to start a business.[112] Acs and colleagues attribute the many low-skilled positions migrants take prior to becoming an ethnic entrepreneur to low education levels making entrepreneurship a necessary employment option rather than an opportunity.[113] In discussing ethnic entrepreneurship in this manner, the migrant is not motivated to migrate in the hope of starting a business; rather, after experiencing the labour market, the migrant is motivated to start a business.

Alternatively, entrepreneurs, migrant or otherwise, can be motivated to start a business for the sake of opportunity, such as to be one's own boss, or after identifying a niche in the market.[114, 115] Specifically focusing on Poles in the UK, research by Harris highlights that some Polish entrepreneurs in the UK post-2004 were more strategic in having a business idea prior to moving to the UK and, building on Lassalle and colleagues' argument, only worked in 3D positions to raise funds to start the business.[116, 117] This would explain why migrants had several low-skilled employment positions – 'any job' – in the division of labour before moving up to a 'better job' and potentially a 'dream job', as described by Parutis's work on Lithuanian and Polish migrants in the UK.[118] In this case, the 'dream job' would be entrepreneurship.

In terms of the workers for the ethnic business, ethnic entrepreneurs will rely on social networks to access the talent pool in the ethnic economy as well as their own personal networks, which may extend back to their country of origin (Evans 1989). The need for co-ethnics can be based on the wages paid as well as promoting the complete appearance of an ethnic business to consumers. From their study on the wages of A8 migrants in the UK, Anderson and colleagues point out that self-employed Poles, which could include ethnic entrepreneurs, often earn more income in the UK, and this trickles down to increased wages for their co-ethnic workers.[119] Depending on the situation of the ethnic entrepreneur's family and their contacts within their social network in the destination country, workers can either arrive in a chain migration fashion, with frequent return visits, to help with the business, or the local, unrelated co-ethnics can be used as the labour pool.[120] Arguably entrepreneurs would be more willing to exploit available family networks, as the immediate costs relating to the migration of the family member will be offset by the amount of work that they will do for the business. In addition, due to the level of social capital among family members, there will be less distrust that an employee will steal or start a similar business in the ethnic economy, thereby increasing competition.[121]

Ethnic entrepreneurs also rely on their bonded social networks as well as the wider Polish community to form the demand for their products. In addition to using the shared language in the Polish store, the migrant is able to find products from the country of origin within the ethnic economy. The migrant who uses the firms in the ethnic economy can catch up on events from the destination country through newspapers and/or general gossip. Maintaining the evolution theme that has been integral to this chapter, over time, the Polish ethnic entrepreneurs in the UK have to consider what will happen to their niche business once their customer base declines through return migration or through cultural integration. Research demonstrates that because of the roots put down within the community (both ethnic and non-ethnic), migrant entrepreneurs are less likely to return-migrate than migrant workers; however, what happens to Polish businesses once the demand for their products fluctuates?[122]

Recent research on Polish entrepreneurs in Birmingham highlights that while these businesses are initially created to serve the Polish community, over time many start to employ non-Polish staff.[123] This staffing change could be in an effort to maintain employment numbers within a changing talent pool, or it could be the first step in diversifying the business. Lassalle et al. focus specifically on ethnic firm diversification through breaking-out into mainstream markets and note that this has yet to happen for Polish entrepreneurs in Glasgow.[124] However, this research also notes that an unintended transition has occurred, with ethnic entrepreneurs who initially served the ethnic economy now serving both the ethnic economy and non co-ethnics. The latter use the shop as a speciality store in the same way a speciality delicatessen may be occasionally frequented.

Owing to the ethnic entrepreneurs' significant ties to the destination country, the chance of return is limited, even if the demand for their products decreases or evolves. The following section will review the motivations for other, non-entrepreneur migrants to stay in a destination country over time. Given the long-term migration of the Polish migrants in the UK thus far, the inclination is to categorize them as 'settlers' or 'stayers'.

Overstaying, Settling and Return Migration

From the classic description of post-2004 Polish migrants in the UK outlined in Chapter 1, Poles were originally characterised as short-term migrants. While this characterisation may have been supported in the pre-2004 period as well as in the period immediately after enlargement, more current literature acknowledges that many Polish migrants are staying in destination countries for a longer term than they originally planned. Increasingly, research on EU migrants in the UK is focusing on the motivations for migrants to stay longer in the destination country in spite of the push and pull factors to return-migrate.

Cook et al. undertook a qualitative study of the Polish, Slovakian and Roma (post-2004) migrants in northern England that focused on the temporary nature of migration, highlighting the fact that many migrants in their sample initially said they were staying in the UK only for the short term but ended up staying much longer.[125] The research focuses largely on economic motivations relating to migrants' occupational mobility and human capital development in providing a temporal approach to migration. Regardless of the economic emphasis, the homogeneity of A8 migrants' occupational mobility, as well as their clear motivation to stay in destination countries, is questioned, therefore challenging the traditional notion that economic migration is temporary.[126]

Taking into account the non-economic motivations of post-2004 Polish migrants to stay in the UK, Thompson discusses their decision to delay their return migration, thereby extending their time in the destination country.[127] Through his work on Polish migrants in Wales, Thompson noticed a definitive social aspect when the migrants moved from being temporary to long-term migrants, despite their initial economic inclinations to migrate.[128] While he mentions the initial economic motivations and the multiple factors that influence the migrants to overstay their expected time in the destination country, even during a recession, emphasis is placed on the 'in-the-moment' nature of the migrants who do not have any clear strategies for their future plans.[129] This 'migratory drift' sheds considerable light on migrants' motivations to change their temporary status owing to family and organisations.[130]

Literature related to the concept of migratory drift in the social context includes the work on 'liquid migration',[131,132] adapting Bauman's[133] earlier concept of 'liquid modernity'. Engerbsen and colleagues in a number of important publications have arguably best captured this sense of post-2004 migration as not only quantitatively different from population movements which followed earlier EU enlargements in its size and scale, but also as a qualitative species because of its 'liquid' form. The EU's open borders have enabled individuals to try out working abroad in other, sometimes multiple EU member states. New forms of technology, combined with comparatively cheap means of transport, often sponsored by staffing agencies capable of facilitating the movement of large numbers of workers across national borders, enable workers to move around the EU whilst still being able to maintain strong links with families at home.

Conclusion

As we will explore in subsequent chapters, one of the clearest findings to emerge from our studies in Wales is that migrants who typically came seeking short-term employment, usually intending to stay less than a year, have often stayed much longer. Migration, as we note in what follows, is a 'numbers game', for social scientists as much as for the public and policy-makers. In the wake of the EU enlargement in 2004, expert predictions on the scale of the migration proved to be incorrect. As time has passed, too, perceptions of the relative 'liquidity' of this migration to the UK have also looked to be on less certain ground. While it is difficult to determine precisely how many migrants are overstaying or settling in the UK, in part because of the subjective form of these categories, what is evident is that many are remaining in the UK for much longer than they originally expected. As in other studies that have been carried out in the UK, our research found instances of short-term, back-and-forth movements between Wales and Poland. Generally, however, we discovered how individuals were transitioning after arrival, setting their horizons, even if loosely defined, on a longer-term stay. In later chapters, we will delve into why we believe this has happened.

This initial review of the migration literature has been necessarily selective, and it has been our intention to draw out some themes to which we will return in later discussions. Significantly, in seeking to understand why migrants have stayed in Wales for longer than they initially intended, we argue that it is necessary to look at the initial period after arrival as a discrete stage in the migratory career. Economic factors are undoubtedly important considerations in weighing up the decision to move abroad for work, but non-economic factors have a critical bearing on decisions to remain in the UK. The supply of steady employment, and the transition from being agency staff to being directly employed, is what makes remaining in the UK possible. Understanding why so many have decided to stay, perhaps the paramount concern for policy-makers at different levels, requires us to look at the experiences of migrants and the transformation of their outlook at different stages of the migratory career.

3

Locations and Research Methodology

Introduction

As we explained at the outset, this book presents, collectively, a substantial body of new data on Polish migration to the UK in the wake of EU enlargement in 2004. The data which are at the heart of this book were collected across three case-study locations in Wales through three independently conducted studies. The three locations, while all in Wales, vary spatially, socially and economically. Cardiff, the capital of Wales, is the urban case-study location. Merthyr Tydfil, a town approximately twenty-five miles from Cardiff, is the semi-urban case-study location. Llanelli, a town approximately fifty-five miles from Cardiff and forty miles from Merthyr Tydfil, is the rural case-study location. Due to the proximity of these three locations, they are referred to periodically throughout this book as the South Wales region. The aim of this chapter is to highlight that despite the proximity of the case-study locations, there are considerable differences among the actual locales and there are also significant variations among the samples of Polish migrants in each location.

Wales has a lengthy history of both inward and outward migration. After WW2, a number of 'Polish camps' were set up in different parts of Wales to accommodate Poles displaced by the war and the ensuing political settlement in central Europe. In Cardiff, for example, 'Newport House', located on Newport Road, is a space for post-WW2 Poles residing in Cardiff to meet and use their Polish language skills. Commensurate examples exist in the other locales. Similar, however, to other studies on links between pre-2004 and post-2004 Poles in the UK, we found no substantive connections between this earlier wave of Polish migrants and the post-2004 Polish migrants in Wales.[1] In addition to this lack of connection between individuals who share a nationality residing in another country, there are other interesting points relating specifically to the Poles residing in Wales in terms of where they are locating themselves within the country. Supporting other research on post-2004 Poles, the post-2004 Polish migrants who arrived in Wales located themselves within cities such as the urban case and other city regions in North Wales; but these migrants also located themselves in non-urban locations, such as the semi-urban and the rural cases.[2, 3] While case studies of individual spatial locales exist such as those on Poles in North East England or in the Scottish Highlands, few, if any, spatially comparative studies exist at the regional level.

The Fieldwork Sites of the South Wales Region

This section will review the economic, spatial and social commonalities and variations among the urban, semi-urban and rural cases. Where possible, specific points in time will be addressed for each of the localities, including: the 2004 EU enlargement period, the data collection period (2008–12), and data for 2015. While the last data collection period ended in 2012, it can be assumed that many of the migrants that participated in the individual studies are still residing in Wales or in the wider UK. As a result, the 2015 information is assessed to highlight how these spaces evolved over a three-year period between the end of the data collection period and the time of writing.*

Urban case

The research for the urban case was conducted in the capital of Wales, Cardiff. According to the 2011 census, the population of Wales was 3,063,800, of whom 345,400 people, or 11 per cent of the population, live in Cardiff.[4] Geographically, Cardiff is a coastal city situated in the South Wales area, approximately two hours from London. Economically, the main employee jobs in Cardiff are in the service sector (87.9 per cent)

---

* While the EU funding to convergence regions will change if the UK leaves the EU, this historical account is still accurate. Migrants, even those that were migrating for economic reasons, were not dissuaded by the destination location, even if it was economically underdeveloped.

LOCATIONS AND RESEARCH METHODOLOGY

which accounts for distribution, hotels and restaurants (20.4 per cent); finance, IT, and other business activities (25.5 per cent); and public administration and health (30.9 per cent).[5] According to the Annual Population Survey, Cardiff is home to a number of universities, and almost 40 per cent of those in the workforce hold a tertiary-level education qualification, in contrast to the 28 per cent in the rest of Wales and 31 per cent in England.[6] Socially, Cardiff is a diverse city with an established history of migration due to the once prominent docklands area in Tiger Bay bringing inflows of migrants from popular port countries such as Somalia, Ireland, Spain and Portugal.[7] This inflow of migrants to port cities is common in other UK cities such as Liverpool, Bristol and London.[8] Equally, Cardiff continues to be the most ethnically diverse local authority in Wales.[9] Through regenerative efforts, the Tiger Bay area is now known as Cardiff Bay, but the wider city still retains a diverse population as it is home to 111 different nationalities.[10] Cardiff's population is also welcoming to migrant groups with 66 per cent of the population considering those born outside the country to have integrated well in the city.[11]

As the Poles in the Cardiff sample were initially motivated to migrate to the UK for economic reasons (discussed in further detail in Chapter 4), it is necessary to look a little more closely at the economy of Cardiff, highlighting the variations to the regional economy over time. Due to variations between EU regional areas and the UK local authorities, the Cardiff 'region' varies at the Nomenclature of Territorial Units for Statistics (NUTS) level and at the local authority level. At the NUTS II level, Wales is divided into two regions, between the East and the West (almost in half) due to the uneven economic development between these two regions. The Cardiff region is located on the east side of Wales at the NUTS II level and, as a result, is categorised as a Regional Competitiveness and Employment (RCE) region. The EU Cohesion policy (outlined in Chapter 1) provides different levels of funding to EU regions based on their economic performance in six-year cycles. For both the 2007–13 cycle and that for 2014–20, Cardiff has maintained its position within the RCE region. While this equates to less potential EU funding, it also highlights the strength of the economy in the NUTS II area.

At the NUTS III level, Wales is divided into twelve regions. At the NUTS III level, Cardiff is a part of the wider Cardiff and Vale of Glamorgan region. This is the base level for NUTS and there is no further specification. In contrast, there are twenty-two local authorities in Wales,

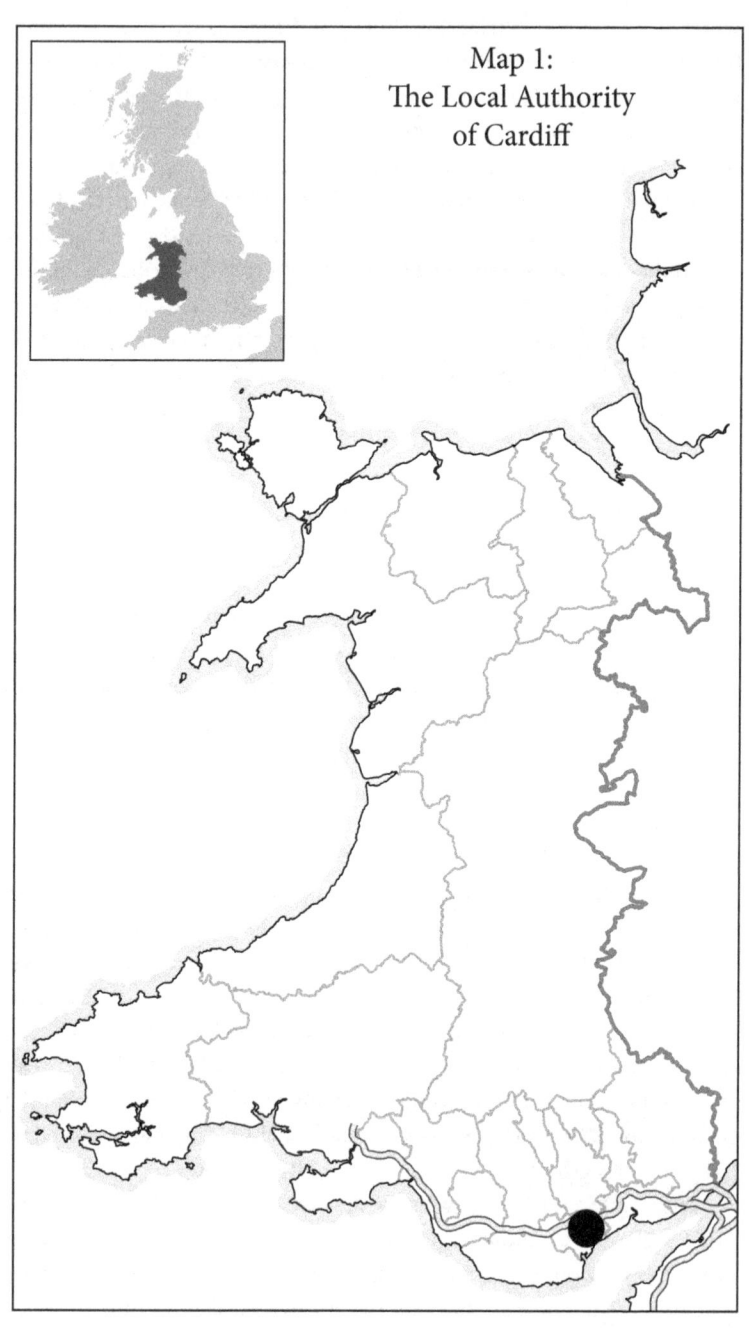

with the Cardiff region in one local authority. While the local authority data are more accurate when discussing the Cardiff region as well as the other regions in this book, because of the varying amounts of data available at the local authority level, both the NUTS data and the local authority data will be reviewed in this section. The map in Figure 1 illustrates the local authority boundaries in the country with the dot indicating where Cardiff is located.

To put the Cardiff and Vale of Glamorgan (NUTS III) level in context economically, with the NUTS II and NUTS I level, there were 724,000 people of working age residing in the NUTS II region in 2015. At the same time, the Cardiff and Vale of Glamorgan region contained 318,000 individuals of working age, or approximately 40 per cent of those residents of working age in the larger NUTS II region.[12] This highlights the concentration of working-age residents in the city region. The GDP of this region has steadily increased from 1997 to 2007, but has continued to decline in the recessionary period.[13] From 1997 to 2011, the GDP of the NUTS III region has contributed 20 per cent of the GDP of Wales.

Similar to the Wales level (NUTS I) and east Wales (NUTS II) level, the GVA (workplace-based) in Cardiff and the Vale of Glamorgan (NUTS III) steadily increased from 1997 to 2008, from 5bn (GBP) in 1997 to 9.5bn (GBP) in 2008. However, the GVA across all three NUTS categories decreased in 2009 as a result of the recession and, after rebounding in 2009 continued to increase in 2012. The Cardiff and Glamorgan GVA in 2012 was $10bn, with the Wales GVA of 47bn (GBP) at the same time.[14]

The unemployment figures for Cardiff are at the local authority level with 239,000 people of working age residing in the area in 2015.[15] Reviewing the unemployment figures for the local authority of Cardiff from 2004 to 2012, the figures have more than doubled, with 4.3 per cent unemployed in 2006 to 9.7 per cent unemployed in 2012.[16] In 2015, the percentage of those unemployed reduced to 8.4 in the local authority of Cardiff.[17]

Despite these economic figures, Cardiff is the only one of the three localities covered in this book that is not an EU Convergence region from 2007 to 2020. According to the Welsh Index of Multiple Deprivation (WIMD) Report, which measures the socio-economic well-being of the population of sub-regional areas within Wales, Cardiff contains some of the less deprived sub-regional areas in Wales.[18] However, there are sub-regional areas within Cardiff that have been found to be the most deprived areas at that level in Wales, such as Butetown. The presence of these deprived sub-regions in the relatively prominent region, points to the unequal distribution of social and economic benefits in the region. This finding has not changed considerably for the duration of the WIMD period.

Moving on to the social characteristics, the city has long been a destination for migrants. The major migrant population in Cardiff, which has historic relevance owing to the initial waves of migrants arriving in the late 1800s and early 1900s, are the Somalis. As a result, Cardiff is home to the largest British-born Somali population in the UK.[19] These migrants originally came to Cardiff to work, and sent remittance payments home.[20] It should be highlighted that they were originally not refugees, and could live and work in the UK without limitations because of Somalia's colonial status.[21] Because of war in Somalia, many of these migrants settled in Cardiff in the long term.[22] Over time, the Somalis' migration status changed; incoming migrants who are not completing a chain migration with existing family in the UK are being considered refugees.[23] It is estimated that between 4,000 and 10,000 Somalis live in Cardiff.[24] The Somalian migrant population has constructed an ethnic community in the Butetown area of Cardiff. This is the same sub-region of Cardiff that the aforementioned WIMD report described as one of the most deprived areas in Wales.[25] As demonstrated throughout the UK, this closed community has not sought to integrate with the wider population of Cardiff, mainly because of lack of employment as a result of low English-language skills.[26] A significant amount of research has been completed on this migrant group in Cardiff. In comparison, from 1 May 2004 –to 30 April 2011, over 2,500 Poles migrated to Cardiff, and little research has been conducted in this local authority on this migrant group.[27]

According to the WRS, the Poles entering Cardiff composed 65 per cent of the total A8 migrants entering Cardiff during this period. The same limitations to the WRS data outlined in Chapter 1 apply here. From the 2011 census, Polish is now the most spoken language after English and Welsh in Cardiff.[28] As a whole, these migrants exhibited similar characteristics to the Polish migrants at the UK level. It should be highlighted that there are no similarities between the type of migration completed by the Polish migrants and the Somali migrants and refugees currently living in Cardiff. To further demonstrate the differences between these migrant groups, the Poles have sought to establish an ethnic economy and live in 'transient' areas of Cardiff characterised by: walking distance to city centre, diverse population, and short-term, less expensive housing rentals. This supports their highly mobile, short-term nature. Similar to Vershanina and Meyer's study in Leicester, the proximity to a Catholic church and Catholic school were also factors in Polish ethnic economy creation in Cardiff.[29] While the Poles have an increased visibility within the Cardiff area through ethnic shops, a proven willingness to contribute to the economy of Cardiff and an established ethnic community within the city, little academic research has been conducted on this group.

Semi-urban case

Merthyr Tydfil is a part of the larger South Wales Valleys (SWV) (*Cymoedd De Cymru*). The 'Valleys' – as they are known locally – are a string of formerly industrialised valleys stretching out from rural Carmarthenshire in the west to Monmouthshire in the east, and from the towns and cities on the South Wales coast to the Heads of the Valleys region in the north. The County Borough of Merthyr extends fourteen miles south from the Brecon Beacons National Park to Trelewis. Once Wales's largest town, Merthyr Tydfil lies at the northern end of the Taff Valley.

As a strategic location in the once thriving South Wales coalfield (SWC), Merthyr has welcomed successive waves of migrant workers from many countries, including England, Ireland, Italy, Russia, Poland and France, with the majority arriving between 1901 and 1911. Many of these migrants initially entered Wales through the port in Cardiff and travelled to the Valleys for the employment opportunities that were offered. At its economic peak in 1913, the SWC employed over 230,000 people and accounted for almost one-third of the world's coal exports.[30] Coalfield employment peaked in 1920, and between the wars around half a million people left the Valleys to look for work in the New World.[31] With the closure of the mines and the exit of the SWC, the region experienced an economic depression that has led to many residents living in the Valleys and commuting to nearby cities for employment. Moving away from its industrial past, Merthyr Tydfil now has a concentration of public administration, health and social work, and IT industries.

Economically, Merthyr Tydfil exists as part of a larger NUTS region as well as a local authority, the smallest in Wales. Scaling back slightly and looking at the position of Merthyr Tydfil at the NUTS II level, it is a part of the west side of Wales, a Convergence Region within the EU's

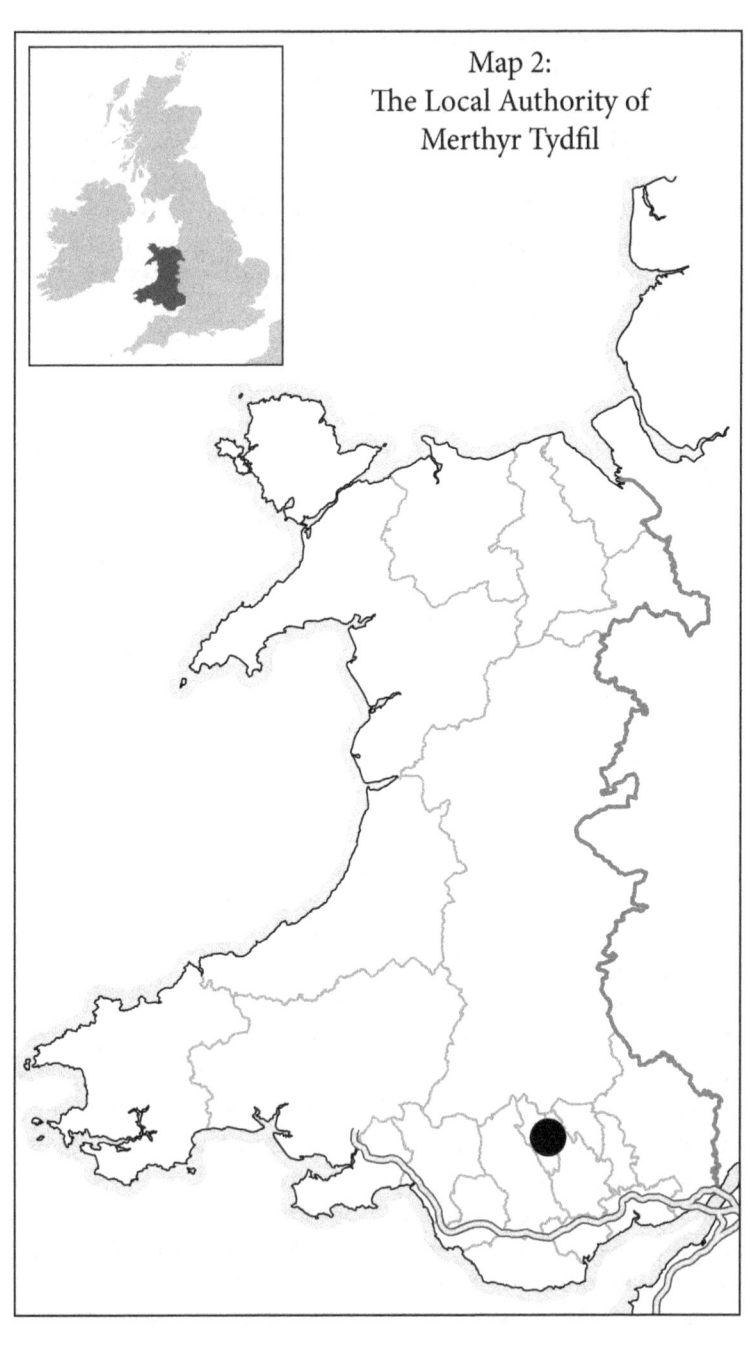

LOCATIONS AND RESEARCH METHODOLOGY

Cohesion Policy (2007–13 and 2014–20), which aims to reduce regional disparities. As a convergence region, the west side of Wales has access to the most funds from the EU as its per capita GDP is lower than 75 per cent of the EU average.[32]

At the NUTS III level, the semi-urban case is located in the Central Valleys region which includes Merthyr Tydfil and Rhonda Cynon Taff. The average qualification of a working- age resident in this NUTS III region is a qualification or some sort, with approximately 18 per cent having at least an NVQ level 4.[33] At the NUTS III level, the GDP of this region has steadily increased from 1997 to 2007 but has continued to decline in the recessionary period. From 1997 to 2011, the GDP of the NUTS III has contributed 8 per cent of the GDP of Wales.

Similar to the NUTS I and NUTS II GVA (workplace-based) figures, the Central Valleys (NUTS III) workplace GVA steadily increased from 1997 to the mid-2000s. However, unlike the NUTS I and NUTS II levels where the GVA immediately declined in the wake of the recession, the GVA in the Central Valleys declined in 2011, rebounding in 2012 with a fifteen-year high of 3.8bn (GBP) in 2012. In comparison to Cardiff and the Vale of Glamorgan GVA in 2012, the Central Valleys region's contribution is approximately 30 per cent in 2012. Interestingly, at the NUTS II level, the West Wales and Valleys region, as a Convergence region, contributes more GVA with 25.9bn (GBP) in 2012 than the East Wales, ECR region with 21bn (GBP) in the same year. Regardless of this comparison between East and West, the Central Valleys NUTS III region only contributes 3.8bn (GBP) GVA, which has only increased slightly over time, with a 2.2bn (GBP) GVA in 1997. The region is attractive to more labour-intensive industries because of the low average wage in the region in comparison to the average in Wales.

Like Cardiff, Merthyr Tydfil is considered one local authority, so data collected at this level are more reliable than the data available at the wider NUTS III level. The map in Figure 2 illustrates Merthyr Tydfil's location in South Wales. The unemployment figures for Merthyr Tydfil are at the local authority level with 38,000 people of working age residing in the area in 2015.[34] Reviewing unemployment for the local authority of Merthyr Tydfil from 2004 to 2012, the figures have more than doubled, with 5.5 per cent unemployed in 2004 and 12.5 in 2012. In 2015, the percentage of those unemployed has reduced to 7.5 in the local authority of Merthyr Tydfil.[35] According to the Welsh Index of the WIMD Report, which measures the socio-economic well-being of the population of sub-regional areas in Wales, Merthyr Tydfil contains the second most deprived amount of sub-regional areas in Wales.[36] This finding has not changed over time.

Due to the precariousness of the labour market in Merthyr, the consequently low wages and its remote location, it is surprising to see an oft-considered economically motivated migrant group locating in the region. Since EU expansion in 2004 there has been another influx of migrant workers from A8 countries into the SWV, most notably from Poland. Merthyr has become the principal destination for Polish migrants in the Valleys, with over 80 per cent of all WRS and NINo registrations made in the region between 2004 and 2011 being made by Poles. The 2011 census confirms this trend, indicating that 5.5 per cent (1,016) of all Poles in Wales are resident in Merthyr – the second highest figure of any local authority in Wales.[37] Polish is now the third most widely spoken language in Merthyr after English and Welsh, at 1.66 per cent of the resident population of 55,500 people.[38] The relative short-term intensity of this in-migration has brought a significant change to a region that has traditionally been less ethnically and racially diverse than other parts of South Wales.

Rural case
Llanelli is a sizeable, coastal town in West Wales situated in the predominantly rural region of Carmarthenshire. It is a locality that has been and continues to be in transition both socially and economically. Historically, migration to the town has largely been from England and Ireland, with labour attracted by its once sizeable steel and tinplate foundries and associated industries, though following WW2 there also arrived a small but influential Italian population. Since 2004, Llanelli has seen a significant increase in its migrant population from Poland, leading it be dubbed in some sections of the media as 'Llaneski'.[39] Simultaneously, the population of Llanelli is ageing, with the migrant population starting to balance the average age of the region.[40]

According to the WRS, approximately 4,525 A8 migrants entered Carmarthenshire from 2004 to 2011, of whom 4,300 were from Poland. Because of the relatively remote location of Llanelli and the lack of major transport links in the region, this figure could be significantly lower than the actual number of Poles entering the region through intra-UK migration. Between 2001 and 2011, Llanelli's non-UK-born population doubled from 2.1 per cent to 4.7 per cent, but what is most striking is the change in the composition of its foreign-born population. In 2001, citizens born in the countries which joined the EU in 2004 formed just 7 per cent of the overall population born outside the UK, but by 2011 this had grown to over 40 per cent.[41] Similarly to other studies on Polish migrants living in rural areas of the UK, Llanelli offers low-skilled employment opportunities and a relatively low cost of living in comparison to larger cities such as Swansea or Cardiff. The fastest-growing sectors in Llanelli are caring and personal service occupations, health and social care associate professionals, and business, media and public service professionals.[42] However, there are some remaining manufacturing opportunities that may be on their way out of the region, with the continuing decline in manufacturing and the growth of service-based industries.

This change in industries highlights the economic transition the region is undergoing. Economically, Llanelli shares a profile similar to that of Merthyr Tydfil. Both regions are located in the Convergence Region (West) in Wales and both have been adversely affected by the decline in industry and manufacturing in Wales. Focusing specifically on the case of Llanelli, it is a part of the South West Wales NUTS III region, which comprise Carmarthenshire, Pembrokeshire and Ceredigion. At the local authority level, Llanelli is a town in the local authority of Carmarthenshire. In comparison, both Merthyr Tydfil and Cardiff had representation at the local authority level; however, at the same level, Llanelli is still part of a wider region.

At the NUTS II level, there were 1.2m people of working age residing in the area in 2015, with the South West Wales region (NUTS III) containing 232,000 individuals of working age.[43] The GDP of the NUTS III region has steadily increased from 1997 to 2007 but has continued to decline in the recessionary period. From 1997 –to2011, the GDP of the NUTS III region has contributed 10 per cent of the GDP of Wales.[44]

Dissimilar to the Wales level (NUTS I) and West Wales and Valleys (NUTS II) GVA workplace-based figures (as well as the other case-study locations in this chapter), the South West Wales (NUTS III) workplace GVA has been unstable from 1997 to 2012. The fifteen-year high was in 2011, with 4.7bn workplace GVA, and the fifteen-year low was in 1998, with 2.8bn GVA. Interestingly, despite this lack of stability in workplace GVA over time, the South West Wales contribution to GVA is higher than

the Central Valleys GVA contribution that the semi-urban case is a part of. It should be highlighted again that the town of Llanelli is one part of the larger NUTS III South West Wales region. This is the same situation for both Cardiff and Merthyr Tydfil in their respective NUTS III regions. While Llanelli will have contributed to the South West Wales GVA, these figures, as well as the other economic indicators outlined in this section, cannot be solely based on the economic performance of Llanelli.

The map in Figure 3 illustrates Llanelli's location in the wider Carmarthenshire local authority in Wales. According to the 2011 census data, the population of the local authority of Carmarthenshire is 183,800 (6 per cent of the Wales population) and the largest town in the region is Llanelli, with a population of 81,245 (44 per cent of the Carmarthenshire population and 2.6 per cent of the Wales population).[45] The unemployment figures for Carmarthenshire reflect the Wales unemployment figures, which are significantly higher than the UK-level unemployment figures. There are 111,000 people of working age in the local authority of Carmarthenshire.[46] Reviewing the unemployment figures for the local authority of Carmarthenshire from 2004 to 2011, they have almost doubled, with 3.7 per cent unemployed in 2004 and 7 per cent unemployed in 2011. However, perhaps in recovery from the recession, in 2012 only 4.4 per cent were unemployed, which was last experienced in the region in 2007. In 2015, 6.3 per cent of those of working age in Carmarthenshire are unemployed.[47]

Specifically focusing on the economic performance of Llanelli in comparison to the economic performance of Carmarthenshire, Drinkwater, analysing data from the ONS, highlighted three main differences: (1) the average weekly earnings, (2) the composition of the industries and (3) the demographic shift.[48] First, from 2010 to 2013, the gross average weekly earnings of full-time workers in Llanelli were less than the earnings of workers in Carmarthenshire. However, the difference reduced over time, with Llanelli workers earning approximately £20 less in 2010 and approximately £6 less in 2013. Second, from 2001 to 2011, the characteristics of the main industries in Llanelli changed considerably, with an 8 per cent reduction in employment in manufacturing and increases in more high-skilled industries such as energy (0.6 per cent), health (1.6 per cent) and education (2 per cent). Similar fluctuations between these industries occurred in the wider Carmarthenshire region. Third, along with the ageing population in Llanelli, inward migration has had a significant impact on the demographics of the area, the economy and the culture. The 2001–11 figures for individuals living in Llanelli but born outside the EU14 was discussed above. In contrast to Carmarthenshire, in 2001 Llanelli had a lower percentage of residents born in those countries which would join the EU in 2004, but had 8 per cent more migrants from these countries living in the locality than in Carmarthenshire in 2011. Because of the lower wages in Llanelli in comparison to Carmarthenshire, and the town's physical location at the far end of the M4, one of the issues to be considered later is how migration was facilitated, especially in the period following 2004, by staffing agencies.

According to the WIMD Report, Carmarthenshire contains some of the least deprived sub-regional areas in Wales.[49] The exception to this is around the Llanelli area of Carmarthenshire.[50] This finding has not changed considerably for the duration of the WIMD period.

Review of Research Methods and Sampling

Urban – Cardiff

The research conducted for the urban case was part of a larger, primarily qualitative study of the post-2004 Polish migrants' motivations and trajectories in Cardiff. The larger study consisted of a participant observation at a local Polish restaurant, semi-structured interviews (2008 and 2011), focus groups, an analysis of Labour Force Survey data, and the dissemination of a questionnaire to the Polish community. While the research presented in this book is solely based on the semi-structured interview results, the interviews would not have been possible without the help of the Polish entrepreneurs from the restaurant acting as gatekeepers to the growing Polish community in the area.

In both 2008 and in 2011, the interview participants were initially contacted through the use of gatekeepers. Two different gatekeepers were used during the course of this study to collect interview participants. The first, used in 2008, was the Polish restaurant owner from the participant observation. The second, used in 2011, was a university researcher who was well connected to fellow Polish migrants working in a hotel in Cardiff Bay. Beyond those Poles that the gatekeepers facilitated contact with, the remaining sample was collected through snowball sampling. This was a convenient way (opportunistic sample) to increase the number of respondents, especially since the interviews were conducted in English. An interpreter was always offered to participants but was never used. All of the interviews were recorded.

The interview sample was composed of thirty-three migrants, with a total of thirty-nine interviews as a result of six migrants being interviewed twice, first in 2008 and then followed up in 2011. There were twenty interviews completed in 2008 and nineteen in 2011. The characteristics of the migrants that inform this sample are as follows:

- Polish migrants who migrated post-2004;
- average age of twenty-five years old, all were under thirty-five;
- slightly more females than males;
- high levels of education;
- mostly high level of English skills at time of interview;
- plan to stay in the UK for longer than they originally expected (initially planned to be short-term migrants but stayed longer).

The questions used in the interview focused on a range of topics including the migrants' demographic information, experience of working in the UK, use of social networks, motivations to migrate to the UK and their future plans.

The interviews conducted in 2011 were structured in a similar fashion to the 2008 interviews. However, while similar demographic questions and motivation-based questions were asked, there were also questions asked about whether the recession had an impact on the migrant's decision to stay in the destination country or on their future plans. In addition, where the migrant was re-interviewed in 2011, there was more emphasis placed on why the migrant had stayed in the UK longer than expected, and what were viewed as his/her future plans. Of the six migrants re-interviewed in 2011, four were ethnic entrepreneurs.

The interview data were analysed using NVIVO 2.0. The nodes used to code the transcripts from the interviews were generated from the data. This analysis was completed in three stages which, while time-consuming, provided precise data focused on changes in lifestyle during the migration period. The data were reviewed three times. As an example, the first review focused on coding general nodes of information that emerged from the data, such as 'migrating to the UK'. During the second review of the data, the existing nodes were narrowed down from 'migrating to the UK' to 'intra-UK migration', from 'migrating to the UK' to 'social networks', from 'migrating to the UK' to 'economic networks', and so on. The third review of the data would, as needed, narrow down these secondary nodes even further such as 'migrating to the UK-social networks-family' or 'migrating to the UK-economic-Poland unemployment'. Through this extensive review of the data the context of the original quotes was retained while focusing solely on the specific issues the migrants were discussing. The data collected in the wider study outlined at the beginning of this section supported the semi-structured interview findings, highlighted in Chapter 5.

Semi-urban – Merthyr

The research conducted in Merthyr Tydfil employed a mixed-methods approach to examine the situations and experiences of migrant workers across a number of interlinked case studies in Wales. The primary focus of this study was to understand the experiences of migrant workers who migrated from A8 and, in the later stages, A2 countries. It should be noted that this research also involved encounters with migrant workers from other localities such as: southern Europe and the Philippines. The case-study locales were not randomly selected; rather, on the basis of the analyses of available data sets, most notably WRS statistics, as well as a number of contextual interviews with key stakeholders at the local, regional and national levels, and an examination of previous studies of migrant workers in Wales.[51, 52] On the basis of this preliminary work, five case-study areas that had witnessed the arrival of significant numbers of migrant workers in recent years were selected, including the following: Merthyr Tydfil, an ex-industrial town in the SWV; Llanelli, a large town located in the south of rural Wales; the small rural towns of Llanybydder and Lampeter in West Wales; Welshpool, a medium-sized market town in mid-Wales; and a string of small rural and coastal towns in North Wales.

There were four phases to the research. First, the WRS data along with the NINo data and census data were analysed to provide more detailed temporal, spatial and social accounts of all migrant workers in the study areas. Second, fifty semi-structured interviews were conducted with various stakeholders, including representatives of national and local government, voluntary sector organisations, health boards, trade unions and migrant support groups, to provide contextual information on the impacts of economic migration in different parts of Wales and the five study areas in particular. Third, with the assistance of local gatekeepers, a face-to-face questionnaire survey of 109 migrant workers was undertaken in the study areas. The questionnaire consisted of a series of closed and open questions that sought to collect a broad range of material on migrant workers, including the migratory journey, employment, home and community relations. The face-to-face surveys that were completed with Polish migrants in the Merthyr Tydfil region were conducted in Polish. The final phase of research consisted of follow-on semi-structured interviews with a small number of migrant workers who had participated in the previous phase of fieldwork in order to explore emerging themes in more depth. Descriptive statistical analysis of the quantitative data from the survey was undertaken using Excel, with the sections of the interview schedule used to structure the analysis. Open-ended responses and the material from the semi-structured interviews were analysed using conventional qualitative techniques of coding and sorting.

The findings from the research conducted in Merthyr Tydfil used in this book are based on a combination of the fifteen open-ended questionnaire responses (2012) of the Polish migrants and the ten semi-structured interviews (2012) that were completed as part of this wider project. The specific characteristics of the Poles in the sample for the semi-urban case are as follows:

- migrants less than fifty four years of age;
- even gender distribution;
- mixed education levels;
- English-language skills poor and often problematic;
- planned to stay for a short time but stayed significantly longer than expected.

In terms of nationality, Polish migrants were the largest group, accounting for 81 per cent of all migrant workers interviewed. However, there was some variation evident across the study areas. Poles accounted for all the migrant workers surveyed in Llanelli, Llanybydder and Lampeter, and Welshpool. By contrast, Merthyr Tydfil also contained migrants from Portugal and the Philippines, and the research in the North Wales study area revealed migrants from several other central and eastern European countries. Turning to gender, women formed the majority of migrant workers in the survey, although there was again variation across the study areas, which would appear to reflect local employment opportunities. The age profile of migrants is skewed towards younger groups, with those aged twenty-five to thirty-four years representing the largest group, and around half of all migrant workers aged under thirty-five years. Lastly, in terms of educational qualifications, the majority of migrant workers possessed post-school qualifications, with 31 per cent holding degrees and 28 per cent having a vocational qualification. The findings from the open-ended questionnaires in Merthyr Tydfil will be featured in Chapter 6.

Rural – Llanelli

The qualitative study of post-2004 Polish migrants that was carried out in Llanelli from 2008 to 2011 focused on their experience in the rural location. In the initial study, the researchers were especially interested in the various channels through which the Poles had come to Wales, and in particular the role of staffing agencies in facilitating this movement. The local press had been picking up on how a particular local employment agency had opened offices in Warsaw to bring Polish workers to Llanelli. In the past, the town's metal industry had been a magnet for migrant labour, but not in significant numbers. As the scale of this employment shrank, Llanelli's rurality – set in the heart of one of Wales's largest and most historic counties – became apparent. The arrival of a quickly swelling Polish population in the town in the months after May 2004, then, came as a surprise. What had brought these people to Wales – to Llanelli? In common with the Cardiff study, the Llanelli study focused specifically on post-2004 Poles. In contrast to the other case studies, semi-structured interviews were the sole method used to collect data. Llanelli was, however, the location in which the largest number of interviews were undertaken in the South Wales region.

The semi-structured interviews were conducted in Polish by a Polish researcher who, working through a key local civil society body, developed excellent networks in the locality. Through a small number of gatekeepers, in 2008, twenty seven semi-structured interviews with Polish migrants residing in Llanelli were conducted. In addition, surveys were undertaken with 114 Polish migrants. In 2011, an additional twenty-five semi-structured interviews with Polish migrants residing in Llanelli were conducted. Again, the aim was to understand why these men and women had left Poland, the immediate triggers which had led them to decide to go and also how they had come to extend their stay. The later study did not involve follow-up interviews with any of those who had participated in the original research.

Across the two studies, and fifty-two post-2004 Polish migrants interviewed in the rural sample, the following characteristics stood out:

- a majority under forty years of age;
- even gender distribution;
- low levels of English skills;
- a majority with high school education;
- after planning to stay for a short time they stayed significantly longer than expected.

As we will discuss in more depth in Chapter 7, those who came to Llanelli did so because of the niche meat-processing and food production industry which had sprung up close to the town. These were people who came knowing that work was available, having learned this either through staffing agencies or through friends and family who had arrived earlier. It is a very different world from that just a short distance away in Cardiff and, in a different way, from Merthyr Tydfil.

Limitations to the Studies

Despite carrying out three studies at roughly the same point in time in the South Wales region, the researchers were unaware of each other's work until 2013. In spite of this, though perhaps unsurprisingly given what was known at the outset about labour migration, the questions the researchers asked their respective samples and the key topics addressed in each locale were strikingly similar.

The authors acknowledge, however, that there are limitations to conducting sociological research in each of the studies as well as to combining three independently conducted studies. Both sets of limitations will be discussed focusing on the following points:

- gatekeeper use and sample creation;
- language of the interview;
- positionality of the researcher; and
- generalising the findings from the studies.

First, each study used gatekeepers and snowballing sampling in the respective localities. While gatekeepers are frequently used by researchers to access vulnerable, or populations hard to access, the use of gatekeepers can have an impact on the sample created. For example, using a young, female gatekeeper with a large number of female friends of the same age will most likely result in a gender-biased sample that does not represent the surrounding population. In this way, the first and second points are intrinsically connected.

Second, the varied interview language used across the studies is a limitation of the research. For the case of Cardiff, the sample size increased through the use of gatekeepers and other participant referrals. An interpreter was offered to participants but was never requested, largely because of distrust within the Polish migrant community. As a result, these participants knew that the interview was conducted in English and their referrals may have been affected as a result. This could explain why the number of Poles in the Cardiff sample had a higher level of English-language skills. The samples in Llanelli and Merthyr Tydfil were collected in a similar fashion – through gatekeepers and referrals – but those facilitators knew that the interview would be carried out in Polish, which can have a similar effect on the composition of the samples from these locales.

Third, the positionality of the researcher in each study varied. For Llanelli, a research assistant who was fluent in Polish, and a fellow Pole, conducted the interviews. In Cardiff, the sole researcher, herself a migrant from outside the EU, conducted the interviews in English. While the language issue has already been addressed, from these three examples the positionality of the researchers and their ability to gather similar findings when asking similar questions in the interviews might be questioned. While it may be the case that the participants would divulge more information to a fellow Polish migrant, it could equally be the case that the participants would divulge more information to a non-Pole. In regard to the latter, Putnam notes in his work on immigrants in America that when 'in more diverse settings, Americans distrust not merely people who do not look like them, but also people who do.'[53] As a result, using a fellow Pole who is a part of the immediate community to interview Poles can be problematic owing to potential distrust amongst migrants with the same background. Alternatively, having a local interview a migrant may not produce the best results as the migrant may depict a more positive experience in order to not upset the local.

Fourth, because of the traditionally smaller sample size accessed when using qualitative methods, researchers are often cited for wrongly generalising their findings to a larger group of people by considering their sample to be representative of the wider population.[54] However, by discounting any qualitative research findings gained from relatively small samples as specific cases that cannot be generalised, the field of sociology is inherently limited. Because of this contradiction, the issue of generalising findings from qualitative studies with small samples has been the focus of extensive sociological research over time.[55, 56] The Payne and Williams (2005) research establishes various conditions which allow qualitative data that are not statistically representative, similar to the data presented here, to be generalised, with specific limits, including: time periods, estimations, specific patterns or tendencies, and subject area.[57] Owing to the variations among the samples collected in relative proximity to one another in the South Wales region, the findings from this book can be generalised to post-2004 Poles in Wales who have stayed in the UK longer than what they initially expected at the time of arrival.

Conclusion

Historians of Wales, studying the changing demographics of the nation over the last century, have typically had to rely on documentary sources to track the experiences of those who have come to the country from abroad. The migration from the countries which joined the EU in 2004 to Wales has afforded social scientists an opportunity to observe this phenomenon at closer quarters. In recent decades, migration has become one of the most highly charged and socially divisive political issues – capable, as in the case of the referendum on UK membership of the EU, of almost determining the political direction of a nation. It remains, nevertheless, a fundamentally human story, one about how people's aspirations and actions are wrapped up in a decision to seek work abroad. As we will spell out in later chapters, they rarely start with the intention of creating new lives and homes in these distant places, but this is what so often comes to pass. It is also a story which connects populations, not least those already resident in the place which comes to receive these new arrivals from other nations. Wales is not one of the UK's natural migration hotspots. The scale of the movement means that it is unlikely Wales will be changed in anything approaching the ways in which other centres have been transformed, over time, by successive waves of migration. For all that, it has been changed, and places across the country where the memory of earlier migrations had slipped have found themselves coming to terms with comparatively substantial populations from CEE member states. The localities which are featured in this book are part of a broader UK experience, where these migrants, in contrast to any previous mass migration, have come to settle in all corners of the country. Our studies are designed to shed light on the encounters of those who have arrived since 2004 and to make sense of this larger human experience at this key moment in European history.

PART II

4

Why Migrate? Motivations and Migrant Decision-Making

Introduction

As a public issue migration often comes down to numbers. It is a subject which the media, public and politicians alike routinely quantify. Politicians, chasing immigration targets, are charged with 'playing the numbers game'. Government agencies marshal considerable resources to create and analyse data on how many foreign nationals are entering the national territory, producing regular digests of the ebb and flow of human traffic across national borders. How many people are moving into 'our country'? How long will they stay? Social scientists are regularly called on to help understand the financial consequences of international migration. What, they are asked, are the costs of immigration for public services in the localities into which migrants move? For example, do migrants pay their 'fair share' of taxes while living abroad?

The question of what compels people to leave their home country to move abroad is also often couched in similarly quantitative terms, and, more specifically, in monetary value. From the pejorative 'benefit tourists' to the more neutral 'economic migrants', citizens of CEE states which have joined the EU since 2004 have been cast as self-seeking economic actors using the freedom of movement afforded by EU citizenship to secure their fortunes abroad. In this way, like international migration more broadly, intra-EU migration is generally understood to be a consequence of 'push' and 'pull' factors rooted in the differential conditions of national labour markets. People will move because it is worth the financial risk, the personal travails and the hardship.

In this chapter, we will show there is plenty of evidence that the lure of better economic prospects is indeed a driver of the migration we have seen into the UK since 2004. However, we also highlight that migration is sponsored by less financially centred concerns. That some migrants, especially younger and often higher-skilled migrants, travel abroad to develop their reserves of cultural capital is well established. Much less, however, has been written on migration as an aspirational strategy among other categories of migrants from the post-2004 accession countries. In what follows, we want to show that the aims are more modest, but no less life-changing for the individuals concerned.

A Culture of Migration?

In the UK, immigration has, since the late 1990s, grown to become one of the major political issues of our time. It is rarely far from the headlines. As debates about the EU regularly demonstrate, it is now integral to our political culture. To begin, we want to look at this subject from a different angle, from the perspective of a country in which the exit of citizens to live and work abroad is a historic strand of the national story.

With hindsight, we know that the largest single wave of migration which the UK has witnessed was not expected. The UK government minister most closely associated with policy in this area at the time, Tony McNulty, subsequently admitted that the government had 'no notion really about how many would come' from the countries which acceded to the EU in 2004.[1] Studies commissioned by the Home Office, while stressing a number of caveats, predicted that the numbers were likely to be relatively small, in the region of 5,000 to 13,000 annually until 2010. Instead, within three years, by June 2007, just over 400,000 Polish nationals alone had made applications to work in the UK under WRS. Estimates suggest the *unofficial* number from the new CEE member states reached nearly one million migrants by end of 2007.[2]

Why was it that the UK became the principal destination for migrants from the CEE member states? On one level, we can say this happened because so few EU states were willing to openly allow the free movement of EU citizens in the wake of enlargement in 2004. The UK was the largest and most flexible labour market open to those seeking to take advantage of the newly acquired right of freedom of movement for EU citizens. Besides the UK, only the Republic of Ireland and Sweden did not impose the temporary restrictions on labour mobility introduced in other 'old' EU member states. Public opinion in other EU member states cast a long shadow over how governments viewed the prospect of increased migration from CEE states. In France, the Polish plumber became a bogeyman in the minds of a substantial section of the electorate, symbolising an expected wave of low-wage labour that swept into the country. In Germany, which until 2004 accounted for approximately a third of all Poles living outside their national territory, surveys showed that an overwhelming majority of citizens were anxious about the impact of increased migration from the accession countries on employment and wages.

Poland is a country in which the migration of its citizens has been a recurring theme of its modern history. At the back end of the nineteenth and the early twentieth century, an estimated 1.5 million Poles emigrated from central Europe to the USA. In their classic study titled 'The Polish Peasant in Europe and America', Thomas and Znaniecki describe features resonant of the 'culture of migration' mapped by later scholars. In the late nineteenth century, they argue, limiting the exodus of Poles, especially in the eastern border territories adjacent to Russia, was critical to the 'national struggle for preservation'.[3] By the opening decades of the twentieth century, international migration had been considerable for an extended period, and leaving Poland to work abroad, whether in neighbouring Germany or in the USA, had come to be seen as 'normal' in some places. Throughout the last century, subsequent waves of Poles arrived in the USA in the wake of World War 2 and following the dramatic political changes in central and eastern Europe at the end of the 1980s.[4]

Over the last decade the departure of so many Poles to countries in western Europe, particularly to the UK, has been reported widely in the media in Poland. Moreover, where once it was hundreds of letters written by migrants living in the USA to family back in Poland which provided the evidence which informed 'The Polish Peasant', today the experience of migration and the stories of migrants has become the stuff of television documentaries, soaps and dramas as well as a stimulus for literature.[5] As a mass phenomenon, post-2004 migration has become part of popular culture. When the big-budget Polish soap, *Londyńczycy* (Londoners), was broadcast in 2008 advertising hoardings carried the strapline 'Wielka Brytania, Wielkie Nadzieje' ('Great Britain, Great Expectations').

We want to argue that this recent migration needs to be viewed as the result of a particular set of economic, political and social circumstances. Here, we follow de Haas's contention that international migration should be 'understood as a constituent part of broader development and change' rather than a response to economic, and specifically earnings, differentials between the home and destination countries.[6] Prior to accession in 2004, Poland had spent the preceding decade undergoing radical economic restructuring, leading to fundamental changes in its labour market. The workforce had gone from being almost wholly employed within the public sector to, by 2004, nearly 70 per cent working in the private sector.[7] While in the years immediately preceding accession Poland experienced a temporary economic slowdown, Polish GDP per capita had grown from just over 30 per cent in 1992 of the then EU-15 average to 43 per cent by 2003.[8] Indeed, over the decade prior to accession, Poland had the fastest-growing economy of the CEE countries which joined the EU in 2004. In 1994, its government applied to join the EU, became a signatory to the OECD and, in 1999, a member of NATO – developments which, collectively, cemented the country's transition from state-planned to free market liberal democracy.

This economic transformation was also underpinned by an accompanying change in political culture. In the case of European integration, the state public diplomacy machinery mobilised to get citizens' endorsement of EU membership, including spelling out the economic benefits for the country.[9] Others have argued, too, that an important element of the process of Europeanisation was the linking of Polish national interests – and the specific interests of constituent groups of Polish workers and citizens – and the country's accession to the EU.[10] Cultural change was arguably even more advanced in the development of a consumer culture. Sociologists have demonstrated how, following the collapse of communism, consumer attitudes changed rapidly, and this was most notably evident in citizens' expectations about their right to exercise choice.[11] In Poland, the Czech Republic and Hungary, lending to households increased by 25 per cent annually between 1997 and 2001.[12] Kurczewski writes of the role of the mass media in stimulating the rapidly evolving consumerist desires of Poland:

> the postcommunist societies from Vladivostok to Warsaw tune in every evening to a culture that is the culture of capitalist societies, regardless of their strata or variants. To more than one person in the countryside,

the heroes of 'Dynasty' are closer than the heroes of the Warsaw cultural or political scene.[13]

Others have analysed the role of a flourishing yet still fledgling advertising industry in Poland at the back end of the 1990s, pointing to how it served to 'educate and cultivate the new Polish consumer into being'.[14]

Desires nevertheless need to be capable of being sated. Sharp national economic growth did not translate into rising standards of living across the board. Inequalities in household income increased markedly in the decade before accession. Unemployment grew, especially in the agricultural and industrial sectors in which the state had been so dominant, with the gap in the employment rate between Poland and the EU-15 average increasing fivefold in the space of just five years from the launch of the country's national integration strategy in 1997. Social scientists have documented the impact of Poland's transition to post-communism in rural Poland, especially the impact of the movement away from state-managed agricultural production on unemployment in these regions of the country. Buchowski goes further, detailing how these economic changes also had a devastating impact on people's sense of belonging both to their local community and their relationship with the wider state.[15] In a similar vein, Rakowski's vivid account of citizens of 'degraded communities', emptied by the departure of state industrial and agricultural production during the economic transition of the 1990s, eking out a living in the face of overwhelming odds, highlights the profound and complex economic and social changes experienced across Poland.[16] As others have noted, in this context international migration offers individuals an opportunity not only to find work but also a mechanism to lever back an element of personal autonomy which had been peeled away by larger political and social shifts.[17]

Long-term unemployment became particularly pronounced. Younger sections of the population fared among the worst, with unemployment among this group rising to 40 per cent.[18] The prospect, too, of EU membership appeared to be a concern for a substantial number of Poles; in 2003, just over a third of Poles expected membership to result in greater losses than gains for them personally.

If concerns about rising prices was one of the underlying causes of this anxiety, the ability to work and live abroad was identified as the major benefit of EU membership. The legacy of the changes Poland had experienced since the political reforms of the 1980s, but most especially those which characterised the decade of economic transition prior to accession, was that the right of freedom of movement became, we suggest, a channel for accessing the means for a way of living not possible at home. Studies have illustrated how fundamentally cultural attitudes and citizens' expectations changed in Poland during this period. Survey work on high school students in Poland revealed that the proportion declaring one of their principal objectives to be to achieve a 'high professional status and to enjoy a career' jumped from 19 per cent in 1994 to 31 per cent in 2003.[19] Others have argued that, among this section of the population, a key cultural factor in understanding pro-migration attitudes is the 'consumerist aspirations integrated into their lifestyle to which this generation is strongly attached'.[20] We will argue below that these aspirations were far from limited to younger Poles.

Using data from the South Wales region, when we carried out the initial round of fieldwork in 2008, we specifically wanted to learn more about the ways in which attitudes to moving abroad for work were informed by the wider backdrop – of political and legislative change – at the moment of accession in 2004. In contrast to the rhetoric among the political class about European 'reunification', for example, was accession greeted as delivering more prosaic benefits in the form of freedom of movement? How, we wanted to know, were decisions about moving abroad shaped by the knowledge that others – many in positions similar to their own – were also reviewing this option or, indeed, had already left?

One of the first matters we want to investigate, therefore, is to ask how the individuals who participated in our studies were making decisions about their own mobility at a time when others – many others – were similarly doing so. Within the wider social science literature, there is a rich vein of work on 'cultures of migration'. Put simply, the essence of these studies is that the likelihood of an individual making the decision to migrate is greater in a locality in which there exists a historical pattern of people leaving to find work elsewhere, including crossing national boundaries. Where migration is part of the social and cultural fabric of a place, those growing up will very likely have to consider whether they will follow those who have laid down the trail, who will assist with the logistics as well as, importantly, provide the encouragement to move.

'Migrants follow pathways to their destinations', Cohen and Sirkeci put it, 'that were charted over the years with the input of earlier movers.'[21]

In his own work on migration from Oaxaca, Mexico to the USA, Cohen describes the 'culture of migration' as comprising three elements.[22] Firstly, it is historic. In Oaxaca, it stretches back to the early twentieth century. Secondly, he argues that the decision to migrate is rooted in individuals' 'everyday experiences'.[23] That is to say, whether or not a person makes the decision to leave is typically informed by local sets of cultural expectations and social practices and negotiated with family, friends and others within their social networks. The household, Cohen – and others (see Massey[24]) – contests is central to understanding migration.[25] People seek work abroad to support families they leave behind, but their move is usually not possible without having been sanctioned and supported by kin and other close contacts who remain. The final constituent element of these local 'cultures of migration' is that mobility is accepted as one of the principal ways in which an individual (and a household) can ameliorate their economic fortunes.

Just as we show in this book the limitations of speaking of 'Polish migrants' as if they represent one homogeneous ethnic population, equally it would be a grave analytical error to reify the notion of a singular 'Polish migration culture'. Numerous studies have underlined how local and regional histories, especially of international migration, labour market conditions and demographics, can create a particular cultural habitus in which inhabitants experience migration and, ultimately, whether or not they become migrants. At one level, researchers have pointed to similar discourses on migration across, for example, small-town locations in different parts of Poland, even though these were framed through the prism of the stories told by and to local inhabitants. Elrick and Brinkmeier, for example, account for differences in the volume of migration flows between two towns, in the west and east of Poland respectively, as due in large part to corresponding differences in the historical experience of migration from both places.[26] As a consequence, they contend, in the town in Silesia, in western Poland, with a long history of moving abroad for work to neighbouring Germany, Poland's accession to the EU in 2004 acted as catalyst for migration, after which personal knowledge of people who had moved abroad became increasingly normal. White, by contrast, takes care not to overplay the notion of unique place-bound migration cultures.[27, 28] Drawing on her extensive experience of researching localities with high volumes of international migration, White describes stories carried from abroad by those who have already left as 'social remittances' which can be powerful agents of cultural change in localities of origin, and explores how these are woven into regional and local norms about migration. She suggests, however, that it may be more useful to look at migration 'sub-cultures' among occupational or socio-economic groups. In our research, perhaps the most striking case of a local 'culture of migration' was the town of Zychlin. Located in almost the dead centre in Poland, approximately 50 km from Lodz and 110 km from Warsaw, it is a town with just over 12,000 inhabitants. It seems likely that the same sense of uncertainty which White describes as hanging over other small towns across Poland, was also a factor in Zychlin.[29] As we explore at various points throughout this book, the insertion of external parties, principally recruitment agencies, into this locality – a factor which Elrick and Brinkmeier also note as relevant elsewhere in Poland – played an important role in bringing Polish labour to Wales.[30] Zychlin is located within the Lodz 'Special Economic Zone', akin to the enterprise zones found across the UK. Importantly, from the perspective of agencies seeking to source labour for work in the UK, the agri-food sector is a significant employer within the region and therefore workers might be attracted by the prospect of similar work for higher wages overseas.

People do still require this 'stimulus' that compels them to migrate. They are leaving family and friends, uprooting their lives to leave for another country, albeit consoling themselves that they would be going only for a short time abroad. For all that low-cost airlines have made it cheaper and easier to be internationally mobile, and that technology has enabled people to maintain relationships over distance, international migration remains a major life decision. One man living in Llanelli spoke especially openly about difficulties which most others shared: 'every time when a person goes somewhere unknown, there are bound to be fears because you never know what to expect. Especially, that it isn't 20 or 100 km from home. It is a completely new reality, new world, new people and there is the language barrier' (Wicek, M).

Often, the impetus to move came from migrants' personal social networks. All those interviewed in the course of the Llanelli and Cardiff studies in 2008/9 and 2010/11 knew people who had lived away or were currently working outside Poland. They were repeatedly exposed to information about migration, about the opportunities – and less so – the challenges of working abroad. In line with the literature on localised 'cultures of migration', we found examples of small towns in Poland where there had, in a short space of time, emerged a collective experience of moving to the UK, and to Wales in particular.[31] Thus, among those who had been the pioneers of the move to West Wales were individuals who had come from Zychlin. Zychlin became the base for a recruitment agency tasked with securing workers for the food processing industry in Carmarthenshire. As this presence became established in the town, it also became a hub for migrants from further afield. One man from the surrounding region told us: 'so everyone went. They laugh that in Zychlin only toddlers and pensioners remained – that there's nobody else. As I'm saying, that's quite a dense gathering of people and they often feel as if they were transferred' (Alfons, M).

This openness to migration was not, however, limited to particular localities. Among those we interviewed in Llanelli participants told us of exchanges with friends, family and contacts who had raised with them the prospect of moving abroad for work. These were men and women who, in most cases, had no prior experience of working outside Poland, but who, after their country's accession to the EU, became swept up in conversations about the money to be made abroad, about the possibilities of turning their fortunes round. Anastazja, a woman who had moved from a small town in north-eastern Poland, not far from the border with Lithuania, to join her daughter already living in Llanelli, spoke to us about her memories of living through the changes leading up to accession. She could, she said, 'remember that everybody's been discussing the opening of the borders – I've never even thought about it ... that I would go abroad.' We heard repeatedly how they were actively encouraged to consider moving abroad. Another woman from a large town in northern Poland, who had been living in Wales since 2009, told us that she 'made the decision because my parents insisted we would give it a go, and also I missed them not being in Poland, so made that decision. Quite suddenly actually. My husband had wanted to come much earlier. I stalled because of the house and my work' (Rachela, F). Others spoke similarly of parents who gave them the nudge to leave the country. Rahel, who had been living in Wales for just over five years when we interviewed her in 2009, had moved from her home in central Poland with her boyfriend, now her husband and father to their two children born in the UK. Travelling with her partner certainly helped, she explained, to remove some of her concerns. It was, however, the encouragement from her parents which really gave her the strength to make the move: they 'simply said themselves that it would be worth going and trying something new.'

When we initially analysed the qualitative data from the first round of data collection, one recurring theme which stood out was how quickly migrants appeared to have made the decision to leave for work in the UK. In practice, as we will comment on further below, they were enabled to move quickly *once* the decision to leave was made. On closer inspection, however, the interviews highlighted that while the gap between what participants recalled as the moment when they made their decision and their departure was often short, they had usually been considering this matter for some time. As scholars such as Massey and Cohen in the USA have noted about Mexican migration, though, in the end, an act undertaken by individuals, it was nevertheless a collective or social action carried out with the blessing, support and encouragement of others.[32, 33] Similarly, when we undertook the follow-up study, we heard account after account of people who had made the decision to leave following the active support and encouragement of those within their personal social networks. Decisions which appeared to have come 'out of the blue' rarely did. Acts which looked, on initial inspection, opportunistic, needed to be viewed through a longer temporal lens.

In line with the 'culture of migration' framework, what, too, became more evident after a more fine grained inspection of the data was that the decision to move abroad had become a widely accepted means of improving an individual's or household's, financial well-being. For those we interviewed in Llanelli, and, in contrast, to the better-educated, and usually younger migrants found in Cardiff, migration came to be seen by people with limited options to reduce debts or even just to provide income as a viable way to improving one's lot. As one man remarked in 2008, 'in some time the prices [in Poland] will eventually fall and the level of life as well ... for this moment the differences are very big and that's why the migration is so big. It's a pursuit of the better.'

It is this notion of migration as a 'pursuit of the better' which we will explore in the next section. As White has noted, migration as a 'livelihood strategy' is an evaluative frame used more commonly to study internal migration as well as migration to Europe from other continents, most usually Africa and Asia. It is deployed less often to analyse migration *between* European countries.[34] We want to show that a migrant's desire to 'do better' does not translate only into hard currency – better wages, money to save or spend back in Poland – but also into terms which might not appear to have a place in our understanding of contemporary intra-EU migration, such as a 'normal life'[35] and 'dignity'.[36]

Money, Motives and Migration

In the period following Poland's accession to the EU in 2004, media reports left little doubt that the principal driver of the unexpectedly rapid and large increase in the number of Polish migrants arriving in the UK was the two countries' divergent economic circumstances. As a headline in the *Daily Telegraph* put it in January 2005: 'It's the economy, *glupi*' (the Polish word for 'stupid').[37] 'Experience suggests', the *Telegraph* added, 'that migrant workers are just that: they come here to work and nothing more.'[38] Higher wages and plentiful opportunities to earn were widely understood to be the catalyst for the migration from the new EU member states. For as long as these differences remain, the *Daily Mail* told its readers, the UK will be a 'magnet for all those who cannot find work or for whom wages are too low'.[39]

In the social sciences, too, there is a long-established tradition of viewing migrants as rational economic actors. At a micro level, differences in wages and income are among the classic 'push' factors which explain international migration. People move to earn more income abroad, often to repatriate earnings to household members in their country of origin. When such differences reduce or the conditions between countries begins to equalise, the level of movement between these places will fall. In the UK, this perspective underlies the speculation about what the impact would be of the 2008/9 financial crisis on Polish migrants in the UK. It is a view which has come to be increasingly discredited by more recent scholars. As Massey et al. note in one of the most authoritative studies in the field, labour market differentials are a necessary condition for international migration to happen, but they are not a *sufficient* factor for people to leave their home nations.[40]

On the surface, our data, especially in Cardiff and Llanelli, appear to lend support to the rational actor approach. When asked about their motives for moving, participants were likely to immediately cite financial factors as the main reason for their decision to leave Poland for work in the UK. However, there were some who spoke of coming to Wales because they wanted to sample life in a different setting, or who made it clear that money was not their motivation. Piotr (M), for example, is a young man in his late twenties who had moved to Wales, giving up a job in his native Warsaw to follow his partner abroad. He was insistent he had not been 'pushed' by financial considerations. For him, the decision 'wasn't dictated by debts, or that I didn't earn enough or . . . I don't know, that I was being chased by a bailiff . . . No. It was more for an adventure.' In Llanelli, certainly, but also in Cardiff, such views were not widely held.

Migrants in Llanelli appeared to be generally propelled by more immediate priorities. Agnieska (F), who had been living in the town for over three years, and had arrived not long after Poland joined the EU, said that his motivation for moving was he 'only wanted to see what it would be like here. I wanted to see how much one was able to earn here, and how much I could bring back with me to Poland.' Others spoke of the need to raise money quickly to meet the spiralling costs of debt repayments in Poland. We have no way of knowing how widespread this particular problem was as only a few mentioned explicitly the burden of loans they were struggling to manage, though in the literature on post-2004 intra-EU migration there are reports elsewhere of this having a wider resonance.[41] Some commented on using migration as means of helping to stay afloat under the weight of personal debts and also that of other family members. Melania, a woman in her mid-twenties who had been living in Wales with her young family for over two years, had moved from south-western Poland along with nearly a dozen other women. In her case, she had to try to get herself clear of financial worries before moving on with her life. 'I was saving', she told us, 'for paying off the debts: my own, my ex-husband's and my parents'.' Another was quite explicit about why she had wound up in Wales: 'I think that in situations where people go abroad and they make money, they earn for many different things. Nobody came here for their own pleasure. Nobody was born and thought "Oh, in some and some years I'll go to Llanelli". They've been usually compelled by their life' (Tamary, F). As we have already noted, we know, too, that in making the decision to leave individuals will use information about the cost of living in Wales gleaned from their personal networks and which allows them to make cost-benefit calculations. That earning more money is a primary motive for migration, then, is not in doubt.

Better wages, some disposable income or the ability to remit surplus earnings to family back in Poland, are, however, far from the only, or perhaps even the primary motivations for migration. Among those we interviewed in Llanelli, in particular, a much more evident pattern within our data was of participants reporting that they turned to migration because they were weary of scraping by on the wages they were earning, typically from more than one job. Money was a source of domestic friction. Life in Poland was a grind, we were told repeatedly, and migration offered an opportunity to escape from the constant chasing and checking of money. Agata (F), a mother of two from central Poland, who in 2010 had been living in Llanelli for three years, explained how she and her husband 'kept having quarrels . . . because basically he didn't earn enough'. Moving to Wales, difficult as she found the prospect, was the solution: 'I was fed up with this constant counting of the money. There wasn't money for this, for that – constant restrictions. How long can one keep cutting down on everything?' In one interview after another, participants similarly explained their frustrations with life in Poland. During an interview over a coffee in a participant's home, Matylda, who had moved from a small town in central Poland, shortly to be joined by her husband and young son, explained how 'in Poland, the people can't afford this. At least in the region I come from, what I can observe. So, everyone shuts themselves off at home. "God save me from people dropping in for a cuppa, because it will cost me money." I used to see it this way!'

These accounts reflected the experiences of many of those we interviewed, and they illustrate the need for caution in speaking broadly of labour migrants being 'pushed' out of their countries by economic circumstances. Most spoke of the challenges of making ends meet in Poland on the wages they earned, but we did not come across any circumstances in which individuals could be described as having little choice but to seek better fortunes abroad.

To raise a point we will pursue further below, our data suggest these moves need to be understood as being born more from aspiration than desperation. 'They call the Poles who come here to work, they call them migrants,' one man said, 'but we've come here "looking for bread", for a better life, haven't we?' (Wicus, M). A man, in his mid-40s and from a town on Poland's Baltic coast, said that his motivation for leaving his home and uprooting his family had been to earn 'better money' but, as with so many others to whom we spoke, the aim was to achieve a more stable and enjoyable lifestyle:

> I wanted to have ... a better life than we had in Poland, a more relaxed one, to be able to make ends meet ... Because, in Poland, I earned some money, so did my wife, but to do anything, to buy things one needed, one had to take credit, or a loan, or the like, because it never was enough. (Wicek, M)

For most of the participants in the case studies in Wales, the UK promised income and employment opportunities which would have been unimaginable at home. Many appeared to have been prepared to make their move on the basis that they could always return if it did not work out for them abroad. They had clearly compared their earnings in sterling with what they could expect to be paid at home, and they were keen to take advantage of the relative strength of sterling against the Zloty. It was evident, too, they had also tried to take account of their in-country expenses, such as rent, food and transport costs, to estimate the scale of the financial returns. The cost/benefit calculations on which they moved was not always based on the most accurate information, even through their personal networks, and it was evident that some were enticed by exaggerated accounts of how much could be earned.

Across the interviews, however, the data show that it was frustration with how, money enabled them *to live* at home which drove the migrants abroad. Rather than reinforcing the neo-classical 'push-and-pull' models of international migration, our data reflect more the arguments of de Haas that migration needs to be understood as an 'intrinsic part of processes of human development'.[42] Even if the need for a short term injection of money was a factor for some, the research reveals that migration was more widely pursued as a strategy for achieving an improvement in *how* they lived by changing *where* they lived.

Social scientists often differentiate between 'lifestyle' and 'labour' migrants. As one sums up the difference, the former is 'not motivated by economic or political factors'.[43] Put a different way, these individuals are unlikely to have been 'pushed' from their home country. For Benson and O'Reilly, in another key study, the term 'lifestyle migrants' refers to 'relatively affluent individuals of all ages, moving either part-time or full-time to places that, for various reasons, signify, for the migrant, a better quality of life'.[44] 'Labour' or 'economic' migrants, by contrast, are defined by their systematic pursuit of work and financial rewards which are greater than those they will receive in their home nation. In practice, as we have found, the distinction between 'lifestyle' and 'labour' migration is less clear-cut.

We repeatedly encountered individuals who talked about their futures, about 'ambitions', even 'dreams'. Sometimes, these aspirations were unspecified, but evidently material in some form. At times, they perhaps only came to light after participants had moved abroad. 'In Poland', a man in his late fifties told us, 'we live in a "crazy way" … here, if one works, one can plan everything, and achieve the aim one wants to achieve, sooner or later. One can put money aside here, buy things one dreams to have, can't they?' (Mosze, M). In other cases, participants came to help them fulfil grander plans. In an interview in 2010, for example, Marcelina, who travelled with her husband from Warsaw and had been living in Wales for over four years, told us how 'we had always dreamt to have our own house.' We asked if the move to Wales was intended to further that goal: 'Yes, we did have dreams like this, and we still do; that, in the future, we will manage to earn enough to have a place of our own, I mean to build our own house.' The decision was undoubtedly difficult for some, as we found, but their desire to effect more leverage over their lives, and for family members too, was strong. 'It is a terrible thing to leave your country', one mother of two children commented in 2010, 'because of such circumstances so that your child could have a better education and better chances for future' (Marian, F). Others made similar statements – that the move was as much about others' as their own plans: 'The main reason? It was simply the fact that I was afraid of the future for my children. There was no future there' (Marcely, M).

A major study in Poland concluded, just four years after accession in 2004, that 'emigration is not an escape from "Polish hopelessness". It rather shows that Poles take the opportunity to fulfil their aspirations also outside the country,'[45] Our research shows, however, a clear pattern that many left because they found the avenues for achieving their ambitions in Poland thwarted by domestic structural, economic and social conditions. We will return to this in subsequent chapters, but it is worth noting at this stage that migrants come here to work, but it is not labour which keeps them abroad, which leads a large number to contemplate longer, even permanent stays in the UK.

Making Migration Happen – Networks and Agencies

Migration is rarely, if ever, an individual decision or act. As the discussion above has already indicated, it is better conceptualised as an instance of collective action, where a range of parties – directly and indirectly – create the conditions for migration. In this final section of the chapter we turn to look at the role of two structures which play a critical role in facilitating migration: social networks and staffing agencies. Social networks have been one of the main objects of research on post-2004 Polish migration.[46, 47] Functionally, they are conduits for vital information about opportunities for work abroad, but, more than this, it is through these channels that individuals are often actively encouraged by friends and family to make the move abroad. Commercial staffing agencies are a very different matter. They are brokers and beneficiaries of international migration. Broadly, where social capital is the currency of social networks, staffing agencies work on hard capital to make migration happen. Since 2004, their role in facilitating migration has become the focus of growing public and scholarly interest. In this final section of the chapter we examine how both structures have been essential in transferring and transplanting migrants from Poland to Wales.

Social networks

Social network use by post-2004 Polish migrants to the UK has led to an unusual distribution of Poles across all parts of the UK. London and the surrounding areas have been the principal magnets for migrants coming to the UK, but research has shown how places with no previous history of international migration, such as the south-west of England and Northern Ireland, attracted significant numbers of post-2004 migrants from Poland and the other new CEE member states.[48] Rural areas, too, saw sizeable immigration, such as in the Highlands of Scotland, the East of England and West Wales. Trevena was one of the first scholars to note that rural localities can create unique challenges for migrants, particularly owing to the nature of local labour markets, which can be seasonal and limited in scope.[49] For example, the food production industry has been one important source of labour for post-2004 Polish migrants and a determinant for their movement to rural parts of the UK, a phenomenon not unlike the situation in parts of Wales.[50] More recently, Trevena, McGhee and Heath highlight how the internal mobility of international migrants is not driven by location *per se* but rather by the availability of work and accommodation.[51] As highlighted by Massey et al.'s work, these are resources often provided, at least initially, by migrants' social networks.[52]

In what ways do migrant social networks increase the probability of international migration? There is now a good deal of theoretical and empirical work on the influence of social networks on international migration, beginning with the early works of Massey et al. and Boyd.[53, 54] As Haug has shown in reviewing this work, studies have pointed to how social networks may influence whether or not people migrate, the destinations to which they move and the type of migration (whether permanent or circular).[55] Still, as Ryan has suggested, there remain important aspects of the bearing of social networks on migration that we do not sufficiently understand.[56]

As we have already noted above, network contacts can act as catalysts for migration, stimulating interest in the prospect of work abroad and offering reassurances of in-country assistance. In almost all of the cases of participants interviewed across the South Wales region, we found a pattern of friends, associates or family members providing the initial suggestion of moving to Wales. A young woman, a number of whose family members had already been living in Llanelli, told us how 'we made the decision because my parents insisted we would give it a go, and also I missed them not being in Poland, so made that decision' (Melania, F). Another woman, who came with her husband, told us how it was her cousin, already living in Llanelli, who was 'the one to gives us the idea [to migrate]' (Julta, F). As we have noted previously, it was clear that network contacts had been telling friends and family about how much they were earning and how much they, in turn, could expect. Luiza, a mother of four children, had moved to Wales to get some quick money after her husband, the principal breadwinner, lost his job through illness. Originally from a small town near Poznan, she explained how her sister-in-law had been encouraging her to join her in Wales: 'she said there was money to earn, bigger money. So I came here because of her' (Luiza, F).

In other instances, it was friends who were seeking to draw them abroad. In some cases, it was possible to see the influence of friendship groups on members: 'I knew another friend and a female friend with children ... [So, there was a group of people, wasn't there?] It was a large group, at least eleven people. [Was it a group, because all the people were from ?] Yes, they were all from my town' (Melania, F).

We found, however, that in many cases, networks do not necessarily act in concert to support a decision to migrate. In few cases, for example, did we find evidence that individuals left with the full endorsement of family. Thus personal networks, including kin, can very often be a barrier which needs to be cleared, in one way or another, before migrating. Our data lend support to the findings of other researchers that gender is an important variable. Women who would be left behind were likely to tolerate a male partners' desire to seek life abroad, perhaps with assurances that either they would return shortly or that they would bring them across at a later point. This pattern of migration where males migrate first and later send for women is common among authorised migrant groups. On the other hand, for women who were proposing to leave families behind to work abroad temporarily, or were the driving force in making the decision, the matter could often generate conflict, in particular with their partners. One woman, for example, whose sister-in-law had been pressuring her to come abroad, said that her husband was deeply unhappy that she was going without him: 'the day I was leaving (Poland), that day was terrible. He just stopped talking and left the house' (Katja, F). Mieczyslawa, a mother of three boys who had been living in Wales for over four years after leaving Warsaw, told us of the conflict with her husband which was the prelude to her decision to leave: 'when he [her husband] learned about it, when I told him that I was going, and it was final – I said: "I'm fed up with this vegetating", then he seemed to be offended a bit: "Why her not me?"' In the end, in those we interviewed, the wish or need to improve their personal circumstances outweighed these pressures. Thus, as one woman told us: 'I decided and I said to my husband – you are either going with me or you are staying on your own, so he didn't have a choice' (Renata, F).

Beyond the support of kinship networks, migrants also encountered other issues when migrating. In the case of a good number of the men and women who had moved to the case-study locations, there are risks associated with making their way in a place in which they had, at best, a limited knowledge of English. This was even the case in Cardiff, where the sample had a high level of English-language skills. These skills were originally untested with native English-language-speakers, creating anxiety for the migrants when initially arriving. The presence of network contacts already embedded in the destination helps to alleviate a source of anxiety and reduce a potential barrier to migration. More generally, too, the presence of individuals in the destination location with whom the prospective migrant has social ties provides reassurance that there will be a support structure in place on which they can draw, including, most basically, for company and security. Patterns observed in other contexts, such as in North America, are evident in post-2004 Polish migration to the UK. Thus, Garip and Asad show how in nearly all of the cases of Mexican migration to the United States which they studied individuals spoke of how network contacts reduced the risk of migration through the assistance they provided in-country.[57] Similarly, Ryan et al. report that among new Polish migrants in London many had, at least initially, relied extensively on social support from close contacts on arrival in London, and, to quote one participant whose experience was echoed across their sample, 'Poles helped me to stand on my own two feet.'[58]

Within the wider literature on international migration, there has been a turn towards 'mobility' as a framing device for analysing the movement of individuals across international borders. 'Mobility', it is argued, better reflects the fluidity of this movement in an age in which, in contrast to earlier periods, it is less likely to be experienced as, or to lead to permanent residence abroad. There is a danger, however, that using 'mobility' as an alternative to 'migration' can downplay the scale and stress of the decision to leave. Especially in Llanelli, data from our research, highlighted that for most migrants the decision to move away from home to another country is unsettling and is the cause of psychological strain. For those with limited competency in English, this arguably increases the feeling of isolation, of being 'alien'. The presence of in-country social networks which they can access increases their resilience to the pressures of migration. A man who had travelled to Wales on his own and without any network in Llanelli spoke of the challenges of balancing the physical strains of labour with the psychological demands of 'loneliness': 'there was this kind of loneliness that there is nobody I know in here. Nobody I could talk to, talk about memories ... There was nobody of that sort in here – and still there is nobody like that in here' (Mosze, M).

In summary, our research highlights how, in Haas's terms, social networks influence migration by both feeding the *aspiration* to migrate and by enhancing the migrant's *capability* to do so.[59] Personal contacts are a powerful source of information about life abroad – the opportunities and returns and how to maximise them. They are far from the only channel of such information, but they are a highly trusted source. We nevertheless found a pattern of individuals being actively encouraged to 'try' moving abroad, sometimes for its novelty, but more generally as a means of acquiring the resources to live in a way which was simply not possible at home. In Llanelli and Cardiff, where most of our participants had been struggling to make ends meet, this was a common sentiment. In addition, in a variety of ways social networks facilitate migration by removing or reducing obstacles which might otherwise be seen as limits to the potential of individuals to realise aspirations through migration.

Staffing agencies: middlemen of migration

In the wake of the unexpectedly large number of migrants entering the UK from CEE states following EU enlargement in 2004, commercial staffing agencies have come under the spotlight for their role in facilitating international migration. British media have regularly carried stories about the role of commercial agencies supplying 'thousands of cheap east European workers' for leading UK retailers, from the clothing to the food industry.[60] There has been a steady stream of items about the recruitment of migrant workers as the country's 'second-class workforce' and about the 'exploitation of migrant workers at top hotels'.[61,62]

The practices employed by some agencies have led them to become the focus of considerable controversy. In Northern Ireland, the Equality Commission launched an investigation in 2008 into the role of employment agencies in recruiting and employing migrant workers. In Wales, staffing agencies were a particular focus of an inquiry by the National Assembly for Wales into the conditions of migrant workers, especially the operation of 'zero hours' contracts.

Studies in the UK have shown how staffing agencies contributed to the way in which, shortly after enlargement in 2004, migrants from the new member states came to be distributed across the UK, including places which had hitherto little history of migration from these regions. Thus Chappell et al. found that almost a quarter of the Polish migrants they interviewed in England identified work arranged by a staffing agency as the reason for moving to work in a rural area.[63] Research on migrant workers in Bristol and Hull reported that in the latter city, the primary channel of recruitment was through employment agencies, even noting that some agencies were unofficially taking *only* Polish workers.[64] Until 2004, Portuguese workers were the established migrant worker community in the meat-processing sector in Merthyr, yet almost immediately after EU enlargement some factories began to use agency-sourced workers from Poland.[65] In 2005, about 1 in 9 workers at a major factory in Merthyr were from Portugal, but by 2008 the workforce of 1,016 also included 448 workers (approximately 40 per cent) from Poland compared to 121 from Portugal.[66] In rural areas, the leverage provided by staffing agencies may be greater still, particularly in localities with little local experience of migration. Jentsch, de Lima and MacDonald, for example, show how recruitment agencies have made the far north of Scotland one of the premier locations for migration from CEE in recent years.[67] Moreover, they show how direct recruitment can replace local social networks, at least with respect to their role in securing employment in rural localities where previously knowledge of employment opportunities would have spread by word of mouth. Over a decade after enlargement in 2004, studies across the EU have shown that Polish migrant workers are helping to meet a continued demand for low-cost, flexible labour.

Staffing agencies are part of an international human resources supply chain. In the shadow of EU enlargement in 2004, these organisations mushroomed to meet the demand for labour from the new member states.[68] To open new markets and attract potential labour, they opened offices in locations across the target markets, not just in major cities, but in other localities too. Agencies operating in different national markets linked up to provide a combined enterprise for sourcing and placing workers. Ward et al. note how in one western Polish town, within a few years after enlargement in 2004, there were forty-five Dutch-owned employment agencies supplying workers for businesses in the Netherlands.[69] In the case of Llanelli, one of the principal agencies which recruited migrant workers states on its website that it was 'one of the first specialist recruitment companies in the UK to recognise the huge benefits skilled and unskilled Central and East European workers could bring to British businesses'.

Such supply chains offer advantages for clients looking for labour at short notice, and a distinct advantage of staffing agencies is that they can, as research has shown, make things happen quickly by covering all necessary travel arrangements, documentation and accommodation.[70] Elsewhere, others have pointed to how staffing agencies may feed off migrant social networks in a variety of ways. Friberg, in an extensive investigation into how commercial labour agencies have facilitated migration into Nordic countries, notes that commercial recruiters based in

Poland often have migration experience and draw on their own social networks to source labour.[71,72] They also deploy the social capital and trust embedded in these relationships to reassure prospective migrants: 'because there is a high level of uncertainty involved for both migrant workers and clients/employers, trustworthiness and a good reputation is alpha and omega for those operating as intermediaries.'[73]

When the original study was carried out in Llanelli, we knew that one locally based staffing agency, in particular, which had opened offices in Poland, was acting as a major supplier of migrant labour to employers in the locality. We were aware that social networks were an important mechanism for facilitating migration, but how had staffing agencies influenced people's perceptions of migration? As part of the initial study, we undertook a survey with 114 participants, and found that 40 per cent knew no one in the locality before making arrangements to work in Llanelli. In total, just over half of the people we surveyed stated they had work arranged through a recruitment agency. Moreover, our qualitative interviews revealed that even migrants who knew someone living in Llanelli made the decision to move on information from contacts that they could secure work through agencies on arrival. Agencies acting as brokers between network contacts was a recurring feature of both of our qualitative studies in Llanelli. Thus participants spoke of friends saying they could 'fix' jobs for them, but as interviews went on it became clear that what they were 'fixing' was an introduction at one of the local staffing agencies.

The interviews highlighted numerous ways in which employment agencies are able to perform a surrogate role for migrants unable to draw sufficiently from the reservoir of social capital that can be generated by migrant networks. For those with minimal English, it makes the decision to migrate less complicated as agencies will make arrangements for jobs and accommodation at the destination, as well as providing Polish-speaking couriers and drivers to deal with immigration authorities and make travel arrangements,. Thus, Lubomierz, a man who had travelled from a small village close to the northern city of Bydgoszcz with no network contacts in Wales, explained how he was not confident he would 'manage with my English. I really wasn't sure,' but it was the attention of his agency contacts which provided the reassurance he needed. After his employer in Poland began to lay off workers, including himself, he told us how he felt he had little choice but to leave. By good fortune, as he clearly saw it, he learned of a local agency which made clear staff would enable him to move quickly and easily: 'I'd been often on the phone to my agency. I'd consulted them lots, to the extent that they even – they are really a good agency – that they even told me not to take any duvet with me, absolutely nothing, because everything had already been ready, newly bought, and waiting for me here' (Lubomierz, M). While not always the case, the deals also offered by some agencies to cover the initial costs of migrating, which might otherwise be a barrier, also clearly made it easier to make a decision to leave: 'They [the agency] paid the flight. I didn't have to pay for anything. So they paid my flight, picked me up from the airport, only then I had to pay. I paid for the flat and travel to work' (Hanna, F).

One of the main reasons so many of the interviewees initially planned to come to the UK for relatively short stays is because recruitment agencies made it possible for them to feel they had little to lose in taking the step. Also, because agencies are able to put arrangements in place at short notice, many of those to whom we spoke were able to make the decision to migrate in remarkably short time frames. Participants frequently spoke of a phone call from an agency and then a hurried departure. As one woman remarked:

> I filled the documents in [the Agency] in Poland and that lady called me at about 3 p.m. on Tuesday so that I came to her in Warsaw because there was to be a transport on Friday. I went there not mentioning anything at home – it was a secret – I went to Warsaw, completed all the formalities and soon there was the transport. (Morela, F)

Others who had searched for employment opportunities via the Internet also reported a quick decision about migration.

We found little evidence of staffing agencies aggressively marketing migration. Arguably there was no requirement for such tactics. Through one channel or another, including referrals from their own social networks, agencies appeared to have little trouble sourcing labour. We came across instances of individuals aggrieved because of what they believed to have been misleading information, such as about take-home wages or deductions from their salaries. Within the wider literature there is no shortage of reports of such practices and, indeed, of more explicit forms of exploitation, but we did not find evidence to suggest sharp practices to be a systematic feature of how these agencies operate. It would nevertheless be short-sighted to see employment agencies as merely intermediaries between employers and prospective employees.

Conclusion

How can we explain the rapid and (comparatively) substantial increase in the number of citizens arriving in Wales from the new CEE member states post-2004? It is a truism to say this happened because the British government signalled that it would put into practice the principle of freedom of movement, one of the foundations of EU citizenship and the European single market. Without the removal of restrictions on the ability of citizens from those states which would join the EU in 2004 to live and work in the UK this migration would simply not – legally at least – have been possible. It is equally stating the obvious to say that the decision of the majority of other EU member states to limit movement from the accession countries meant that more citizens from these states ended up in the UK than might otherwise have been the case. That Poland, in the immediate run-up to accession, was experiencing an economic slowdown which further depressed employment levels, especially among the young, also undoubtedly served to make working abroad an option to be considered more seriously.

Poland's entry to the EU, our research shows, was accompanied by a high level of interest in the possibility of moving abroad for work. Though our data on participants' views in the build-up to accession is limited, it does nevertheless highlight how migration became a topic of conversation, the subject of plans and the focus for ordinary people's aspirations. At this point, as well as in the next few years after accession, close contacts were often influential in encouraging friends and family to take advantage of the newly acquired right of freedom of movement. It was not just individual citizens, however, who were seeking to capitalise on this change. Poland saw a rapid increase in the number of employment agencies scrambling for labour either to place with foreign employers or to send abroad, a factor which has had an important bearing on the demographics of migration in the UK.

In this chapter we have set out the case for taking account of noneconomic factors as drivers of this migration. Our argument is that the initial migration of Poles to the UK needs to be analysed in the context of a particular process of cultural, political *and* economic development in

Poland, set, in turn, within the wider framework of the country's integration into the EU. Participants' accounts of their motives for leaving Poland are peppered with references to wage differentials and the challenges of meeting the cost of living at home. The underlying cause of their decision to look for better opportunities abroad, however, appears to be rooted in a frustration with the inability to make the kind of life they desire in Poland. In moving out of Poland, they were seeking ways of fulfilling aspirations for a different way of living, rather than persisting with a status quo which earlier generations would have had little opportunity to change. To understand not just why so many left, but also, as we will discuss in chapter 8, why so many are prepared to commit to a long – even permanent – stay in the UK, it is necessary to recognise how a desire to live life differently shapes the decision to leave home.

5

Polish Migrants in Cardiff: Changing Motivations in a Diverse City Environment

Introduction

In the review of the three case-study localities in Chapter 4 we outlined the reasons why post-2004 Polish migrants decided to migrate to Wales, how this migration was enabled and how these migrants lived once they arrived in Wales. When they made the initial decision to migrate to the UK, most migrants in the Cardiff sample were economically motivated; their sole intention was to enter the UK for a short period to earn money in a low-skilled job (often despite their high level of education) before returning to Poland. Migration was facilitated through social networks, and the nature of this group's economic priorities largely continued once they arrived in Wales. As we observe throughout this chapter, this group of economically motivated migrant workers has evolved into a group with complex motivations and reasons to stay in the UK, many of them staying in Wales for many years longer than they initially expected. Indeed it was only after living in Wales for some time that non-economic motivations had an impact on the group, thus highlighting the complexity of migrant decision-making processes overall.

The information in this section thus takes into account a number of changes to the migrant way of life in Cardiff over time, including changes to work and employment opportunities, changes to social networks alongside changes in education and language abilities. Interestingly, many migrants decided to stay in Cardiff for the long-term for reasons that were present prior to their migration, but it was only by living in Wales that they have been able to compare and evaluate this against their quality of life in Poland prior to migration. The aim of this chapter is to explain this group's time in Cardiff – including employment, family, friends, human capital development and future plans using the data collected over time in 2008 and 2011. As outlined in Chapter 3, on the whole the sample of Poles in Cardiff were well educated, had high English-language skills, and relied largely on their social networks. Comparisons between the findings from this locality and the findings from the other case-study localities (outlined in Chapters 6 and 7, respectively) will be discussed in Part III of the book.

Accommodation and Community Building

Initially many of the Cardiff Poles used their transnational social network, or the network of family and friends they had from the country of origin, to find accommodation. Transnational networks are of the utmost importance during the initial phases of migration, as ties to a migrant's country of origin are still strong and migrants are limited in the number of people they know in destination countries. 'Finding accommodation' in Cardiff was facilitated by social networks in one of two ways. First, migrants found a place to stay through friends or family members already residing in Cardiff, whilst continuing looking for their own place. Second, contacts were made through a transnational network to ask for recommendations in specific areas of the city or with people needing a roommate. Either way, involvement in social networks was necessary in the short-term.

Initially all migrants in the sample lived in areas of Cardiff that had a high number of Poles and other migrant groups, including Canton and City Road. As will be discussed below in relation to the ethnic economy, it was in these areas where the first Polish shops opened in Cardiff. Both areas supported the growth of the new migrant population because they had plenty of rental accommodation in close proximity to the city centre, making walking or biking to Internet cafes and employment opportunities much easier. For these reasons, City Road is a diverse migrant hub, housing Poles and other migrant groups as well. Canton has many of the same qualities, but the area is less of a migrant hub than City Road. While Poles in the Cardiff sample had mixed feelings about Catholicism, many who initially resided in Canton mentioned the close proximity of Catholic churches. Recognising the growing demand from the community of Poles in Canton, services were eventually held in Polish at local churches. As Gabriella (F) notes: 'It's nice to have a church service in Polish. I get to practise my religion and it has become sort of a meeting point.' The church in Canton also had a school attached to it, which in turn became a magnet for Polish students over time.

After they had been living in Canton and City Road for some time, many Poles started to move out into other areas of the city, but they continued to seek low-rental properties and/or shared accommodation. It was only after they had accumulated sufficient savings and had started to consider staying in the UK for the long term that they began looking for higher-priced, better- quality accommodation. This was particularly the case for the Poles on City Road, who were keen on the close proximity of the area to the city centre and the robust local employment and entertainment options, but who no longer wanted to live in a transient neighbourhood. While many were not seeking to buy property, thus indicating long-term settlement plans, there was a definite movement in this direction, if not yet fully formulated in the migrant psyche.

Employment in the UK

While their primary concern during initial migration was finding accommodation, the second concern was finding employment. Upon arrival, all migrants in the sample sought positions in low-skilled, 3D ('dirty, dangerous, and dull') employment.[1] Unlike their accommodation, which was largely facilitated by social network contacts, initial employment was found by applying for 3D positions after arrival in Cardiff. This work included (but was not limited to) waiting tables, hotel housekeeping, seasonal agricultural work and childcare. At this point, regardless of their individual characteristics and background, many Polish migrants were not concerned with their career; having an income of any kind was their primary concern. This urgency was often based on a variety of factors including: initial location upon arrival; economic motivations for migration; short-term plans to stay in the UK; and the rate of currency conversion between the GBP and the PLZ.

As discussed throughout this book, all migrants in the Cardiff sample initially planned to migrate to the UK for short-term economic reasons. When first entering the UK, migrants in the Cardiff sample wanted simply to find immediate employment in order to earn as much money as possible during their short, planned stay in Wales. Over time, however, earnings acquired by migrants were used to move out of the social network-affiliated accommodation. Nevertheless, regardless of their human capital levels, many continued to work in 3D employment, often for several different employers, because of their short-term ambitions and the conversion of their income on two levels: (1) between the GBP and the PLZ; and (2) between what they were earning in Wales and would expect to earn in a similar position in Poland. For example, many of the migrants in the Cardiff sample were fully aware of the currency conversion rate, particularly early on in their migration period, when they were willing to utilise a circular migration pattern. As a result, many Poles did not view 3D jobs in Wales in the same way as a British labourer.

The findings from the Cardiff sample regarding the incentives of migrants to take 3D employment are similar to the findings from a larger study of Polish migrant workers in the UK.[2] According to this study, Poles were getting paid slightly above the minimum wage (£4.85 in 2005) at £5.00 per hour in hospitality positions in the UK; based on a thirty-five-hour week, this would bring an income of £700 a month, which was less than the average worker in the same industries during that time.[3] Putting this into context, the same positions in Poland would bring an income of £255 a month at this time.[4] While the currency conversion rate between the UK and Poland varied significantly between 2008 and 2011 as a result of the recession, the perception among migrants was that they were still doing better economically in the UK. This simple assessment does not take into account many other economic factors such as the cost of living and purchasing power parity, but it explains why short-term migrants viewed this employment positively at this time.

As indicated, many migrants in the Cardiff sample had several 3D positions – often between five and seven – before advancing in the labour market. The vast majority used their local social networks to get better jobs after residing in the UK for some time. Local migrant networks were composed of friends and family in the destination country. This not only implies a change to social network composition, but also a change to the reason why the social network was used; it is thus less about lowering risk during initial migration and more about increasing returns through better employment options. The local social network is then used by the migrant to move up the division of labour, based on reputation and social capital accumulated with friends. Furthermore, because of the similarities between social networks and recruitment agencies in lowering the risk and the initial cost of migration, it seems clear that few migrants in the sample used recruitment agencies to facilitate migration. The use and importance of social networks is also evident in the non-ethnic economy and the ethnic economy.

Ethnic Economy Construction and Employment

The term 'ethnic economy' takes into account the spatial, economic, and social aspects of a migrant community.[5] As defined by Bonacich and Modell, the ethnic economy is composed of 'an ethnic group's self-employed, employers and co-ethnic employees'.[6] The ethnic economy differs from the ethnic enclave in that there is no defined area; it also differs from the informal economy, in which there are no taxes.[7] An ethnic economy emerged in Cardiff after the first wave of Poles arrived in 2004. While there was a small community of post-WW2 Poles in existence prior to 2004, this community was not significant in the emergence of the Polish ethnic economy in Cardiff in the post-2004 period. The pre-2004 Polish community in Cardiff would meet informally at the 'Polish house' on Newport Road, but this was mainly to maintain their Polish language skills and it was not the basis for chain migration in the post-2004 period.

The post-2004 Polish ethnic economy in Cardiff transitioned spatially, economically and socially over time. Spatially, it was originally based in the City Road area as well as the Canton area of Cardiff. For the same reasons that a large number of Poles decided to live in these areas, ethnic businesses also decided to locate there – walking distance to the city centre, a diverse population and short-term, less expensive housing rentals. Canton is less diverse than City Road and has fewer short-term housing rentals, but it is close to the city centre and near to both a Catholic church and a Catholic school. Economically, the businesses that comprise the ethnic economy grew over time in number and labour needs, starting with Polish food shops and growing to Internet cafes and Polish hair/nail salons. Socially, the Polish ethnic economy in Cardiff created a social network for new Poles entering the region. The businesses themselves served as places where Polish migrants could catch up on gossip from home, seek employment, use their language skills, and, for some short-term migrants, live in the same way as in Poland, i.e. with the same food, language, etc.

Ethnic Entrepreneurs and Co-ethnic Workers

One of the key components of the ethnic economy is the ethnic entrepreneur.[8] While there is a significant literature on why ethnic entrepreneurs start a business in the destination country, there is less information available that focuses on how ethnic entrepreneurs act over time.[9] This section will review why the migrants in the sample became entrepreneurs and how their social network supported their entrepreneurial endeavour.

The migrants from the sample in Cardiff who became ethnic entrepreneurs, contributing to the ethnic economy in the region, do not have significantly different profiles from those who chose other employment options or non-migrant entrepreneurs. The ethnic entrepreneurs in the sample initially migrated to the UK for economic reasons, used their social networks to facilitate accommodation in the UK after migration, and had several 3D jobs in the non-ethnic economy. The difference between the ethnic entrepreneurs and the other migrants in the sample is in what they did after having several 3D jobs. According to several studies, entrepreneurs seek entrepreneurship either out of necessity, because they do not feel that they can progress in the division of labour using human capital, or for opportunity, because they would like to be their own boss or because they see a niche in the market for their products.[10, 11] However, like non-migrant entrepreneurs, including those in the informal economy, ethnic entrepreneurs' decision to start a business can be complex and may not be easily broken down into either necessity or opportunity categories.[12]

All of the ethnic entrepreneurs in the sample mentioned opportunity-based reasons for starting a business; however, through reviewing both what the migrants said and their work patterns, this opportunity-based response came after the migrant had several different low-skilled positions in the destination country. The line between opportunity and necessity is blurred as the conditions of the migrants' previous jobs or their prior experience in the UK labour market could have incentivised them to be their own boss. This is noted by Cyryl (M) and Borys, 26 (M), who had several jobs working as tomato pickers, cashiers and eventually met on a construction site. After they were made redundant, they decided to start a business and work for themselves in construction. Similarly, Tomek (M) had experienced poor working conditions while in the UK and was looking for something more, finding it through entrepreneurship. Interestingly, none of the entrepreneurs had owned businesses or attempted self-employment prior to migrating, largely owing to a lack of finance. These findings blur the boundaries of this dualistic approach as the entrepreneurs could have started out as necessity-based actors, due to their time at the lower end of the division of labour, and transitioned to opportunity-based actors when realising the benefits of being their own boss.

Beyond starting their businesses, the only other way that ethnic entrepreneurs vary from other migrants in the Cardiff sample is through their extensive use of their social networks. The Polish ethnic entrepreneurs utilised their social networks, both local and transnational, more than any of the other migrants in the sample when setting up their business, acquiring their labour and establishing their customer base. Regardless of the type of business started or the level of integration between the business and the Polish community, none of the entrepreneurs in the sample received financial help from banks, the government or lending organisations to start their business. Rather, their businesses were largely financed through their social networks and their savings.

Even though the migrants did not receive financial support from these organisations, Amelia (F), a nail salon owner on City Road, did apply for a loan:

> I tried to take a loan in bank but they told me no because of the credit crunch loans went to people from this country not to people from outside because of the risk that I could leave ... I talked to my parents and they decided that they could help me with money to get the business started. (Amelia, F)

Amelia's attempt at obtaining a loan was denied mainly because of the credit crunch and possibly her assumption that the rejection was based on her migrant status within the UK. Other migrants, Borys (M), Cyryl (M), construction business owners, and Kinga (F), a Polish restaurant owner, mainly financed their businesses through their personal savings accrued while working in 3D jobs in the UK.

The entrepreneurs also utilised their social networks to find workers for their businesses. This is the case for the entrepreneurs whose business caters mainly to the ethnic community. This specific type of entrepreneur utilises local and transnational social networks to find co-ethnic employees. According to Julia (F), a Polish food store owner on City Road, 'I find most of my employees from the local area ... We also have a board to advertise other jobs in Polish for Poles that employers post ads on often.' This is the same situation for Maja (F), a hair salon owner in Canton, who noted: 'When I first opened I hired girls that spoke Polish in the area.'

For the entrepreneurs whose business caters to the wider community, or whose business has diversified over time, co-ethnic workers are still utilised; however, these workers are not necessarily chosen from the surrounding ethnic community. As needed, both the transnational and local social networks are utilised by the entrepreneurs to staff their businesses. Maja, another entrepreneur with several business sites in the South Wales area, has a slightly different approach to finding staff. Initially she had one hair salon catering to Polish people; but, over time, with the opening of more of her salons, she has utilised her extended local social network as well as the local social network of her British fiancé to find English-speaking personnel. As her business diversified to meet the rising customer demand of the non-ethnic community, her labour needed to diversify as well to service this changing demand.

This change in labour needs could be indicative of the diversification of Maja's business, potentially through the rising English-speaking demand by her customers, or perhaps also through the reduction of Poles in the community. In 2008, there was only one other ethnic entrepreneur-based business that was searching for non-Poles and Poles, Kinga's restaurant. The hiring of non-Poles was economically motivated and was for the front-of-house staff to give customers the impression of a European rather than a Polish restaurant. The Poles, who were part of the entrepreneur's transnational family social network, were the kitchen staff. They used their shared Polish language to communicate with the chef. Interestingly, when the family members had to return to Poland, additional co-ethnic workers were recruited, but from Poland instead of the surrounding Polish community.

The ethnic entrepreneurs also tap into their extensive social networks to increase demand for their products. Co-ethnic consumers were willing to pay slightly more for Polish products purchased at an ethnic business instead of going to the larger British supermarket for a similar item. This economically irrational action was explained through the shared language that the short-term Polish migrant could use in the Polish store when talking to Polish staff. Based on this assessment of the entrepreneurs' consumers, to further meet the needs of their customer base, the new entrepreneurs were motivated to locate their businesses within the ethnic community in Cardiff. However, the changing times are demonstrated by new entrepreneurs that have opened their businesses since 2008 and mainly market themselves to the non-Polish community in Cardiff.

By 2011, the spatial characteristics of the Polish ethnic economy in Cardiff changed owing to the reduction of new, short-term Polish migrants and the introduction of longer-term migrants who were staying in the area for years instead of months. With this change, social networks and ethnic products, which made the migrants' initial transition to the UK easy were no longer relied upon as the migrant became more familiar with the surrounding area. As a result, the ethnic businesses located in Canton either closed or relocated to the highly transient City Road area of Cardiff. Poles continued to reside in Canton because of the proximity of the Catholic school and church; however, these Poles were becoming more familiar with the local shops and no longer relied on the ethnic economy businesses on a regular basis. Furthermore, the Polish businesses which initially clustered on City Road, regardless of their product, started amending their business strategy. Realising the changing demand for their ethnic products and services, the ethnic entrepreneurs diversified their businesses, hiring English-speaking staff and catering more to the British consumer.

The business diversification of the Polish ethnic shops in Cardiff occurred mainly in salon and spa-type businesses, as is evidenced by Maja and Amelia. Maja diversified her hair salon by employing English-speaking staff to target British consumers despite originally marketing the salon as a 'Polish salon'. In addition, Amelia, a newer entry to the ethnic economy, opened a nail salon that employs solely Polish migrants but markets solely to British consumers. The ethnic businesses that will find diversification the most difficult will be the Polish food stores, as they greatly rely on Polish migrants as their customer base.[13] The niche for these businesses is Polish food, so in some cases the diversification could be to a speciality deli; however, given the number of Polish ethnic stores that comprise the ethnic economy in Cardiff, all of the food stores will not be sustainable in the long term. Based on the ethnic economy definition outlined in the introduction to this section and the diversification strategies being implemented by Polish ethnic entrepreneurs, the 'ethnic economy' in Cardiff has been, and continues to be, in a period of transition.

Traditionally, the ethnic entrepreneurs would also be considered long-term settlers in the destination country with the business anchoring them to the area and making them different from the average migrant. However, because of the ethnic economy transition, and the number of other non-ethnic entrepreneurs in the Cardiff sample that are staying in the destination country significantly longer than they originally expected, there are no differences between entrepreneurs and non-entrepreneurs on this point.

Migrant Labour Market Mobility

Taking into account the entire Cardiff sample, both the ethnic and the non-ethnic economy, the Polish migrants seek low-skilled employment when initially migrating regardless of their human capital development (both language and education). After having several low-skilled positions, usually in 3D jobs, they begin to move up the division of labour. This labour market mobility largely depends on the migrants' simultaneous advancement of their language skills and, in some cases, their education acquisition while in the 3D employment.

Examples of this ascent in the division of labour abound in the Cardiff sample, regardless of the characteristics of the migrant when first migrating to the UK. For example, Donata (F) and Zuzanna (F) had excellent English-language skills and undergraduate degrees from universities in Poland but, when first arriving in the destination country, they took jobs in the service industry. Once their confidence grew in using their language skills through daily interaction with English-speaking customers, as well as taking additional courses in their spare time, they began to ascend the division of labour. Donata went on to work in a bank and then as a diversity officer helping other migrants. Zuzanna went on to work as a secretary at an insurance company while also volunteering her translation services to other migrants. Eventually, albeit by slightly different routes, Zuzanna started working at the same diversity outreach organisation as Donata. In addition, Cyryl (M) and Borys (M), the construction entrepreneurs, had virtually no English-language skills when originally migrating to the destination country. As a result, their first job was picking tomatoes and other seasonal work. Through learning and developing their English-language skills, they were able to work in the construction industry and eventually start their own business.

Alternatively, the ascent in the division of labour occurs for migrants such as Dawid (M) and Emilia (M) who do not acquire English-language skills but who acquire social capital through advanced engagement in the local social network and the ethnic economy in the area. This is the case for the Polish co-ethnic workers that contribute to the ethnic economy in Cardiff. From the findings, the main reason that the co-ethnic workers were interested in ethnic economy employment was due to their lack of interest in acquiring English-language skills and the widely held view that co-ethnic employment offered more opportunities to engage with co-ethnics. The actions of the co-ethnic workers in having several 3D jobs prior to entering ethnic economy employment, despite relatively high qualifications, demonstrates that their language skills were insufficient for progression in the traditional labour market. Therefore, the alternative ascent in the division of labour for a migrant not interested in learning the local language was ethnic economy employment, facilitated by their social network. Whether or not the co-ethnic workers, as a subsection of the sample, were unwilling or unable to develop their language skills is unknown.

These examples highlight the variety of ways the migrants in the Cardiff sample ascend the division of labour and further our understanding of the role of the ethnic economy in the region. It should be noted that all of the migrants in the Cardiff sample had several (between five and seven) different 3D jobs before beginning their ascent, which traditionally begins eighteen months after arrival in the destination country and ends on reaching employment commensurate with their skills and education. It can be argued that the migrants in this sample who improved their position over time, were motivated to do so as a result of both necessity, in terms of saturation of the labour market for 3D jobs by new migrants, and opportunity, as they had more local knowledge of the labour market and language skills than a new migrant.

Human Capital Development

The acquisition of human capital by the migrant, whether intentional through schooling (qualifications) while in the destination country or through total immersion in the destination country (language) was a major issue for migrants in the sample.

These migrants approached their human capital development in Wales in different ways based on their pre-migration attainment and future employment goals. Pre-migration human capital development varied, with some migrants having high school education and advanced English-language skills (ethnic entrepreneurs), others having university degrees and low English-language skills (co-ethnic workers), and yet others having University degrees and advanced English-language skills. In addition, future employment goals dictated their human capital development while in the destination country. The ethnic entrepreneurs sought to develop their language skills more to meet the needs of a potential diverse consumer base. The other migrants, despite their high levels of both education and language when initially migrating, sought further education and language endeavours in the destination country in order to find work commensurate with their level of human capital. Even the co-ethnic workers in the ethnic economy, who were able to live and work in Cardiff without having English-language skills and had no immediate need to develop their skills, developed some language base through total immersion in an English-speaking country. This is evidenced in their ability to participate in an interview with a non-Polish speaker.

It should be noted that the 'future employment goals' were considered employment in the destination country but could also include employment when or if returning to the country of origin. For example, Wiktoria (F) mentioned that despite having a Master's degree from a university in Poland and the beginning of a career as a manager in a hotel in Cardiff, she went on to develop her human capital in Cardiff. She accomplished this development through finishing a Master's degree at a British university as she felt that this would open up her prospects if she ever did decide to return to Poland or migrate elsewhere. Many other migrants in the sample mentioned their desire to gain a degree in Britain as well. From their demographic information, this group had degrees from Polish universities but could not find employment in Poland in their field. This incentive to gain a university degree in Britain highlights the migrants' perception that a British degree is needed for high-skilled employment in both Poland and the UK.

The future employment goals of the migrants were also met by language acquisition. This was particularly the case for Donata (F), Zuzanna (F) and Gabriela (F) who had university degrees from Polish institutions before migrating, as well as high levels of English-language skills. They actively sought to develop their human capital through complete immersion in an English-speaking country to raise their confidence levels when conversing with native English- speakers. The way these three migrants actively sought this immersion highlights the difference between this group and the co-ethnic workers who almost accidentally picked up the language during their time in the destination country. Interestingly, Donata, Zuzanna and Gabriela independently started taking courses in translation at university level and completed degrees in translation at varying levels.

While these are specific cases of human capital development by migrants, they demonstrate the variety of ways that migrants actually develop their human capital over time in the destination country. For some of the migrants, it was a part of their plan when they arrived (Donata and Gabriella), other migrants advanced their human capital to transition out of 3D employment (ethnic entrepreneurs), and others (co-ethnic workers) had jobs where there was no incentive to develop their human capital.

Migrant Identity

As evidenced in the migrants' transition from the use of a transnational social network to the use of a local social network, the longer the migrant is in the receiving country the greater the chances of expanding relationships beyond the co-ethnics. The increase in the migrants' co-ethnic connections could also be through the human capital development that the migrant achieves in the UK, whether intentionally (schooling) or unintentionally (total immersion). Looking at it from the migrant's point of view, their identity may change as a result of integration in British society and an increase in cultural capital. However, given the constant pull from the sending country, the migrant's identity will be in a state of flux, neither fully removed from the sending country nor fully absorbed into the receiving country. To further complicate the matter, as the migrant in question is participating in intra-EU migration, the 'EU citizen' identity is also assigned. Taking this into account, can the migrant hold multiple identities – Polish citizen, Polish migrant in the UK (Polish-British/ Polish-Welsh), EU citizen – simultaneously?

The Cardiff sample never explicitly mentioned their 'identity' nor did any of the migrants refer to themselves as 'EU citizens'. However, the migrants in the sample did allude to their identity when discussing other topics, including the cultural variations between the UK and Poland and their family. A subsection of the migrant sample was interested in using their Polish language skills to retain their culture while in the UK. This is interesting for two reasons. First, the migrants that form this section establish the link between culture and language, which greatly impacts on the migrant's identity when in the destination country. Second, because of the migrants' family dynamic, both cases in this section were migrants who had children while in the destination country. Based on this, using the language and retaining the culture is not considered a symptom of homesickness; rather, it demonstrates the potential future plans of the migrants in returning to Poland to pass on their culture and their Polish identity to the next generation.

> There are no specific plans to go back but we [husband and I] still speak Polish in the house with the kids even though we all know English. Maybe someday we will all go back. (Gabriela)

> I'm from Poland and when I say 'bread' in my language I can smell it; when I say it in English it is not the same ... I have a little girl now and I would like her to speak my language and see my homeland. (Amelia)

By preserving their culture through language and passing it on to future generations, Gabriela's family utilises language as a social aspect that may inform their return migration in the future. In meeting with Gabriela in 2008 and 2011, there was a visible shift at the later time towards a more British way-of-life; however, even though her outward appearance may have changed her persona, links to her native culture and identity are still present through her language use. This is particularly interesting as Gabriela has sought to further develop her English-language skills while in the UK for her translator job. Alternatively, Amelia comments on the relationship between language, culture and identity in relation to the memories conjured up when using her native language. Like Gabriela, she has a child born in the UK and feels that language will help the child retain its 'Polishness' when growing up in the UK. Although slight, and potentially because she has not lived in the UK for as long as Gabriela, Amelia differs from Gabriela in the way they reference their country of origin. Amelia refers to Poland as her 'homeland'. This reference could also define the difference in Amelia, holding on to her migrant identity while being a business owner, and a shift in Gabriela's migrant identity over time.

Other migrants in the sample discussed the cultural shifts in Poland since joining the EU, which made it more appealing for them to return. These migrants cited the capital of culture awards and increased population diversity in major cities through tourism and business as reasons to embrace their Polish identity while abroad. Yet other migrants in the sample preferred British culture and felt that it was much more open than in Poland, particularly regarding religion and tolerance. While these migrants are no less Polish, given their exposure to the British culture and their perception of British culture, these migrants appear to be most likely to adopt the 'EU citizen' identity. The variety of responses demonstrates the complexity of migrant identity and the very individualistic approach that needs to be taken when discussing Poles who are living abroad for the long-term, but not necessarily settling in the destination country.

Role of Family and Future Plans

Thus far the role of family has been discussed in a multitude of ways including the composition of the local and transnational social networks of the migrants, the basis of an ethnic business, and the construction of migrants' identity. This section provides further insight into the role of family for the migrants in the sample, particularly how the relationship between family members changes over time outside Poland and the migrants' use of their families as a reason not to return- migrate to Poland.

The vast majority of the migrants in the sample were planning on coming to the UK for a short time when initially migrating. It was only after living in the destination country that their motivations changed to include staying longer than expected or even long-term. Owing to the changing plans of the migrants, the role of family would also be expected to change as it would be easier to leave the country of origin for the short term instead of longer. Regardless of the length of time the migrant is away from their family, many migrants in the sample utilise advances in telecommunications technology to keep in touch with their immediate family while in the destination country. Martyna (F) notes: 'I keep in touch with my family a lot on Skype and Facebook.' In addition, the Polish shop owner Julia relates her lack of homesickness to staying in touch with family through the Internet: 'Not missing family because can be in relatively good contact with them through the Internet.'

As cited by Martyna and Julia, although they are physically away from their families, the migrants have regular communication with them through social media websites and Internet calling, thereby reducing the social distance between them. This could lend insight into the lack of homesickness for family. While migrants that are in the UK in the longer term may have the telecommunications facilities to make this contact from home, this may not be the case for short-term migrants, or for migrants when they first arrive in the destination country. Based on this, Tomek (M) saw the gap in the market and makes it easier for migrants to keep in touch with their family through his Internet café aimed at the Polish population in Cardiff 'With my business, other Polish people can contact their family as I know what it feels like to be away from home.'

The changing role of the family could be viewed positively, where migrants look forward to reconnecting with their immediate family; it could also be viewed negatively, where the migrant prefers life in the destination country without family. For some of those using family as a reason to stay in the UK, it is because their immediate family has chain migrated with them. Jan (M), a hotel worker in Cardiff Bay, is an example of this: 'My parents moved here about two years ago as they are both retired so they live here with me. I don't think I'll go back [to Poland] because there is nothing there for me.' Jan had economic motivations to migrate initially, and he perceived his family as the only reason he would return-migrate, but with his parents now in the destination country, he is complete. By saying that now that his family is in Cardiff he has nothing in Poland, Jan indirectly places considerable weight on the role of his family in his decision-making process.

The migrants' 'new' family members or connections made with other people in the destination country, were also mentioned as having a major, positive, role in the migrants' future decision-making. Zuzanna notes that 'My fiancée is Welsh and he doesn't mind Poland but we probably won't go there.' Other Poles have started relationships with fellow Poles, but the urge to remain outside Poland is still there: 'Now I live with my Polish girlfriend [Masia] and she is part of my plans as long as she doesn't want to go back [to Poland]' (Igor).

These quotes demonstrate that the migrants' newly constructed family in the UK play a significant role in their future plans. For example, in the interview with Zuzanna, her Welsh fiancé was definitely an anchor for her in the UK, but not only in relation to return migration. Zuzanna, had set up a freelance translation business so that she could take the business anywhere if she decided to migrate to a third country or return-migrate. Here Zuzanna is further refining her future plans by specifying that if she can get her fiancé to move, she would not choose Poland. Wiktoria is in a similar situation with a Serbian fiancé that she met in the UK, and she has gained a Master's degree. Whenever they decide to move, it will not necessarily be back to Poland or even to Serbia.

Igor mentions his relationship with Masia in regard to his future plans. These are two Polish people who did not know each other in the country of origin, met in the destination country and formed a relationship. It should be noted that of all the relationships discussed thus far in this section, this is the least developed. Igor puts significant weight on this relationship as he originally migrated to the UK for economic means, and the social network that facilitated his migration was largely based around his previous Polish girlfriend. In addition, Igor is not interested in returning to Poland as he views it as intolerant, while Masia is interested in returning at some point. Even though the person the migrant is anchored to is not family by blood, they are more than friends and could eventually become family, so that the relationship can be a significant determining factor in migrants' future plans.

Other migrants in the sample view their families in Poland in a negative light, and this incentivises them to stay in the UK longer than expected. This is the case for Donata (F) and Angelika (F), two Polish migrants to the UK who are also lesbians: 'I'm a lesbian and they [my family] do not approve ... (Angelika), and 'I don't see eye to eye with my parents as I'm a lesbian and they are not understanding ...' (Donata). As a result of their families' intolerance regarding their sexual orientation, both currently view their families as reasons to remain in the UK. Interestingly, neither of these migrants mentioned their families' intolerance as their initial reason to migrate to the UK as they both had economic motivations.

For the migrants in the Cardiff sample, the main factor in their future plans – both positively and negatively – is their relationships with their family in Poland as well as in the UK. This is a of particular importance as the main reason that the migrants originally left Poland was for economic gain; but over the course of their time in the UK, non-economic factors, many of which were present during their initial migration, have become the deciding factor regarding return migration. This is evidenced in Donata and Angelika's explanation of their parents' intolerance as well as other family-related matters discussed in this section.

Conclusion

This chapter has highlighted an array of economic and non-economic motivations that migrants participating in the sampled non-ethnic economy and ethnic economy of Cardiff have during their migration period. Through reviewing their evolving motivations over time as well as across different subject areas, this chapter explains what life is like for short-term migrants who stay in the UK much longer than they expected.

Across the entirety of the sample, the migrants' original motivation is based on their perception of what is available to them in the country of origin alongside their perception of the lifestyle they can have in the destination country. The poor economic conditions in Poland and the pull of expected high financial returns in the UK were sufficient motivation for them to migrate. This migration was supported by their use of their transnational social networks to find accommodation when initially migrating. With reduced contact over time and increased integration into British society, the Poles in the Cardiff sample increasingly rely on their local social network the longer they remain in Cardiff. While the Poles in the sample sought their original 3D employment through traditional means, their local social network would eventually support many of the migrants' labour market mobility in both the ethnic and the non-ethnic economies.

The future plans of the migrants are the most ambiguous section in all of the migration period. This ambiguity could be associated with a number of factors, including, but not limited to, the following: the uncertain economic times, the changing situation with family or simply the unpredictability of the future. It should be highlighted once more that these future plans are an evolving concept that can continue to change over time. This has previously been demonstrated with the migrants originally intending to migrate for the short term but allowing this complex range of factors to influence their motivations to stay longer.

This chapter has provided an overview of how the Poles that contributed to the Cardiff sample lived, economically and socially, in Wales. By reviewing their responses throughout their time in the UK, the complexities of their migration and the subsequent actions in the destination country have been highlighted. It will be interesting to return to these complex motivations and actions in later chapters, comparing this urban case in Cardiff to other cases in Wales.

6

Polish Workers in Merthyr Tydfil: Happily Resigned to Life in the Valleys?

Introduction

The South Wales Valleys (SWV) were a key global hub for coal production during the nineteenth century, and Merthyr thus has a strong historical legacy of industrial decline and decay.[1] As demand for coal declined dramatically between 1940 and 1980, unemployment rose beyond the UK average.[2] Parts of the area suffer from a duality of deprivation, with social problems associated with declining urban areas existing in the midst of isolated rural communities.[3] The Valleys region has one of the highest proportions of Jobseeker's Allowance claimants in the UK, and there are persistently high levels of unemployment and ill health.[4] Financial exclusion is a major problem. The average household income is below the national Welsh average[5] and the global recession has had a further disproportionate impact on communities across the Valleys.[6]

The County Borough of Merthyr, the smallest of twenty-two Welsh unitary authorities, extends fourteen miles south from the Brecon Beacons National Park to Trelewis. Once Wales's largest town, Merthyr Tydfil lies at the northern end of the Taff Valley, approximately thirty miles northwest of Cardiff. As a strategic location in the once thriving South Wales Coalfield (SWC), Merthyr has welcomed successive waves of migrant workers from many countries, including England, Ireland, Italy, Russia, Poland and France, the majority arriving between 1901 and 1911. At the start of the twentieth century, the Dowlais Iron Company in Merthyr Tydfil recruited workers from the Basque country in Spain as the local labour pool dwindled as men left the Valleys to fight in the Boer War.[7]

Later, when the arriving Spanish workers were to some extent fleeing the Franco dictatorship in search of a better life, Davies argues that they may also have been recruited for exploitative purposes, namely to undercut earnings and reduce the strength of the unions.[8] As we observe in this chapter, similar concerns have been expressed in the early decades of the twenty-first century.

At its economic peak in 1913, the SWC employed over 230,000 people and accounted for almost one-third of the world's coal exports.[9] Coalfield employment peaked in 1920 and between the wars around half a million people left the Valleys to look for work in the New World.[10] Though nowhere near earlier levels of migration, since EU expansion in 2004 and 2007 there has been another influx of migrant workers from CEE countries into the South Wales Valleys, most notably from Poland. Merthyr has become the principal destinations for Polish migrants in the Valleys, with over 80 per cent of all WRS and NINo registrations between 2004 and 2011 being made by Poles. The 2011 census confirms this trend, indicating that 5.5 per cent (1,016) of all Poles in Wales are resident in Merthyr – the second highest figure of any Welsh LA. Polish is now the third mostly widely spoken language in Merthyr after English and Welsh, at 1.66 per cent of the resident population.[11] The relatively short-term intensity of this in-migration has brought a significant change to a region that has traditionally been less diverse than other parts of South Wales.

Over 85 per cent of our Polish sample had been resident in Merthyr for between one and five years; one had recently arrived and one had been there for more than five years. While these data are indicative of ongoing returns and arrivals among Polish migrants, in recent years there has been an increase in Polish families with children and extended family members in Merthyr, many of whom have long-term plans to settle. Over 65 per cent of the sample was married or cohabiting and living with family members, and a quarter had extended family members living with them or nearby.

Accessing the Local Labour Market

With the influx of CEE migrants to the SWV region post-2004, employment agencies servicing the region switched their focus from Portuguese migrants – who had hitherto filled most vacancies in food and meat-processing factories – to Polish workers in order to challenge the established organisation of the Portuguese community and lower production and organisational costs. While the number of Portuguese migrants has continued to decline since then, the number of Poles has continued to increase, but competition between the two groups for jobs in local factories, and among local consumers for migrant businesses, remains strong to this day.

From 2007 until the scheme closed in 2011, over 90 per cent of WRS registrations in Merthyr were for factory-based occupations.[12] In 2008, one meat-processing factory had over 600 migrant workers out of a workforce of 1,000, with the number of Poles increasing steadily. There were also small numbers of WRS registrations for health-related jobs, including doctors and consultants, teaching assistants, sales assistants, cleaners and domestic staff. As well as factory-based occupations, the Merthyr sample included an ESOL teacher and a youth worker, although these had started their careers in meat and food-processing factories in Merthyr. The benefits to local employers and to the local economy of employing 'hard-working' Poles in low-paid occupations was discussed by a number of Poles. As Judyta (F), who first came to Wales in 2008 to work on a voluntary placement after studying in Czestochowa in southern Poland, noted:

> This is the reason that the owners are looking for people from Poland ... because they know that they are hardworking people and they are able to work for this money. So they are definitely contribute economy because they are working for the country. They pay taxes and in this way they help out this country.

The vast majority of Poles in Merthyr generally are recruited for and seek low-skilled employment in local factories, irrespective of their human capital. Around 40 per cent of Polish migrants surveyed finished their education at high school, while 60 per cent had a combination of undergraduate, postgraduate and vocational qualifications. Some Poles have tried and failed to find work that matches their qualifications. For some this is problematic. For many others, however, having any job is just as important as having a job they are qualified for. Junya arrived from Nysa in south-west Poland in 2010 with her daughter to join her husband, who had arrived earlier for a prearranged position in a local factory. As she stated, finding any kind of work was the most important thing as far as she was concerned: 'For me important is just to have a job, doesn't matter what kind of field.'

Few Poles had difficulty finding employment in Merthyr, and around a third had arrived for a job prearranged by a family member, friend or agency. The rest had travelled because friends and/or family had indicated that jobs were available; one migrant arrived on a voluntary placement. As in the case of Llanelli and the sourcing of labour for food-processing firms in West Wales and Anglesey, initially we find agencies playing a key role recruiting Polish labour in Merthyr. In the immediate aftermath of EU expansion, agencies such as Staffline played a significant role in recruiting Poles to work in factories owned by Vion foods (recently taken over by Two Sisters) and OPChocolates. These factories continue to recruit Poles through agencies, though agencies have a less central role than they did a few years ago. Many established migrant workers are now employed directly by local factories through contacts within the migrant community. As we will note below and also point out in the case of Llanelli in particular, the change from agency work to being a direct employee of a local firm *can* be a turning point in the migratory career and a catalyst in the process of settling in Wales.

Very often, however, it is still difficult for migrants in Merthyr to get a job for which they are qualified: 'When I passed from Staffline to the factory they gave me one paper and this paper they asked about your degree and I put I am an engineer and I do this ... I put everything but no, they are not interested' (Tymon, M). Significantly, even if they are employed directly by a company rather than by an agency, some Poles indicated that they are still treated in the same way: 'It's not good in Staffline. But with the company it's the same problem, if you speak with a manager or supervisor they speak with you the same, "Oh if you don't like it, there's the door" ... it's not good' (Tadeusz, M). Nevertheless, even if there was a sense of resignation over aspects of their working life, many Poles also spoke of the benefits of life in Merthyr, as Bolek (M) noted, thus indicating the changing motivations and understanding of their migratory plans and career: 'I'm aware that my wage is not the highest. I know it's one of the lowest which you can get here, but I have enough money for everything and it is completely different than it was when I lived in Poland.'

Migrant Labour Market Mobility

Agency work is generally little understood by those doing it, and over the last decade the language barrier has let agencies get away with a great deal. One aspect of the temporal process by which Portuguese workers became established in Wales prior to the arrival of Polish workers in 2004 was union membership, yet this proved to be their undoing. As the power of Portuguese workers in the workplace increased, the response of the factory owners was to replace them with non-unionised Polish workers. Since 2004, however, the power of all workers in the food- and meat-processing sector has declined as widespread opposition to union membership has emerged in companies running factories across the sector; this has made it difficult to get an overall picture of what is happening in local factories in places such as Merthyr, and to deal with claims that migrants are being exploited.

The issues faced by Polish workers in Merthyr are also obscured by a number of contradictory discourses. Inside the occupational spaces of the factory, for example, Poles are often viewed as 'good workers' vis-à-vis the locally available workforce. Outside the workplace this enhances the perception that migrants are job takers and benefit cheats.[13] Tannock argues that by promoting and accepting such discourses in Merthyr, coalitions of employers, state agencies and civil society organisations have reframed labour market conflict as a matter of local worker deficit and poor labour supply rather than poor job quality.[14] Arguably it is within the tightly defined spaces of the meat-processing factories in Merthyr and places across Wales that the underlying discourses of civil/uncivil, good/bad and moral/immoral come to the fore.[15] These regimes and coalitions are also one of the major contributory factors behind the movement of migrant workers around Wales over recent years to find more favourable working conditions. Portuguese workers had been dismissed by nationality en masse because they were members of a trade union, while more recently arrived Polish workers were not.[16] Some years ago, when Polish migrants started arriving in greater numbers, small numbers of Portuguese workers also started leaving North Wales to look for work in places where more trade union- friendly regimes was operating. Some arrived in Merthyr only to find out that it was the retail union Usdaw – rather than T&G (now UNITE) – that had been allowed into the factory, primarily, it appears, because they have little influence in the meat-processing sector.[17]

Many of the problems Poles have encountered in Merthyr over the last decade are thus closely connected to working practices in local factories. Initially it was concerns over overtime, wages, holiday entitlement and accommodation tied to agency employment that created major problems for Poles.[18] Zero hours contracts, which enable employers to send workers home at short notice when there is no work, were also problematic. However, while many of the earlier problems faced by Poles have declined as the use of agencies has dropped off, the zero hours contracts have in turn become used and established in factory practice. When factories are working flat out at Christmas, workers must work seven days a week or they risk losing their job. At other times, similarly to the experiences of migrant labour in West Wales, when orders are scarce, workers are sent home with no pay. As Jaceka (F) who arrived from South West Poland in 2007 after studying for a Master's degree in Physics pointed out:

> If the factories have got a lot of orders they ask us to work seven days a week without any days off and we just have to go to work because otherwise the supervisor was coming to us, to our home, and just knocked to door and took us from the house. But when the factory didn't have enough orders we need to stay at home even seven days a week – it's the other way around.

A number of Poles stated that their contracts are unlimited or continuous, which effectively means open-ended. In practice this allows factories to legally end their employment at any time, therefore giving them great flexibility at the expense of the labour rights of the Poles. The effects of these new contract arrangements illustrate the changing nature of the problems Poles face in Merthyr as a result of recent and ongoing policy changes. If a migrant worker is put on limited hours at short notice they are often unable to claim benefits, even if they have recourse to public funds, because they need to be unemployed for a longer period of time before making a claim.

Many Poles think that the hours they work and the wages they receive are normal for the work they do. As Alexsy (M), who struggled to get enough hours on a regular basis, confirmed:

We should have guaranteed forty hours per week. The agency had been told at the beginning. After few months I worked only one or two days per week ... but I wanted to work more and often. Sometimes we came to work and after one hour the agency sent us home, because was no work. They did whatever they want with us and didn't treat us fair.

Aside from the perceived unfairness of this contractual arrangement, our research also highlighted the social and psychological effects of the chaotic existence which, we found, was often, characteristic of the experience of the early phase of migration. Even so, as zero hours contracts have been adopted within factories as standard practice, this situation and the consequences for migrant workers have reappeared in a new form in live funding cuts, austerity measures and issues associated with no access to public funds.[19]

While 80 per cent of the Merthyr sample found that they are generally better off in Wales than in Poland, the effects of this often fragile financial existence can create problems. In the initial 2004 period, many Poles were sending a large percentage of the weekly wage home to support their families in Poland whilst struggling to make ends meet in Merthyr. Today the problems Poles face still revolve around the family, but as many migrants now have near and extended family members living with them or close by in Merthyr the nature of the problems they face have also changed. Some Citizens Advice Bureau (CAB) workers argued that the employment-related problems faced by migrant factory workers in Merthyr have declined over recent years. Some interviewees argued that the number of complaints faced by local meat-processing factories was so high five years ago that they were forced to act and develop better occupational and human resource management practices. This may be true to some extent, but, as indicated, the nature of the underlying problems and ways of working have also changed. Some stakeholders recognised this and suggested that as organisations such as CAB have had their funding cut their capacity to understand the problems faced by migrants and offer help and support has, much like unions, declined significantly. Many migrants now go elsewhere for support and advice. Indeed, while Poles still face many problems in Merthyr and across our other cases, they now rely on their own support networks and specialist migrant-focused agencies instead of organisations such as CAB. As a local stakeholder confirmed, 'informal networks establish to fill the gap that's created when a service like CAB is no longer working ... so they [Poles and migrants generally] ... go down to somebody else somewhere else and get the kind of support [they need].' This situation was evident in the number of Poles openly discussing the help they receive from organisations such as the Polish Association of the Valleys and initiatives such as Glamorgan GATES – a funded outreach project at the University of Glamorgan that was overseen until 2012 by a local social entrepreneur from Merthyr; we will return to this issue below.

CAB interviews also indicated that debt was a major problem for the low-income Polish families working in local factories. When they are in work, many migrant workers have been entitled to tax credits and housing benefits, but if they have been put on short hours or lost their job their finances often fall apart very quickly as they struggle to pay regular bills. These problems are often compounded by the fact that some family members – often more recent arrivals – are not entitled to benefits. Some Polish couples are thus being pushed into hardship: the person in work loses their job and the other is not entitled to benefits, so the couple collectively have to manage on the benefit entitlement of one person. As money gets stretched too far, the payment of rent and council tax is often overlooked, thus pushing Poles into the hands of unscrupulous doorstep lenders and aggravating the problems with debt.

Inside the Workplace

We have established that employment practices underlie many of the problems Polish workers face. But what about working conditions inside the factory? We have seen already that migrants are often presented as 'good workers' vis-à-vis the local workforce, who have long being refusing to do 3D work in local factories. While many migrants accept their situation with a sense of resignation, some Poles in Merthyr also spoke of their isolation in the workplace and of how they keep to themselves to avoid the day-to-day interactions of factory life.

> You know in the factory the problem is that the people don't have qualifications and some people speak with you ... but with me there are three people work with me and some others speak with me and I

have an education but when I go to eat my lunch I stay alone, you understand. I don't like confusion. (Anatol, M)

A number of educated migrants also spoke of the need for forced isolation simply to avoid the everyday misunderstandings and disagreements that emerge in the workplace, very often through the use of language. The prevailing assumption that migrants from one country are a homogeneous group is also misleading in this context, with class being a significant factor in the day-to-day existence of factory life. Talented and qualified migrants often find themselves in the midst of co-workers that they have little in common with except their occupational role. The recession, which struck following the global financial crisis of 2008, also had an impact on the availability of work in Merthyr and the surrounding region. During our research it became evident that work was not as easy to secure in local food and meat-processing factories as it once was; some migrants suggested that during this time there was more demand to speak English than there had been previously. This new emphasis on English-language skills could be due to the recession reducing the number of positions available but it could also be due to the growing supply of Poles in the region, or a combination of both factors. Others remarked that the shortage of jobs created more tension between migrants of the same nationality. Again, as we note in the next chapter on Llanelli, the competition for scarce resources during periods when work is less readily available also has the effect of closing off flows of information about opportunities.

Over time, a small number of Poles move on to occupations outside of the factory. In general, however, opportunities for employment outside the food- and meat-processing sector are limited, not least because many jobs require a level of English-language that many Poles simply do not possess. The implications of not having such skills, particularly when they first arrive in Wales, were widely recognised by Poles. As Alina (F) stated: 'I worked as a packer in the meat factory. It was different, completely different. It was my first work when I came to Wales because I couldn't speak English.' A small number of Poles in Merthyr move on from production line work in factories to become heads of a production line team consisting solely of Polish workers. Despite this type of occupational progression, the type of occupation is controversial and was seen by one local stakeholder to be a big impediment to integration. As the local authority worker stated: 'So, say you'll have three lines of Polish workers and a Polish supervisor, two lines of Portuguese workers with a Portuguese supervisor. So, there's no need to communicate with each other.' Occasionally the lines will be mixed, but they are kept separate when numbers allow. While such practices reduce the likelihood of migrants learning English, some stakeholders argued that it is difficult to change if employers find it beneficial through increased efficiency.

Social Networks – Beyond Initial Migration

The number of friends individual migrants have in Merthyr from their home towns and regions in Poland varies from very few up to fifteen or more. While some migrants stated that they do not have time for friends, due to the pressures of work, others indicated that they go out to restaurants and pubs in Merthyr town centre to socialise with friends from Poland. Sometimes these relationships emerge though contacts and acquaintances made outside work, at the Polish Community of the Valleys Association (PCVA) for example. Andreka (F) arrived from Kalisz in central Poland in 2008 looking for work, and she now regularly attends PCVA meetings, which has led to new friendships and social outings. As she stated: 'I socialise with other people from my home country. We meet each other every 2-3 weeks or once a month. The place it depends, sometimes we go to our friend's house and sometimes we go out to restaurants or pubs.' Beyond socialising, social networks are engaged by migrants to address other needs. It often appeared during fieldwork that the only permanent way out of factory life in Merthyr was through self-employment and/or entrepreneurship, and it appears that Poles often go into business because they know they have a ready supply of Polish workers to help them out in the early days of their business venture. Walking around the town visiting shops and businesses, we talked to numerous Polish entrepreneurs about these issues and how business success is initially dependent on their social networks.

Working conditions in local factories were also noted as a motivating factor for setting up a business. Asked what had been her motivation to become a mobile beautician, Ania discussed the problems shift work created for her family life: 'Because my husband was working three shifts, I couldn't find a job with one shift when I had my daughter. So, because I was doing nails since I came to this country ... he said 'why don't you open a business' and I said, 'Well, why not?' and that was the start.' Many mobile businesses are thus set up out of necessity, either because a migrant cannot get a job, cannot get enough hours or does not earn enough to survive from their main job.

Two Polish entrepreneurs had set up a business in partnership in Merthyr because of the growing Polish population and the increasing demand for products from home by Polish workers in the area. They had initially opened up a shop in nearby Caerphilly, only to find out that there were not as many Poles in the area as their Internet research had led them to believe. With the business struggling, the two entrepreneurs decided to move the shop to Merthyr, where the Polish population was well established. As one of the team said, 'Even though we know there's a few stores there already ... I am quite surprised, for a small town like Merthyr there is a population [of Poles] so big' (Izaak, M). Iwo (M), another Polish entrepreneur who arrived in 2007, made a similar point: 'When I've come here, four to five years ago, I'm not even sure if was one Polish shop. At the moment there are three to four Polish shops. I know that is some Polish hairdresser, so definitely Polish people are running more and more businesses.' The socio-economic situation in Merthyr and the surrounding area presented many initial opportunities for Polish entrepreneurs to find a market niche and provide goods and services (both on and off the high street) to fellow migrants. More recently, successful migrant businesses have also attracted customers from among the local population. As a Pole with numerous business interests in the town Andrzej (M) confirmed: 'That's why I like it, the locals are interested in what we sell and the national foods, most of them try different things on holidays so they are not scared of trying something new.' However, competition for the Polish pound is strong in Merthyr. Tesco stocks an increasing range of Polish products and a Polish shop owner stated that he has to adapt his product ranges regularly if he is to keep his customer base happy.

Despite Merthyr's historical legacy of social and economic problems, there have also been signs of change over recent years. A number of migrant entrepreneurs and local stakeholders spoke about the ways in which migrant entrepreneurs and new migrant businesses had played a significant role attracting a new clientele to Merthyr, people who not so long ago would have avoided the town. The interaction and competition between Polish and Portuguese entrepreneurs has been a major driver of change in this sense. At the bottom end of the high street a number of migrant businesses have sprung up over recent years, and just outside the town centre, adjacent to St Mary's Church, a glut of Polish businesses emerged. There have been many other migrant businesses in and around Merthyr over the last decade, including a veterinary practice, a garage run by eastern European migrants and various mobile businesses.

There is a general perception that these businesses have made a contribution to the social and economic regeneration of Merthyr over the last decade. As a local authority stakeholder said in 2012, 'It's more multicultural if you like which for somewhere like Merthyr Tydfil is quite unusual because the Valleys' mind-set is the norm you know so I think people are excited to see changes you know in the foods they can taste and the dining experiences they can have.' As policy change and funding cuts emerged during the recent recession, a number of specialist migrant-focused and migrant-led organisations sprang up in Merthyr. Glamorgan GATES, a funded outreach project at the University of Glamorgan until 2012, was widely recognised by Poles in Merthyr for the range of help and support it provided. The social entrepreneur who ran GATES has recently set up a new venture ,Y Bont (The Bridge) Culture Hub, to provide a similar service to help foster integration. Y Bont emerged to enable individuals from all cultural backgrounds to be aware of their rights and responsibilities, to access services and engage in learning, training, work and arts-based experience (see chapter 10).

As noted already, the Polish Community of the Valleys Association (PCVA) also plays a significant role in the Polish community. The Chair of PCVA illustrated its role clearly: 'We help support people and give advice and information about living and working in Wales, but also we are trying to integrate people from Poland who live here.' As public sector organisations such as CAB have been forced to make cuts, the work of these organisations and social entrepreneurs has become increasingly significant. As a local stakeholder in Merthyr noted, 'What happens is informal networks establish to fill the gap that's created when a service like CAB is no longer working ... [as it once did] ... so they [migrants] ... go down to somebody else somewhere else and get the kind of support [they need].'

Similar developments can be seen in the use made of different venues in Merthyr town centre. Polish migrants have tended to use the Polish Association of the Valleys as a central focus for their activities, while the Portuguese community often congregate at the local tapas bar. Asked where they go for information on any number of local issues, migrants often gave answers along the lines of, 'Oh, I just go down to X and ask Y.' Very often the individuals providing this type of support and advice are closely connected to prominent social entrepreneurs and local migrant networks.

Nevertheless, long working hours in factories and poor wages present significant barriers to integration. As the local priest in Merthyr pointed out when discussing his attempts to increase the number of Poles attending mass, 'they work over the weekends, they work anti-social hours they work at night time, which means they can't come to anything or won't come to anything and they won't mix.' This was confirmed by Alina (F), who stated: '[I]n the factory we work a lot of hours . . . so you don't have a lot of time to do much more. If I start at seven then I finish at twelve and then I start at five o'clock the next day.' Despite such problems Church remains important. There is Polish mass at St Marys Church on the first Saturday of every month, and this is well attended at certain times of the year, particularly at Easter and on Christmas holidays, when Poles travel to mass to meet up with other Poles and visit nearby Polish shops.

Conclusion

In 1999, Merthyr was named the unhealthiest town in Britain, and social problems associated with poverty, illness and long-term unemployment are clearly evident in the experiences of Polish migrants, particularly in their interactions with younger people and those that, discursively at least, are seen to be in competition with them for jobs.[20] Even so, our research suggests that migrant workers in Merthyr get on as well with local people, as they do with other groups of migrant workers. However, it is also clear that this situation masks certain differences and tensions both among and between migrant groups, with competition between Polish and Portuguese workers remaining strong to this day. Migrants from both groups also highlighted recent tensions within their own groups over jobs, particularly, as noted, between established workers and newcomers. There is also an assumption that migrant groups are homogeneous in terms of class and background, which, as we have also shown, is far from the case.

It is clear that the relative short-term intensity of in-migration into the Valleys, particularly in Merthyr, has, for a time, had a profound impact on the town, bringing a significant change to a traditionally less diverse region of South Wales. However, it is also clear that many local people see migrant workers as a threat. As well as being seen as job takers, there is a general perception that migrants also get preferential treatment from service providers. This can be the source of tensions, and some migrants had experienced verbal abuse in the street. Some Poles were particularly wary of abuse and the threat of violence from young people in the town centre, especially at night. As one noted, 'I would never go out at night alone, even if it was to a shop around the corner.' Many of the problems encountered appear to be class- and gender-based and/or generational. As another Pole stated, 'people from my neighbourhood, mainly older people are very nice ... but younger generation from my work or neighbourhood have a prejudice against people from different countries.' It should be noted, however, that these incidents were not commonplace. When they do occur, migrants link the underlying attitude back to the groups they are seen to be in competition with for local jobs, rather than as overt expressions of racism or discrimination. Indeed, given Merthyr's many long-standing entrenched social problems, discrimination, racism and crime were not as evident as one might imagine, and it appears that many Poles are happily resigned to life in the Valleys.

7

Polish Migrants in Llanelli: What Happens after the Initial Migration Period?

Introduction

In the wake of EU expansion in 2004, Carmarthenshire became one of the unanticipated hotspots in Wales for labour migration from CEE countries. In particular, it was the town of Llanelli and the surrounding Gwendraeth Valley which emerged as the destination for those who moved from towns and cities on the new eastern borderlands of the EU. In a matter of a few months, a town popularly known as 'Tinopolis' because of its long history of mining and metal manufacturing quickly came to be dubbed 'Llaneski' in some parts of the tabloid press due to its new association with the phenomenon of CEE migration, especially from Poland.

As one of the principal centres of industrial production in Wales, Llanelli had long attracted migrant labour to its industrial foundries and factories. Then workers from Ireland and Italy as well as other parts of the UK swelled the local workforce, attracted to the town by plentiful work and good wages. Llanelli is, however, no longer a natural magnet for large-scale migration. A good deal of the industrial production once undertaken in the town, employing tens of thousands of workers, is now done elsewhere or employs a substantially smaller workforce. How, then, did Llanelli became a hub for migration from the new EU member states?

In answering this question we show that as in Cardiff and Merthyr Tydfil migrant social networks feed international mobility. They act as circuits for the flow of information about migration opportunities both from contacts living in Poland and those working abroad. In the case of Llanelli, however, we will show that a critical factor was the intervention of temporary staffing agencies in facilitating migration. As we mentioned in Chapter 4, studies in other parts of the UK have highlighted the importance of commercial organisations not only in making migration possible, but also in *sponsoring* the movement of individuals across the EU. This is the first study to examine their role in Wales in bringing migrant workers into the country.

We will also explore how those who have moved have been changed by their experience of migration. Money and work are what motivate most to move, but when we look at why migrants stay, these factors are only part of what persuades them to remain abroad. In the majority of cases, it is the change in migrants' broader outlook and lifestyle which makes them want to stay. None of this diminishes the significant challenges all face in adapting to life in Wales, but the longer an individual is abroad the more they come to see migration as a positive change in their circumstances. We begin by introducing the migrants' access and initiation into the local labour market. The review of the locality which these men and women have made their home was outlined in Chapter 3.

Accessing the Local Labour Market

Since 2004, those who left their homes in Poland for West Wales have been drawn by similar opportunities to relieve financial pressures and, as many see it, to make a 'better life' for themselves and their families. Like migrants of earlier generations, they, too, have come to plug gaps in the labour market. Now, however, they have come to perform tasks which, it is claimed, local workers are unwilling to undertake in sufficient numbers.

As noted already, in Llanelli we find a more prominent role for staffing agencies in moving labour. The food-processing industry on the fringes of the M4 corridor may provide employment to a sizeable body of labour, but these are comparatively niche labour markets. In this context, staffing agencies act as a critical broker between prospective employees and contractors seeking the type of worker they claim cannot be sourced locally in sufficient numbers. While the role of staffing agencies as facilitators of migration in other countries has been widely documented, their place in moving migrant labour to localities which had not previously had any notable history of settlement from the CEE countries is one of the most striking features of the migration to the UK after 2004.

The significance of temporary staffing agencies in enabling migrants to secure employment in Carmarthenshire is especially marked in the case of those who arrived shortly after Poland joined the EU in 2004. As reported in Chapter 4, among those surveyed in Llanelli in 2008, just over half stated they had work arranged through a recruitment agency before coming to Wales. In practice, the number of migrants gaining work through staffing agencies – whether before coming to Wales or on arrival – is likely to be much higher. Opportunities for employment outside those sectors in which migrants are predominantly employed are limited because they require a level of competency in English which most of those who come to Llanelli do not – certainly initially – possess.

Frequently, participants spoke in quite matter-of-fact terms of how staffing agencies orchestrated their move to Wales. Thus Marta, who had (in 2008) been living in Llanelli for just over a year, explained that personal contacts pointed her in the direction of staffing agencies who made her move happen. Initially, her father had told her he could find work for her husband in Wales, but when this failed to materialise friends pointed her in the direction of a local staffing agency which had previously facilitated their own move to the town. Thus her husband moved initially with the agency and she followed shortly afterwards with their young daughter. She told us how the subject of work abroad, and especially how agencies could broker moves, was discussed frequently within her close network of friends: 'We would get to know from our friends ... that there are agencies. And from friends we got to know that there were those agencies and we went there, left CVs, filled the forms.' In many interviews, participants spoke of this process in strikingly straightforward terms. Marek, who was interviewed in 2011, and who uprooted from his home town just south of Warsaw in a matter of weeks, explained that he had 'simply learnt [from a friend] that there was a recruiting agency in Lublin, and simply went there, got a job and was sent here by the agency'.

As we showed in Chapter 4, temporary staffing agencies make migration happen by reducing barriers to mobility. They make it feasible for individuals to 'try' life abroad, which is certainly how the majority envisage their plans pre-departure. Accommodation, travel and documentation are all arranged through these commercial middlemen. They will often cover the costs – at least upfront – of getting to the destination. In Llanelli, CSA Recruitment is a staffing agency, which has grown in scale from the opportunity to recruit labour from Poland, with an office in Warsaw employing a dozen staff to coordinate the recruitment and movement of workers for employers in Carmarthenshire. CSA describes itself as 'one of the first specialist recruitment companies in the UK to recognise the huge benefits skilled and unskilled Central and Eastern European workers could bring to British businesses'. Among those whom we interviewed in 2008, CSA had been the primary staffing agency in facilitating migration to Llanelli. It is also an agency which has come under the spotlight from media, trade unions and politicians for the contracts on which migrant workers are employed.

Most of all, of course, agencies provide employment. Their particular value to the migrants who came to Llanelli is that they offer work, which can be largely done alongside other workers from Poland. Though migrants do encounter members of the local population in work, they will spend much of their working day with other Poles. Among those we interviewed in 2008, the overwhelming majority stated they had, at best, very limited competency in English before coming to Wales. Therefore, they need to work in environments in which they are unlikely to need to speak English; staffing agencies meet this requirement. Without the intervention of staffing agencies, we can say with some certainty it is unlikely the region would have experienced the scale of migration it has seen since 2004.

For those who came in the first year after Poland's accession to the EU, companies such as CSA were critically important in enabling migration. Among those arriving later, family and friends play an increasingly important role in bringing new migrants to Llanelli. Among those interviewed in 2008, many were pioneers, the first among their family or friendship group to migrate to Wales. It is not long, however, before a system of chain migration through migrant networks is evident in bringing new arrivals to Llanelli.

Thus, with those who took part in the second round of interviews in late 2010 and early 2011, it was more typical to have work arranged through personal networks. Maria, for example, a woman in her late twenties, arrived in Wales in 2007 with her boyfriend at the time, who had been contacted by a friend already living in Llanelli to say that there was a job for him. Ewa, who had been in Llanelli for just over a year when she was interviewed in 2011, was living in the town with six other members of her immediate family; in her case, it was her father who moved first to Wales: 'My father worked here, through the agency, he set us up with work, otherwise we wouldn't have come here, just like that without work and plans. So we had the job lined up for us.'

For men and women eager for better prospects, the promises and offers of assistance from family and friends abroad can be difficult to resist. Lukasz, for example, was a man in his mid-fifties who had been living in Wales for two years when he was interviewed. He described how a succession of temporary labouring jobs and financial pressures, had combined to make him contemplate leaving his home just outside Warsaw to seek work abroad. Like so many others, it was a call from his brother, already living in Llanelli, which provided the final impetus he needed. "Simply, my brother called me: Come over to me because I've found a job for you." Simply this way, and that's why I came.' Established migrants, through networks which they have developed over time, can find opportunities for family and friends, but it is firms such as CSA on which most rely for work in the area. Even when participants spoke of family or friends 'fixing' openings for them, mostly what they were arranging was an 'introduction' to the staffing agency.

Migrant Working in Llanelli

Those who have come to Llanelli are employed in a range of largely low-skilled roles, including construction, agriculture and social care. Among the largest employers are the meat-processing and packaging firms Dawn Pac and Dunbia, both of which are, in turn, suppliers to major retailers such as ASDA and Marks and Spencer. This sector has grown significantly for some decades, and migrant labour has been a key ingredient of this success in recent years.

For all of the ways in which staffing agencies are able to reduce the barriers to migration, new arrivals still face significant challenges in attempting to settle in Llanelli. Their lives are punctuated by disruption. Accommodation provided by agencies is rarely suitable for anything other than an immediate stop-gap, and most are quickly looking to find somewhere better. More than anything, it is the struggle to achieve a regular working pattern which governs their daily existence, certainly for the early phase of their migration.

Participants spoke of waiting for mobile phones to ring to learn, at short notice, they were needed for a shift. One man, Klemens, who had been living in Llanelli for just under two years recounted his experience of working with agencies: 'one of us was called and a lady or a guy said that there were no orders and they had to cancel us that day. And there were times that we'd have received a similar phone call four times a week and go to work only once.' Another man, Ludwik, who had also been living in Llanelli for just under two years when he was interviewed in 2008, had left a factory job in his home town in north-western Poland to work in the meat- processing industry in West Wales. Though he had a close relative already working in the same plant, he had clearly not been forewarned about the irregular nature of employment as an agency worker. Like many others during the initial period abroad, he explained how it was impossible to settle into a routine because he did not know his working hours from week to week, and even from day to day. He similarly explained how he would be 'ready to go to work and suddenly the phone rings that I'm not going or sometimes I was supposed to have a day off and there's a phone that I'm going.' These are very representative accounts of what is for most of those arriving in Llanelli a normal part of their early migratory career.

The effects of this chaotic existence were evident. Participants spoke of how the unpredictability of work affected their lives. The case of Katja, who moved to Llanelli (later to be joined by her husband) in early 2007, was typical of accounts relayed by others across both studies. As she told us in 2011: 'I worked very irregular hours. There was work, and then there wasn't any work. You would wait for the phone call. You couldn't plan for anything.' For most of those arriving to work in Llanelli, too, their contracts with local employers are short-term, lasting no more than three months at a time. Only after a year do some of the larger employers consider putting migrant labourers on permanent contracts, but most will continue to rely on the orders to keep coming in to remain in employment. Some participants spoke openly of feeling misled about how the labour market would be in Llanelli. Agency staff in Poland had, they said, told them there would be more work than they had secured. As Jakub remarked about the female employee in the staffing agency back in Poland who had 'sold' the move to him: 'Well, she did lie a bit. But she has to. If she didn't, who would come here?' Contracts, which they thought had promised forty hours of work weekly, worked out differently in practice once they arrived in Llanelli.

Participants spoke, too, of the demands of their working environment and its toll on them. The daily routine was, for some, draining, and work was a 'treadmill', as another man who had been living in this way for nearly four years remarked. For those involved in food processing, the long hours of repetitive labour, working at what they said was an often demanding pace on production lines, could be stressful. In many interviews in 2008, when we asked more specific questions about working conditions, there was a definite recognition they were employed for labour in which, they believed, others were simply not as productive. When Adam, a man in his early thirties from a small town in central Poland, arrived in Llanelli, he joined a substantial group who had moved at an earlier point from the same locality ('when I first came here I could see lots of old friends, former classmates, friends'), and employers, he believed, took on Poles because they would push themselves harder than local workers. When we spoke to him he was employed in a large meat processing plant, and told us quite plainly that 'some companies prefer to take a Pole rather than a Welsh person. They have learned to appreciate our work. We're more efficient than people from other countries.'

The conversations in 2008 were peppered with references to tensions among workers, which, for the most part, was the normal workplace strife over hierarchies and personalities which exists in many organisations. In both studies in Llanelli it was evident that though Poles do tend to work together, where they do work alongside locals there is a degree of resentment over their perceived easier treatment by line managers:

> A Pole works three times as much as a Welsh. A Welsh will stand next to a conveyor belt, laugh; he is allowed to. A Pole is not. He mustn't. Not Poles. A Pole has to work. I mean, a Pole has to work, because everyone wants to earn money, don't they? And, as for a Welsh, he somehow doesn't care. (Lucjan, M)

A small number did, however, address work-related difficulties using the framework of equal treatment of Poles. The payment of an overtime rate, for example, was raised explicitly in a number of interviews. Lech, for example, relayed an account of a particular conflict about differential rates of pay between agency worker and direct employees of the food-processing factory in which he had worked for two years. He had wanted to show that Poles recruited through a staffing agency were not employed in a 'work camp', as he emotively put it. In contrast, others explained that, much as they were unhappy with the arrangements for working overtime, they were not comfortable raising it with line managers who were charged with getting them to stay. Jerz, who had arrived in Llanelli in early 2007 from a large town near Kracow, remarked that he and his friends were disgruntled about how their line manager made them stay beyond their normal working day – without, he claimed, overtime payment. They hadn't complained, he suggested, because 'we were too afraid to lose that job. We were intimidated.'

For much of the time, those we interviewed in both 2008/2009 and 2010/11 were working mostly with other Poles. There is no evidence that employers seek to recruit only migrant workers for work in the food-processing sector in the locality; senior managers from CSA and Dawn Pac are on record as stating they cannot find local workers in sufficient numbers to fill posts. It was nevertheless common for co-workers to be co-nationals. Some of the participants said this was because they were doing jobs locals did not want. Milosz, who had been employed through an agency in this sector commented that he worked only with other Poles 'because none of the Welsh with their senses would. The temperature in there is −5. I have to wear two pairs of gloves to run the documents. I'm being chased for everything.' Mostly, whatever the difficulties between individuals, participants were comfortable with the broadly Polish working environment because their English-language skills were generally low. Luiza, who had moved two years previously from Lodz, told us that she had moved because it was difficult for women to find work in her home city. Like many others to whom we spoke who believed they had not sufficient competency or confidence in English, she also illustrated how being employed alongside fellow Poles was a preference. Currently employed in a food-processing factory, she told us that she had been offered a job in 'an English work' but turned it down because 'I think I got scared a bit cause only English people work there.'

Though the food-processing sector in the locality cannot be properly described as constituting an 'ethnic economy', for Polish migrants it is the market in which they are most likely to be hired and, as we have said, there are limited opportunities for working alongside locals. It was clear some workers had direct experience of circulating between employers in this sector, even actively choosing to leave one factory for better work and wages in another. The availability of work and the ability to work in a largely Polish environment undoubtedly contribute to the fact that relatively few of the workers change their job. In our 2008 survey in Llanelli the majority had not changed jobs more than once, and nearly two-thirds of these had not left the job for which they were initially recruited. At best, they were employed by organisations that initially recruited them through staffing agencies. Their experience of how precarious their situation is, should the work dry up for longer periods than they can tolerate, combined with an awareness of how difficult life had been for many back in Poland, definitely keeps most focused on retaining their current contract or securing the next one.

More than this, there is a clear understanding they will struggle to find work outside the sector in which they are employed. Most spoke openly of wanting to improve their employment status and earnings, as well as, in some instances, of matching their job more appropriately to their skills. Among those we interviewed in 2008, there were nevertheless few cases of individuals successfully making the transition into the mainstream economy. Where they work alongside locals, they do so often as agency workers recruited along with other migrant workers. The transition from agency worker to direct employee therefore represents an important career turning point not only in wages and security, but also in status.

Their ability to speak English at a level which would allow them to make this transition is the single greatest obstacle to finding work which is more secure, better paid or just more in the vein of what they might like to do in the longer term. Michal described how it was the 'language barrier' which was the 'only thing stopping me from changing the job, 'cause I've got sufficient skills to make much more money. I've got welding, mechanical skills. I'm also a professional driver – I can do everything. It's just the language.' Until they are able to improve their proficiency in English, they are dependent on work which they know could, for most, end at short notice.

In spite of this, we found almost universal agreement that the labour market is better than in Poland, even if the availability of work, and, for some, the nature of the work, is not what they might wish. Most had left Poland at points in their lives at which they were experiencing personal troubles, normally as a consequence of financial difficulties. In Poland, they might have been struggling to find work, or had to hold down two, sometimes three jobs to make ends meet, and most seem to have been barely managing to make ends meet. In Wales, by contrast, they may have been earning more for similar or shorter hours or succeeding in getting by on one job, albeit one they would wish to change for a higher salary or better conditions.

A small number of participants in both studies had clear plans to improve their status. In 2008, our sample was overwhelmingly composed of migrants who had exited the education system at the end of secondary school, with some leaving before this point. Few had studied at university, though some had followed vocational training programmes. Those who had studied at university had managed to find employment outside the food-processing sector, in environments in which they formed friendships with members of the local population. There were examples, too, of others who were looking to improve their prospects by studying for British qualifications, which they believed would enable them to find better-paid, more secure employment. In most cases, the plan, where there was one, was to improve competency in English. Their likelihood of staying in the UK was, they knew, contingent on having the requisite language skills to work outside the migrant economy. Again, Katja, who had been living in Llanelli for four years at the time of the interview, was aware that the options open to her and her husband were limited 'because of the language barrier. We are so handicapped because of that. It makes me really cross.' Another woman, who had given up a job working in a bank in Poland and persuaded her son to move with her to Wales to earn more money, explained that her intention was to 'master the language up to a certain standard, in a year or two, then ... probably look for another job among the British or Welsh'.

If only a minority were actively seeking to manufacture a life change through the acquisition or enhancement of skills, few had not been changed in a quite fundamental way by their migration. In sharp contrast to those who had migrated to Cardiff, almost none of the migrants who had moved to Llanelli had done so as a life experience. Indeed, Krystyna remarked that 'nobody came here for their own pleasure', adding that they 'they've usually been compelled by their life.' While money may be the primary motivation for migration rather than the development of human capital, changes to their pattern of life brought about by moving abroad play an important role in encouraging individuals to suspend or stretch into the distance their exit strategies. Migrants might come to work, and without it they will leave, but it is the way of life which makes them want to stay. This is a theme to which we will return in Chapter 8.

Being a Migrant

For all that their migration may have been driven by a simple economic exchange, it is also a fundamentally human experience. In the public debates about numbers, costs and benefits to the host country, it is easy to neglect the human aspect of the great trek of recent European migration. These are men and women who have left homes, often left family, in search not only of work but also of solutions to stark personal problems. The changes to their financial circumstances are nevertheless only part of a much larger transformation. Moreover, to see the change in crude terms as due to differences in the cost of living between the place they have left and the one to which they have moved is to miss that the biggest change, at least as far as this locality is concerned, is the difference in *how* they live.

There is little doubt that among the most difficult challenges is the need to renegotiate relationships on a number of fronts – with those with whom they had been thrown together in temporary accommodation, with new workmates, with family they had left behind and also those who either came with them or who followed after. They are strangers making their way in a foreign country who, much as some may try to avoid it, have no choice but to adapt to an unfamiliar cultural terrain. None of it is straightforward. Relationships creak, and sometimes sunder, as a consequence of the physical separation which migration brings. Competition for labour and other valuable resources almost always breeds a degree of mistrust of those outside an individual's immediate circle of family and friends.

Maintaining contact with friends and family in Poland is necessary for many because of what they have left behind, but it also helps to offset some of the strains of adjusting to life away. While they are abroad they will be in contact with friends back home through email, Skype and assorted electronic fora, such as Gadu Gadu, as well as on the phone. More mundanely, satellite television also allows migrants to retain a familiar link to Poland. When we undertook the second study in 2010/11, Polish-language programmes on televisions in living rooms sometimes formed the backdrop to interviews. For all that they have left Poland, modern technologies facilitate the organisation of transnational communities.

Migration will have significant, even long-term effects on families in which one or more member moves abroad. For those left at home, there are concerns about migration, and they would make clear their desire for the separation to end. Anna, a woman in her late twenties who had been living in Llanelli with her husband for over four years when we spoke with her in 2011, told us about how she suspected her husband limited the frequency with which he called his mother because she continually asked him to come home. More often than not, however, they had actively supported the move. Parents encouraged their children to try working abroad to address their financial difficulties. Family roles, too, were reorganised to accommodate mothers or fathers moving to Wales on their own. In a time and place in which such moves were common, and even, for many, something of which they will have had personal knowledge, this is not surprising. It is still nevertheless a wrench for migrants to adjust to what one man who had lived away from his family for four years called 'the heartache of the separation'.

As they forge a new life for themselves in Llanelli, however, they must rely on their local networks. On a practical level, where individuals come with friends or already have contacts living in Llanelli, they can secure immediate accommodation and gain referrals to prospective employers through these personal contacts, as well as benefit from insiders' valuable knowledge about work that might pay more or where conditions might be better. Often, too, they can reduce expenditure by sharing rental costs and, as numerous participants did, jointly purchasing a car to give greater choice over where they lived and worked. Also, even where individuals arrive alone, relationships are forged with fellow migrants who share their lot, either in the workplace or in the often cramped living conditions they experience on arrival in Llanelli.

Networks tend to be clustered around small groups with little meaningful contact with other small groups or diffuse networks. The bond between network members is intensified by the high levels of suspicion of fellow Poles beyond their close personal contacts. Miron (M) succinctly captured what for many of the participants is a concern which does not go away – competition for scarce resources:

> Let's say, they've got a job and we've been looking for a job. There are people we used to work with and someone found a job and we asked him about the address where he has found that. And he was going in circles around the topic, but didn't say exactly. It's just like he doesn't want to tell us 'cause he thinks then when we go there I'll apply and maybe he'll lose his job because of that. And that's the way it is.

Another man, Lukasz, explained that aside from his close friends, the other Poles he knew 'keep everything in secret, their job and everything ... if they have got a job they won't be willing to help anyone else to find a job there cause they're afraid of their own place.' Individuals do benefit from information or openings obtained by network contacts, who in turn gain this information from other sources. Among our participants, however, only a few spoke of making new friends in Llanelli who gave introductions to others who could provide work. This is not a phenomenon unique to Llanelli, but the town is not a labour market like Cardiff, with its wider range of opportunities. Indeed, some attributed it to a culture of 'getting by' which they bring with them from Poland and which is intensified in circumstances in which they lack the language skills and networks to make their futures less contingent on matter beyond their control.

In these conditions, the support of family structures becomes all the more important. The presence of family in Llanelli mitigates some of the challenges of settling. Among those we surveyed in 2008, just under a third had kin networks in the town before they left Poland. The psychological anxieties about leaving the familiarity of home were, understandably, lessened by the knowledge that family would be there to support them when they moved. On a practical level, too, having family already living in Llanelli helps new arrivals to get over some of the obstacles which others before have learned to negotiate, from securing work to opening a bank account and registering at a doctor's surgery.

That migrants encourage their kin to follow them to Wales is nevertheless only partly due to their desire to create something approximating what they had left behind in Poland. Rather, it would be more accurate to say that they want their family with them because of a firmly-held belief that their life abroad would trump the circumstances which most had experienced in Poland. Time after time, we were told that family life is better in the UK. Most struggled to get by in Poland. Krystyna had initially moved only with her son, leaving her husband and daughter behind in Poland, but the family was reunited after two years of living largely parallel lives. She described the difficulties for families like hers in Poland in making ends meet from one month to the next: 'without a family, one would have problems to earn a living earning the money I used to earn there ... that's why there are quarrels and there are divorces. But here, if there is work, then basically one afford some decent life.' Younger couples, in particular, noticed the benefits of being able to afford to live alone as a unit, where in Poland, because of the cost of living, they might have to live with one set of parents. The support the state gives to families undoubtedly helps. We spoke to parents who were in receipt of welfare benefits, but this is only one element of what was seen as a more effective structure of support. Those with children cited examples of their children receiving healthcare which was superior to that which they had experienced in Poland. Schooling, too, was largely viewed as better, and as their children made swift improvements in their English-language skills this was seen as further evidence that the family had reaped wider benefits from moving abroad.

The most profound change, arguably, is even more personal. Almost without exception in both studies in Llanelli, each of the individuals we interviewed spoke of being transformed by moving to Wales. For all the pressures of adapting to life abroad, including the demands and uncertainties of their working conditions, they believed their lives had been qualitatively and unexpectedly improved. They talked about being less stressed, of life being less frantic and of feeling they could enjoy themselves as they had not been able to before they moved. They compared what one man referred to as the 'rat race' in Poland to the 'comfort', 'calm' and 'normality' of life in Wales, as others variously described their time in Llanelli. Money is undeniably important. Not worrying about bills as they had hitherto done makes them feel as if a weight has been lifted from them. They compare themselves to the locals, who, they say, do not 'worry about what tomorrow brings'. Perhaps the most remarkable commentary on the perceived stark differences between lives in the UK and Poland came from Kazimierz, who had been living in Llanelli for over six years:

> I'm an old-fashioned man. We can put it this way because I can remember the communist era. This communism has been condemned until today, but basically I still can see it. It's like a reference point, that people used to live a more dignified life than now. And, basically, what is starting to happen there, then I think that here, the UK, is like the old 'Komuna' that we used to have in Poland ... We had this peace of mind then ... And this peace of mind, I think, is probably the most important for everyone from our generation.

Such nostalgia was not too far out of line with the views of many. In contrast to the conditions that caused them to leave home in search of work and better wages, participants remarked that locals do not, as one woman who had (in 2008) lived in Llanelli for two years said, 'care about tomorrow too much. They've always got jobs and they'll always be able to provide for themselves' and they are not, as another observed, afraid of 'what tomorrow brings'.

Conclusion

When we undertook our studies, Llanelli had not replaced migrants' home villages, towns and cities in their affections. Their inability to converse with the locals was a daily reminder that they were outsiders. More often than not, however, they did not class themselves as migrants, or at least they did so less than when they arrived. They commented that locals had, by and large, not made them feel like strangers. Also, most were not prepared to commit to remaining permanently in the UK. They might not have been able to foresee when they would return to Poland, but they knew that remaining in Wales was contingent on factors beyond their control, principally the availability of work. Thus they nevertheless live an in-between existence which is shaped by their experience of migration. They may feel an attachment to the country they left, but Llanelli had become for many a second home. Visits back to Poland served to remind them that life had not stood still there when they left – friends and family had moved on, just as they had for them in Llanelli.

PART III

8

'Migratory Drift' (or Why Migrants Nearly Always Stay Longer than Planned)

Introduction

We began Chapter 4 by saying that for public and policy-makers alike immigration is a complex subject which is invariably boiled down to numbers and a few associated questions. Paramount among these, perhaps, is the issue of how many migrants (usually from selected states) are living in the country at a given time. This is the one issue that grabs the headlines, consumes editorials, exercises political leaders and, opinion polls would suggest, is on the minds of a substantial proportion of the British public. It clearly occupied the minds of many voters during the 2016 referendum on UK membership of the EU. It was one of the primary issues on which the Prime Minister at the time, David Cameron, claimed to have agreed important concessions in the lead-up to the referendum. One opinion poll after another, however, revealed that a substantial proportion of the electorate wanted much more robust assurances that freedom of movement into the UK would be dramatically curtailed.

Following EU enlargement in 2004, and after it dawned on voters that the projected number of migrants arriving from the newly joined CEE states had vastly exceeded experts' estimates, the other question which was asked was: 'How long will they stay?' The widely held assumption was that these were 'temporary' migrants, attracted by the prospect of better jobs, here to plug short-term gaps in the labour market. This was a view which was not dissimilar to the disposition of those arriving in the UK from the new EU member states. It was also a perspective which, as it turned out, was not any more accurate for having been held on both sides.

It is expected that anywhere from 30 to 50 per cent of the migrants that entered the UK from Poland since 2004 have left.[1,2] This still leaves a substantial foreign-born population. As studies across the UK have shown, many migrants stayed long after they – and 'we' – had expected them to return to Poland. What forces determine this pattern of migratory behaviour? Why do migrants commit to a migratory career which can routinely last for years rather than months, and what factors shape their decisions about returning to Poland or making their home, on a more permanent basis, in Wales?

Though the focus of public and policy debates is more usually focused on the subject of 'how many', it is arguably the question of 'how long' which is politically and sociologically of the greatest import for both migrants and local resident populations as well as for political authorities at this time. The arrival of large numbers of migrants in a short space of time presents its own challenges for already resident populations, for services and for governance. Substantial populations remaining for a long period of time – measured in a handful of years at a minimum, and in many cases longer – raises questions about how authorities should approach the thorny dilemma of immigrant integration into the mainstream population. In the following discussion we ask why so many migrants in our studies in South Wales stayed long after the point when they had expected to return to Poland. We anticipate that this answer will lead to a more detailed discussion in the next chapter, as this phenomenon may have a considerable impact on the integration of Polish migrants with British society.

Migratory Patterns and Policy

Prior to Poland's accession to the EU in 2004 it was widely expected that the lowering of legal restrictions to the mobility of Polish citizens would result in a wave of new international migration. In neighbouring states, fears about the movement of cheap Polish labour following accession were stoked by centre-right parties. In France, during the debate on the European Constitution in 2005, the Polish plumber became a bogeyman in the minds of a substantial section of the electorate, symbolising an expected wave of low-wage labour which would sweep into the country.[3] In Germany, which up until 2004, accounted for approximately a third of all Poles living outside their national territory, surveys showed an overwhelming majority of citizens to be anxious about the impact of increased migration from the accession countries on employment and wages in the country.[4]

Studies have highlighted how 'freedom of movement', one of the cornerstones of EU citizenship, and specifically the right to seek work abroad, was enthusiastically sold by Polish policy-makers and media alike prior to Poland's accession in 2004 as one of the principal benefits of EU membership.[5] Coping with the fallout from a hard transition to a market economy in the 1990s, successive governments sought local agreements with other European states to allow for short-term mobility of Polish citizens to work abroad as trainees or seasonal labourers to ease labour market pressures during the transitional phase. Research has also shown how Polish government policy during negotiations on EU membership, and in particular in the lead-in to accession, has been viewed as a continuation of this earlier policy.[6] The Polish government's policy, however, in sharp relief to the view in many 'old' EU states, was informed by estimates that the size and scale of this movement was not expected to be significant. This was a view also shared by many social scientists at the time.[7,8]

There was also a widespread acceptance that much of the mobility would be short-term. Indeed, studies prior to enlargement pointed to what would probably be a high level of labour market volatility. Surveys carried out in the late 1990s in those CEE states which would later join the EU reported large numbers of individuals who would move to west European member states for short periods of time, ranging from a 'few weeks' to a 'few months'.[9] Wallace, drawing on survey data on would-be migrants' intentions, assessed that migration from these countries would largely 'take the form of short-term, circulatory commuting where people can travel more easily'.[10]

Since 2004, numerous investigations of migration from the 'new' to the 'old' EU member states have found evidence that temporary, circular migration is indeed one of the dominant types of migratory behaviour. One of the earliest studies drew a typology in which three of its principal migratory types were differentiated by strategies which were nonetheless forms of short-term mobility.[11] Thus 'storks' are usually seasonal workers employed in low-paid jobs, 'hamsters' leave with the intention of a single visit during which they will accumulate capital to be used at home, while 'searchers' move abroad with little plan beyond staying for as long as they wish – only 'stayers', as their name suggests, fit the bill of what might be seen as a more conventional form of migratory settlement.

Others have identified temporary, circular migration as a strategy to cope with structural problems linked to Poland's transitional economy. Thus Okolski refers to the rise of 'incomplete migration' as one of the standout trends in the movement of citizens from CEE states.[12] This phenomenon, she argues, is 'quasi-migratory' in that individuals engaged in this activity will be abroad for periods of time, not necessarily following any regular pattern, and while away will maintain frequent and 'steady' contact with home. Fihel and Grabowska-Lusinska found evidence of 'back-and-forth' migration as a strategy for individuals either struggling to secure regular employment in Poland or who wanted a more flexible, albeit irregular, form of employment to help maximise income.[13, 14]

Engerbsen and colleagues in a series of important publications have arguably best captured this sense of post-2004 migration as not only quantitatively different from population movements which followed earlier EU enlargements by its size and scale, but also as a qualitative species because of its 'liquid' form. The EU's open borders have enabled individuals to try out working abroad in other, sometimes multiple, EU member states. New forms of technology, combined with comparatively cheap means of transport, and often sponsored by staffing agencies capable of facilitating the movement of large numbers of workers across national borders, enable workers to move around the EU while still able to maintain strong links with families at home. Moreover, this migration is more individualised, less network-driven, with younger migrants less inhibited by family commitments in Poland. The result, they argue, is that the 'new migration is more like transnational commuting than a migration which includes settlement in the country of destination.'[15]

In line with the emphasis on this migration as 'incomplete' or 'fluid', other researchers have additionally pointed to how many of those moving abroad are reluctant to set any fixed timescale on their return. Thus, their research on Polish migrants to London led Eade and colleagues to conclude that a peculiar feature of the migratory careers of younger migrants in particular was that they were actively pursuing a strategy of 'intentional unpredictability'.[16] In the Republic of Ireland, Moriarty et al. deployed the concept of 'deliberate indeterminacy' to describe the disposition of migrants who neither saw themselves as returning in the short-term to Poland nor as settling permanently abroad.[17] Drawing on the findings of a number of studies carried out in Wales, Thompson uses the notion of 'migratory drift' in a similar fashion to refer to how migrants become 'blown off course' from their original, short-term migration trajectory, but still hold to a desire to return, at some point, to Poland.[18]

Over a decade on from Poland's entry to the EU, however, there remains a very sizeable Polish-born population in the UK. The 2011 census showed there were 600,000 Polish nationals living in the UK, with official estimates putting the number considerably higher.[19] Many of these may well be pursuing a migratory strategy which is conditional and provisional, and a good number of those represented in this return may be migrants who are still wedded to a 'back-and-forth', circular pattern of migration, but what of the prospect that the longer migrants remain the more likely they will be to 'settle', even if accidentally rather than by design? A survey by Ipsos Mori in 2014 found that among their sample, only 11 per cent described their residency in the UK as 'temporary', while over three-quarters said their stay in the UK was 'permanent'. The same study found that 40 per cent intended to apply for British citizenship. Home Office data show that while the number of Polish nationals actually becoming British citizens represents a small proportion of this overall population, grants of UK citizenship to former Polish nationals have grown from just under 500 in 2009 to over 6,000 in 2013.

Studies of migration have long recognised that migration which starts as 'temporary' may evolve into a more settled, long-term, sometimes permanent settlement abroad. Sui noted how the sojourner came to complete a 'job' but over time became 'vague and uncertain about the termination of his sojourn because of the fact that he has already made some adjustments to his new environment'.[20] More recently, Castles and Miller, in a major study, remark how many start as temporary migrants subsequently go on to bring over partners, have children who are born abroad, and, after a while 'settlement takes on a more permanent character.'[21]

More than a decade after the EU's expansion in 2004, research has emerged which points to evidence of this pattern in the case of Polish migration to other EU member states. White's careful and extensive studies of Polish families in the UK has provided one of the most robust counters to the stress on 'fluidity' and temporariness which characterises a good deal of the work on post-2004 Polish migration.[22] She argues that there is undoubtedly evidence of circularity, but she found also that migrants wearied of mobility, and sought stability, which many found after a phase of 'double migration'.[23] Here, migrants who had returned to Poland and experienced a 'failed' return migration, because they may not have found suitable work or because they remain frustrated with the pace of change and opportunities in Poland, look again at returning abroad, but this time to settle. Often, White points out, these individuals are at a point in their personal biographies where they actively want to settle and to begin to make more certain plans for their futures.[24]

In other work, Ryan, who, like White, has been one of the leading British social scientists working in this field, was among the first to begin to detect patterns of settlement emerging among those who had been in the UK for a number of years.[25, 26] In one of her later studies, of Poles who had been living in the UK for approaching a decade or more, she observed how attitudes towards their migratory careers, their relationships with families and friends in Poland and their networks in the UK evolve over time, leading to a gradual process of settlement. These findings are not, either, peculiar to the British context. Drawing on research in Norway, Friberg describes how migratory careers can unfold over three main stages, from the initial period after arrival through a period of transnational commuting and, finally, to more permanent settlement abroad.[27] Not all migrants, he stresses, will move through these stages, but, as with White's findings, he shows how many migrants who have overstayed reach a point where they must either return to Poland to reunite with families, because they cannot maintain the fluid, transnational form of living, or the families will move abroad and commit to life in a new environment. Again, Engbersen and colleagues in other works have written about migrants electing to settle in the Netherlands for the medium-to-long term being influenced by their relative level of socio-cultural integration into Dutch society as evidenced through contact with Dutch natives or speaking Dutch in their workplace.[28]

The findings of our studies in South Wales, which we will present below, fit a wider pattern of a migratory career, which can, and often does unfold over stages. It is a process marked by personal adjustments and evolving commitments. We begin by asking how so many of our participants stay after the point when they had otherwise expected to leave, and after which they are 'drifting'. In our studies, the majority of our participants spoke of settling in Wales for the long haul, but few spoke of remaining for good. In many cases, those to whom we spoke came to Wales not intending, they said, to stay longer than a few months. We spoke to few individuals who came with a clear plan to migrate to the UK and stay or even intending to base themselves in the country for an indefinite period. Our samples included a small number who stated they came with no fixed timescale for returning to Poland. Most, however, said they intended to come for a short period and then return. In practice, few did. Why?

The Initial Phase of Settling In: Six Months after Arriving in the UK

It is, we would suggest, necessary to look at migration as a process which, after arriving in the destination country, unfolds in stages over time. The first period, the initial period of six months or so immediately after moving abroad, should be treated as a very particular stage because most migrants noted that before leaving Poland this was the timeframe they had envisaged being away. Thus, we need to ask what occurs during this phase of the migratory career which leads many to stay longer.

The reasons for this behaviour are often assumed to be rooted in economic forces. Since migrants have been attracted by the promise of higher earnings, by the differential labour market conditions between Poland and the UK, then as long as their earnings expectations are met they will remain, which, broadly speaking, they are doing. Most, however, have to abruptly confront the reality that there will be less money than they had expected, prior to departure, to have at their disposal. There are fewer hours available to work, work is not as regular as they had been led to believe, deductions from pay are unexpectedly higher, and what they need, especially food and housing, just costs more than they had previously calculated. Most, it would seem, nevertheless remained fixed on the prize for which they had come, and interviews highlighted the commitment of migrants to securing the job which would deliver the better remuneration which they so clearly sought.

Balanced against the financial gains are not inconsiderable hardships. Numerous participants spoke of the psychological strains of adjusting to life abroad, of the loneliness of making their way in unfamiliar terrain, and, especially among those we interviewed in Llanelli, without a level of competency in English to help negotiate their way through new challenges. Indeed, in some respects, instead of asking why migrants stay so long, the sharper question might actually be why they stay at all. In the different localities, participants commented on the difficulties of being thrown together with other migrants with whom they would not ordinarily have chosen to live, and often in conditions, which simply had to be endured until they could find somewhere better. Moreover, in both Cardiff and Llanelli participants complained of their working conditions. They spoke about their lives in this period immediately after arrival being governed by waiting for phone calls to tell them whether or not they were required in work, conditions which made it difficult to establish any routine to their lives. In Llanelli, where the majority of the participants were employed in meat processing, they remarked on the impact of working for long hours in cold conditions on their physical well-being. Generally, with the possible exception of the small number of participants who had prior experience of working abroad, most are forced to hastily come to terms with an initial arrival period marked by additional mobility, upheaval and a sequence of personal challenges which they must overcome.

In these circumstances, and even allowing for the dogged commitment to higher earnings, it is not immediately obvious why so many should end up staying so much longer. What other factors contrive to ensure that migrants will almost always drift beyond the period when they expected to have returned home? A recurring motif of many of the interviews, though it was especially pronounced among participants living in Llanelli and Cardiff, was that the decision to leave home was driven by a desire to live differently. Participants' accounts of their motives for leaving Poland are peppered with references to wage differentials and the challenges of meeting the cost of living at home. As we argued at the outset of the book, the underlying cause of their decision to look for better opportunities abroad, however, appears to be rooted in a frustration with the inability to make the kind of life they desire in Poland. A lack of work or a shortage of money meant that choices about how they wanted to live were denied to them. In moving out of Poland, they were seeking ways of fulfilling aspirations for a different way of living, rather than persisting with a status quo which earlier generations would have had little opportunity to change. Much as migrants routinely spoke of short timeframes for their migration, most were likely, even before they had left, to drift beyond these limits – they were moving, in many of the cases we considered, because they did not feel they could make it in Poland.

To understand why migrants almost invariably drift in this way we must additionally investigate more closely the social dimension of migration. As we discussed in Chapter 2, studies of migration personal social networks are often analysed for their role in facilitating mobility. Through these channels migrants learn about opportunities for work abroad, and are often able to access in-country resources, such as accommodation, through friends and relatives who have already moved away. Social scientists have also studied social networks for their value in providing psychological and emotional support as well as practical assistance, a feature which has been noted, very specifically, in the case of recent Polish migration to the UK. It is our contention that these networks also function as ties that bind people to the migratory career.

Many, in different ways, have staked reputations on staying. The majority of the participants had friends and family living in the localities to which they were moving who had evidently gone to considerable trouble to arrange jobs and accommodation. Some were clearly doing so as part of pre-migratory agreements that when they joined up abroad they would share costs. Others had travelled with friends and family members on the understanding they would support each other while living in Wales. After arriving, and especially after experiencing living in accommodation pre-arranged by employers or agencies, there is a strong desire to seek alternative rented housing, something which can only be afforded in concert with others. Some had even come directly with young children, preferring not to leave them at home. In other instances, once family join them or once the migrant opens a business – which we will further discuss below – the likelihood of return at any point soon diminishes markedly. Matylda, for example, who had moved to Wales from a large town in central Poland, told us how she had initially come on her own but was later joined by her husband, who very quickly gave notice to his job on Poland; they had, she said, 'put it all on one horse – to come here and live here'.

The arrival of children early after settling in Wales, which, again, we will explore more fully below, is game-changing for many migrants. Marbeta, a woman in her mid-twenties from a small town in Silesia, explained how she had moved to Wales two years previously on her own before being joined, not long after, by her family. In particular, when her son arrived after she had been abroad for only six months she felt she now had to take into consideration his interests: 'I had come in July and my son went to preschool in September, as he was three years old. He really started enjoying himself and it made me starting to think about staying here, more than myself sitting here on my own.' Lena, who had initially left Lodz with two female friends in 2007 (and had therefore been living in Wales for four years when we interviewed her), spoke about the often conflicting pressures from family. Her husband had initially been resistant about her leaving, but she was insistent because she felt the opportunities to earn income necessary to support her family's future prospects. Support from her parents, however, who were encouraging her to try her luck abroad, was crucial to her decision to stay away in spite of the challenges she was experiencing: 'My family offered their support and not only was it an emotional support but also financial. My dad came here and brought me money and I rented a flat here on my own and they came afterwards. It was then I made a decision that I would be staying on.'

In a different way, others had invested in proving they would stay the course. Some younger participants were clearly keen to prove to parents they had the resilience to stay abroad and to demonstrate their ability to live independently. A number of the female migrants we interviewed spoke of disputes with husbands who did not want them to leave, but of being resolute despite this opposition. In both instances, to return would have been to lose face with both immediate and extended family. Mieczyslawa, for example, who had moved from Warsaw in her mid-forties, relayed an account which was quite typical of female 'pioneers' who had moved without their male partners. The decision to move, she commented, was 'more my decision because my husband [facial gesture indicated that he was not pleased with the proposition] ... Also, my mum would say "you won't manage", "you won't manage this." They were more "no" ... I'm sure they wouldn't have let me go if my daughter hadn't been here.' In the end, not only did she leave, but her husband and her son, joined her within six months, unable, as she said of her husband, to manage matters in Poland on his own.

Social networks are more usually analysed as enabling, but we should also understand them as conferring obligations and therefore as constraints on action. We encountered few migrants who were 'free agents', seemingly unencumbered by interests tying them to others. Mostly, these were men and women for whom migration was either partly a product of responsibilities to others or which engendered commitments of one form or another. In exploring why, in spite of what the large majority believe before they migrate, they almost invariably will stay much longer than they had planned, it is also important not to underplay the psychological strains of their experience when they move abroad. As we have noted in earlier chapters, migrants typically do not have in-country networks beyond a very small, select group of contacts. Often they are isolated from the majority population culturally and linguistically, and they are very conscious of being seen as 'immigrants'. Their links with compatriots tend to be hampered by a variety of factors, not least the drive to limit access to scarce resources, such as employment opportunities, to their close contacts and, often, a broader distrust of other migrants. Whatever the reasons, the effect is that resilience is achieved through the support of their closest contacts with whom they are thrown together by the shared experience of migration. Thus, though studies of social networks conventionally look at the way new migrants are beneficiaries of these channels, our research highlights, too, a flip side – how, at the very earliest stage, they create ties which, in turn, maintain a longer-term commitment to the migratory career.

The Transition Phase: Drifting Through Migration

In many of the interviews we undertook across the three localities we were told repeatedly by participants who had stayed long after most had talked about leaving that they were no longer making fixed plans. They were here 'for the moment', but would see what the future would bring. The attitude of Adam, for example, was typical of the majority of the participants. He had moved to Wales thinking he would stay for six months, but at the time of interview had stayed for a further three years. He believed he would return to Poland at some point, but had given up working out when this would happen. During the interview he had said he would remain in his current job 'until the end', but when asked when this would be he said: 'I can't tell, because I don't know. I am just not thinking about going back at this moment. I intend to stay here for quite some time.'. Likewise, the interview with Anna, who had been living in Wales for just over two years when we interviewed her in 2009, illustrated the futility many interviewees saw in trying to make plans for the future. A woman in her late thirties, divorced but with an adult daughter living in Poland, she had come to Wales and found a more rewarding lifestyle, in spite of separation from her family. A steady supply of work, disposable income and a new relationship had created an unanticipated commitment to Wales. Consequently, she was open to the future:

When I first came here, I was thinking about a half a year to a year and then I would come back. Now I've been here two years and I've had moments that I'd say to myself – I'm staying here till the end, although I didn't really believe in what I've been saying. Now I'm saying that I'm not going to stay, but who knows what I will be saying in one and a half or two years.

Like those, then, who spoke openly of viewing migration as a kind of personal experiment, these individuals also talked about waiting to see how things would bear out, of 'living for the moment'.

What we term 'migratory drift' should not be understood as aimless behaviour. Rather, we use it to refer to the situation of the majority of those we interviewed who left Poland not intending to stay abroad and who, for the large part, were not unequivocally bound to the objective of living permanently in the UK. In these instances, they have been 'blown off course'. What factors shape the decision-making and influence the length of time migrants remain abroad? In what ways do these differ from those forces, which are the catalyst for early drift?

At one level, Polish citizens who have come to the UK stay, in part, because they can. EU citizenship provides a legal framework for migratory drift. Where their predecessors who came to the UK prior to 2004 may have lived with the risk of being deported if they overstayed, recent migrants can drift because they are not legally compelled to make a decision to leave. Those who had experience of migration before 2004 referred to this as a factor in prolonging their stay in the UK. Magda, for example, who had been in the UK for five years, told us how when she first arrived she was going to 'stay only till the summer vacation and go back. But as I'm saying, our accession to the EU probably helped me to make that decision. There were no longer problems with visas, or a legal job, so it was easier later.' More generally, interviewees spoke of how their country's membership of the EU allowed them to choose when to leave and removed the hurdles of securing a visa to work abroad. Thus Maria explained that at the time Poland joined the EU her thoughts were that she 'won't have to be applying for a visa any more or do things like that. That I will be able to think of a country and go there.' For another young woman the issue was equally straightforward: 'I've got a choice. I can be here, I can be there' (Kamilla). As numerous studies have shown, Polish migration to western Europe did not begin in 2004 – it had been developing incrementally over the previous decade. There is nevertheless little doubt that in a number of important ways EU membership lifted barriers. In particular, as we note at various points in this book, the key difference is that EU citizenship gives migrants a greater degree choice about whether or not to remain abroad.

That they are not legally required to return after a defined period of time in the UK may explain why they *can* overstay but it does not, of itself, account for *why* they do so. Migrants come knowing, it would seem, their new citizenship rights gave them the flexibility to make choices. Some were evidently prepared to stay indefinitely, but in most cases it is something participants decided once they had been abroad for a period of time. Having work, being busy, managing families and a variety of personal commitments can make time go quickly, but none of those to whom we spoke were without an awareness of the passage of time. As our interviews revealed, they actively reviewed decisions to stay in Wales, extending timeframes contingent on their circumstances. Our research points to at least three factors which inform migrants' actions, all of which are, importantly, products of their life abroad, and more particularly of the experience of having been settled in Wales for a number of months. These are the main cause of longer-term migratory drift.

First, migrants overstayed because, at a minimum, their ability to find work and earn money enabled them to fulfil their expectations about how they believed life should be lived. In all localities, the ongoing ability to earn higher wages abroad was a critical factor in ensuring that migrants remained in Wales. However, the participants' interest in money, we found, was about much more than what they could save. It was also about how it enabled them to live. The core message which came from the studies in the three localities was of participants' weariness with being able only just about to cover their costs, and with the pinch of rising costs in Poland. In each locality, participants routinely spoke of how in Wales they pay bills more easily and, consequently, worry less about the future. Tomek, a middle-aged man from a small town close to Lodz, was very typical of many of those we interviewed. He had left Poland having struggled to run, for the previous five years, his own business, and had been living in Wales for two years at the time of his interview: 'Life's different in here. You can make a living – maybe you can't really spare too much, but you don't have to be counting money – whether it will be enough from 1st to 1st [one month to the next] – you know?' Another recurring theme, to which we will return below, is that those who moved often spoke about being able to plan for the future. In Poland, one father of three in his late fifties commented:

> we live 'in a crazy way', and here one lives a stabilised life ... one is not sure what's going to happen the following day, do they? And, here, if one works, one can plan everything, and achieve the aim one wants to achieve, sooner or later. One can put money aside here, buy things one dreams to have, can't they? (Natan)

Across the different localities, it was evident that migrants monitored comparative economic conditions back in Poland. While in a number of interviews rising prices and the wider recession in the UK were giving some cause for concern, the situation was still perceived to be better markedly than in Poland.

As they settled in Wales, even through the turbulence of the early months of their migration, participants began to see the opportunities for a different way of life. Perhaps not surprisingly, the differences are characterised in financial terms, in having a degree of choice about how money is spent. Often it was the mundane, everyday practices and costs which exposed the differences between their new lives abroad and those they had left in Poland, such as having more time and money to socialise. Having disposable household income was a welcome novelty for many participants. Matylda, a woman in her forties, noted that while living in Wales she could 'afford to enjoy a cup of coffee, go out with friends to a pub. Simply, they can afford this. In Poland, the people can't afford this. At least in the region I come from ... So, everyone shuts themselves off at home.'

For those with children, or for older migrants, once they have cleared the initial six months or year abroad, and particularly when they have a more secure contract (often directly with an employer rather than through an agency), their thoughts turn to larger aspirations which they felt were beyond them in Poland. Owning a home, perhaps the most symbolic form of putting down roots abroad, loomed large in the hopes of a good number of this group of participants. 'We would like to have a house here too,' one woman told us, 'we would like to buy a house here. But, it is our future plan. If we really decide, for one hundred per cent, that we want to settle up here, then we would like to buy ourselves a house, not to rent as we do now' (Natka). As we have noted, for almost all migrants their first year abroad is marked by challenges, not least of which is the quest for secure employment, but when they have reached this point they begin to entertain a lifestyle which would not have been possible in Poland. Parents bringing children, in particular, start to contemplate what the prospects would be for their children growing up in Wales as opposed to Poland. One man, for example, from a small town on Poland's Baltic coast told us about how his views began to change once his wife and two teenage children joined him in Wales. The work he got abroad changed everything. After a year or so, and having now been joined by his wife, their thoughts turned to making a longer commitment to being abroad and the prospect of enjoying a lifestyle they could not entertain at home: 'if one could buy something, then one would have a place of one's own. It would be joy, one would feel completely different inside . . . [So, the new aim is to have your own place here?] Yes, me and my wife, we would like to have our own flat here' (Nelek).

Beyond starting a family or owning a home, many migrants also sought to establish roots in the UK during this drift phase by setting up small businesses. These were established in the ethnic economies in both Cardiff and Merthyr after the migrant had had several low-skilled jobs in the British labour market. As a result, the businesses, often started with funds saved through the previous jobs and with support from family, were set up through a combination of both opportunity – realising the niche in the market – and necessity, because of little scope for advancement in the labour market. For example, Kamilla worked as a nanny, waitress and cashier before she considered opening a Polish shop in the centre of Cardiff. The funding for her business came directly from her savings, but she received significant support from her family, particularly during the early stages of her business development. During this early time, her brother would drive a truck to Poland to load up Polish goods to sell in the store. Over time, they arranged for their own suppliers, but the initial family support was integral. Kamilla's path to entrepreneurship in the ethnic economy in Cardiff is similar to the other ethnic entrepreneur encounters in Cardiff and Merthyr. Regardless of the incentives to start a business, having one will root the migrant in the area similarly to owning a home or having children.

That many migrants come to have a more positive outlook about their futures is just one facet of what our research suggests is a second major factor contributing to migrants' commitment to remaining abroad. If many of the participants are unrealistic about how long they will stay, they are also often unprepared for how much they will be transformed by the experience of migration. Specifically, the interviews reveal men and women adjusting to profound shifts in the temporal rhythms which undergird their lives. At first, our data suggest, this adjustment seems to come, at least in part, from observing the locals at close quarters and the comparisons migrants draw between their compatriots in Wales and in Poland. In Llanelli, in particular, where we explored the field of behaviour in public places, participants frequently remarked on how much more tense and stressed Poles are than the local population. This could be observed in a variety of everyday settings. Sometimes their comments are about general differences in public behaviour which they frame in terms of ethnic difference. Shops or the public spaces in the town centre are among the few places where most Poles have the opportunity to observe the local population. Participants made frequent references to small gestures and commonplace social practices they notice in these settings, such as greeting someone in the street, engaging in 'small talk', waiting 'patiently' to be served in shops and having conversations with checkout staff. Locals, they observed, did not appear to feel the pressures of time in the same way. Nelek, a young man who had been living in Llanelli for just over a year, spoke at numerous points about differences he had observed in watching his compatriots and locals at close quarters. Poles, he said, would work harder because that was what they had been used to doing, but partly also because they were worried about not having work, something which was noted by numerous participants. By contrast, he remarked, 'British people are very calm. You can see that on the street. British people walk calmly, look, watch, think and Poles, they will rush into a shop, look around quickly and go further. Nearly running. At shops, mainly, markets, streets. You can see that.'

The roots of the reputedly different behaviour that characterises the local population are seen to lie in their distinctive habitus in comparison with Poles,. Stanislaw, who had lived in Llanelli for over two years, commented, when asked what he liked about the town, that it was largely the general attitude of the locals he appreciated most: 'this calmness is what I like, one should not worry, there's always tomorrow. I think that in most cases they do feel like this.' By contrast to the conditions that caused them to leave home in search of work and better wages, participants remarked that locals 'don't care about tomorrow too much. They've always got jobs and they'll always be able to provide for themselves,' and they aren't afraid of 'what tomorrow brings' (Marcely, F).

As they cleared the travails of the opening stage of the migratory career, the transition to a new stage appears to be marked by a recalibration of their temporal rhythms. Agnieska, who had been living in Wales for four years, explained that she also adapted quickly to the temporal differences: 'Why did I stay? I really enjoyed the rhythm of the life from the beginning ... I had a job, a place to stay, the rhythm of the life ... I just got into the rhythm.' Ewa similarly explained that she had learned to live at a different pace, modifying her behaviour through observing the locals: 'There's time for everything ... I live here totally different, almost like they do. I don't get irritated. If I don't make it today, I'll do it tomorrow.' One man, Justyn, who had been in Llanelli for two years, suggested that the longer Poles lived in the town the more likely they would be to let go of the 'weight' brought on by the way their lives had been governed by a temporal regime based around trying to make ends meet. 'Having time' was, for many of those we interviewed, a powerful factor shaping their decision to remain abroad. Financial capital is what makes it possible for migrants to stay, but there was a widespread perception among participants that staying in Wales enabled them to bank 'time', too, and that this was something which had been a similarly scarce commodity in Poland.

The third factor we identified as contributing to migratory drift brings us back to the concept of commitment. As we explained above, migrants may arrive with ties to others which make it difficult for them to exit in the short timeframe most had initially set for their sojourn in Wales. Equally, they may also, as we noted, have made 'side bets' with others which, if they were to return early, would have compromised their reputation and their relationships with individuals not necessarily directly involved in the migration.[29] We found similar ties emerging after participants had been abroad for a year or so (though sometimes less in numerous instances) which made it likely there would be an ongoing commitment to the migratory career. Importantly, these are interests which were not present either before leaving Poland or during the initial phase of migration.

Among the most significant of these is the arrival of family members in Wales. Even though the migration of a man abroad, for example, may have been sponsored in part by collective family interests at home, such as earning much-needed additional income, the arrival of his wife in his new locality almost certainly commits him to a longer phase of migration. Linking with relatives, but especially with partners, brings into play the interests of these others. These new arrivals make their own connections and develop their own affiliations with the locality to which they have moved, and these become part of the constellation of factors which maintain the commitment to migration. As with those parents whose children were born in Wales, not all of the ties are imported from Poland. For those who endure long periods of separation from their families, the routine they fashion in Wales brings its own commitment. Mosze (M) notes: 'I've already acclimatised here enough . . . I treat it here like my second homeland, don't I?' New friendships, relationships and marriages are made in Wales, which in turn generate commitments unanticipated at the outset of the migratory career.

Perhaps the most powerful set of new interests to emerge which committed participants to staying abroad was the arrival of children. One mother from Warsaw, for example, who had been in Wales since 2006, told us how the arrival of her youngest son had impacted on her and her husband's future plans. She was forthcoming about the strains of living abroad – not just being parted from members of the extended family, but also the anxiety when work dried up – but had come to see Wales, after nearly four years away, as her home. The presence of her son meant she couldn't now see when they would return, even if she lost her work:

> we wouldn't shorten our stay here because, as I've said, I wouldn't sacrifice my child's education. I would simply go on benefits. Then I would have to do so till he finishes his education. Unless, it happened later, after my son had finished his schools, then, I don't know what would be my husband's decision. (Mieczyslawa).

Melania similarly explained that it was seeing her young son settle happily in primary school in Wales which led her to revise her ideas about staying abroad; when she became pregnant with a second child she felt doubly compelled to stay in Wales: 'when he started his school I told myself that we would stay until he finishes his school, but I got pregnant and had another child, so I had to change my decision . . . therefore we decided that we would stay for good.'

After the often difficult first six months or even a year away from Poland, most are drifting, eking out a new life for themselves abroad. Years, as we found, pass, taking them further away from the lives and interests they had in Poland. Partly this is because life abroad fulfils personal aspirations about the 'good life' and, compared with home, there is little contest. It is also, we suggest, because once the upheaval of their initial period of settling in has passed, they discover an unexpected new rhythm in everyday life which gives them time they lacked in Poland. Finally, our studies lead us to conclude that this drift is also a product of emergent commitments which mark a new phase in the migratory career and which consequently lead them to revise decisions about returning to Poland.

The Final Phase: The Indecisiveness of Deciding to Stay or Return

The majority of those we interviewed reached a point when they no longer spoke about having a clear deadline for returning to Poland. Over time they had drifted away from their former habitus, even if this left them with some misgivings. A man in his late forties from a village to the south of Warsaw explained how for him and his wife time abroad was putting distance between them and their former lives in Poland: 'every year when we go there, there is always ... we are a bit more as if not from there. Yes, like from a different story' (Lubomierz). Others recounted equivalent experiences: 'The first week I feel it is great to see everybody again, but by the second week I get tired of visiting everybody. During the third week, I just want to be back home in Wales and have my peace and quiet' (Maurycy, M). Voicing sentiments expressed by many of those who had overstayed, Marzanna, who had also been living in Wales for four years with her husband and young family, commented how even though she enjoyed her holiday in her old home, she, too, looked forward to returning to Wales: 'even just to sit down on a bench near one's block of flats, to stare at the stars above. But, to tell the truth, when the holiday was drawing to the end, my thought were here, in this place here.'

While they made regular contact with friends and relatives in Poland, watched Polish television and kept up to speed with news about Poland via the internet and ethnic shops, their own links became, over time, less tangible, especially as, correspondingly, they forged new lives in Wales. Longin, who had left his job in Warsaw four years previously with his partner to find work abroad, put it especially well when he remarked that he had begun to lose a sense of what life in Poland was 'really' like:

> How to put it? Talking about it now, not having been there for the last four years, Poland to me is a bit like fiction now ... I can hear from the people who have been to Poland: 'Oh, the prices have gone up', or the like, or I can watch it on TV, but I haven't experienced it directly myself for the last four years ... I sometimes pretend to myself I say the same, but still it's all fiction, at the moment, Poland. You know, abroad, the biggest patriots are the migrants.

Among those we interviewed, the majority spoke about trying to remain for further lengthy periods in Wales, even intending to settle long term. Their changing personal relationships with family and friends in Poland also served to highlight the extent to which, without realising it, they had drifted away from connections, which had previously been so immediate. Pointed remarks by friends when they had been home about how much they had changed heightened their sensitivity. More generally, they cited examples of how they had drifted away from people with whom they had once been close. Longina, a woman in her thirties from Lodz, spoke of others who had returned to Poland, only to come back again, as well as those, too, who had said they would remain in the UK until 'something suddenly snaps in them and they pack up their stuff and go back to Poland'. She was, she commented, trying to be more measured, not least because of her son. She had settled in Wales, and while she was missing her family back in Poland, she knew, she said, that while she had been abroad, everyone's lives had moved on:

> They have their own lives there now ... That after such a long time, it is not realistic anymore because they have their own worlds now. Although we are still in contact, we can't wind time back. One can't go back. Even if I returned there now or tomorrow, one knows that our previous relations will not be restored. I'm fully aware of this.

For some participants, the effect of this drifting was that it left them feeling they had neither a clear mooring in either Poland or Wales. Rather, they saw themselves as caught between two commitments. Liwia, who had been in Wales for over six years, almost since the point when Poland joined the EU, still didn't feel as if he was settled in the UK. In large part, this was due to the ongoing separation from his wife, who wanted to come to the UK (because she liked the 'laid-back attitude here'), and his youngest son, then fifteen, who wanted to stay in Poland. His eldest son, with whom he had lived for a while in Wales, had now set up his own home with his own young family elsewhere in Llanelli, leaving him feeling torn between work and his family. Consequently, when we asked him if he saw himself as a 'migrant', he remarked that, instead: 'I call myself a temporary employee. I'm suspended in space ... basically, I have something to do, a task to fulfil to somehow, somewhere to obtain money, achieve some goal, and simply go back.' Lubomierz similarly saw himself as neither tied exclusively to his new home nor as having the same relationship he once had with his home in Poland:

> The people who have worked here for some longer period of time, they don't really have their own place now. Because regardless how many years we will live here, we will never be here at our own place. We'll always be foreigners here, and in Poland we don't feel like at our home any more, only like some strangers. I mean, I see it this way, to tell the truth. I don't have my own place now, because I've got two homes.

For the large part, however, participants were committed to staying in Wales for further lengthy periods of time. Some had given up on planning to return. As we have already noted, having children with them in Wales is a commitment which has a strong bearing on the likelihood of parents committing to stay in Wales. Thus, a woman in her mid-forties from Warsaw who had all of her three children living in the UK, including two with her in Wales, told us how: 'we say, with my husband, that we want simply to live here, because anyone who comes here, they always say that they are returning in a year's time. We don't say this anymore. We want to live here and that's it.' Through their school links, their expanding personal networks and participation in a range of organisations, children also allow parents to expand their personal networks, which, in turn, strengthens their links in Wales,. This was the same experience for entrepreneurs as well. They started something new in the UK and they were doing well as a result. They did not want to return to Poland as life in Wales became comfortable and enjoyable.

We nevertheless found few examples of participants cutting ties to Poland to make their commitment exclusively to Wales. A woman from the Warsaw region, who had initially moved on her own before being joined by her husband and teenage son, was one of a small number of exceptions, explaining how they had sold their former home in Poland because her son said he did not want to go back: 'We don't want to go back there either, and, practically, selling this flat ... We came here, looked at each other, and I said: "We have broken away from Poland"' (Matylda). Rather than grand gestures, we found that the process by which most migrants formed attachments to their new homes happened by stealth. New routines which became familiar over time, new associations which blossomed into firm friendships, changes to lifestyles which were once novel ossified into habits – the realisation that they want to remain in Wales creeps upon them gradually. Few set out with the intention of making Wales their home, but over time this was the outcome. 'I just stayed by chance,' said Maurycy (M) from Warsaw describing a common experience of incremental integration, 'and when I stayed, the school happened, and then when I started speaking English people didn't treat me like a Pole, but in a normal way and this is the feeling.'

This is not to argue there is an inevitable link between length of stay and likelihood of settling abroad for the long term. In spite of their declarations, the interviews were peppered with caveats. 'As long as' certain conditions prevailed, 'for the moment' they were not considering returning, 'at present' their plans were to stay in Wales, and 'as of now' they were clear about their intentions. Even among those who spoke of settling in Wales, perhaps even, as they put it, 'to the end', they were equivocal about what 'the end' point would be and when it would come. In almost all of our interviews, we found evidence of an awareness that their base in Wales lacked a solidity which they would otherwise have had in Poland. Much as they might wish to stay, circumstances could, they knew, change quickly, and we suggest they lived in the shadow of that knowledge. Some claimed to be ducking the issue: 'We are not thinking about it. We are living for today. We aren't thinking about what is to come' (Melania, F).

In other cases, participants' responses made clear the contingency of their decision-making. 'At present', said Agata who had moved to Wales four years earlier from her home village in the countryside outside Cracow, 'we don't think about returning to Poland. I don't know, we've decided this way. We'll live here, work here, as long as the work is available. Till they have enough of us' [laughs] and Krystyna told us she would 'stay here as long as I am able to live the life I've lived here so far.' A young woman named Agnieska who had been in Wales, said that remaining would depend on 'how long my work will last, if my boss is happy with my work and it depends how much money I would be able to save up in five to eight years'. Another woman Oliwia spoke of staying in Wales unless one of her parents got sick in Poland and she would then return to care for them. Some spoke of trying to hold on until they could return to Poland for their retirement, but, again, they knew this was contingent on the continued availability of work.

Our studies across three localities in South Wales found a majority of participants committed to remaining in Wales not only for longer periods than they had envisaged on leaving Poland, but also to a largely undetermined future duration. Those who had laid down substantial roots, especially through children migrating to live abroad with them or new relationships forged in Wales or starting a new business, were almost invariably those who spoke of staying for the longer periods. As we have discussed in other chapters, competency in spoken and written English also has an important bearing on migrants' outlook because of the additional opportunities to access resources otherwise closed off to them, not least opportunities to gain more secure and better-paid employment.

Conclusion

We found that migrants are able to overstay or 'drift' for a range of reasons. Most particularly, they can do so because they have work or, should a contract be terminated, can find alternative employment relatively soon and, in contrast to many migrants from outside the EU, there are no compelling legal reasons why they need return. We found relatively few cases of individuals who were actively and positively choosing to stay *because* of their job, with the exception of entrepreneurs who had created openings for themselves and now had business ties to the localities in which they lived. Instead, work was, for the most part, a means to a better end. Similarly, the comparative ease with which migrants move between the EU's member states is a crucial structural enabler of migratory drift, but this is about what makes possible this type of migration rather than what causes individuals to commit, in varying degrees, to an extended migratory career. To understand why most migrants drift, often for many years, we identified three main interconnected factors.

First, a consistent line of action in the form of a migratory career, even one which progresses in stages, is in part a result of personal investments individuals have made through their relationships, or commitments, to others. At the outset, individual migrants are likely to have a good deal at stake in ensuring they persist with staying abroad, even when confronted with the difficulties most face after arriving. The decision they made to leave Poland will rarely have been made in isolation, and whether because of personal debts to others who have helped or because they have staked something of their reputation in leaving, these commitments act as constraints on their actions. Once they are joined by family, or new relationships are formed abroad, the complexity of these commitments increases in magnitude. This is because their actions are informed by interests extraneous to their original decision to migrate rooted as they are in experiences specific to the host society. Social networks have rightly been the subject of a good deal of analysis in the study of migration, but they are more usually framed in terms of how they *enable* migrants to move and to remain away. We have looked at the same relationships from a different perspective: how ties to others *commit* them to the migratory career.

A second factor emerging from our research which contributed to migratory drift was how, again over time, migrants adjusted to a different mode of life abroad. 'Integration' – as evidenced by growing familiarity with English, their exposure to and use of the language in their daily lives, personal connections to members of the local population or by how they accessed news about the host society rather than about life in Poland – was uneven across and within our sites. Especially in Llanelli, but also in Merthyr Tydfil, most of those whom we interviewed spent much of their lives speaking Polish. Their personal networks were largely, if not solely, fellow nationals. They had nevertheless acclimatised to the different rhythm of life in Wales, and this clearly exerted a considerable force over their outlook. Though better wages enabled them to worry less about the temporal pressures to which they were used in Poland – the weekly bills, the monthly rent or repayments – it was their experience that life in Wales, broadly, ran at a different, more welcome pace than in Poland. That many of those who, by objective measures, would be regarded as living in the shadows of the local society felt transformed by their experience of living in Wales might not be viewed as 'integration', but it is nonetheless a powerful form of adaptation.

Finally, we have argued in this chapter that to understand why so many migrants stay it is necessary to take account of the cultural and social, and not only the economic context, in which migration occurs. In the case of Poland, in the near-decade-long build-up to accession, it was not just the country's economic and policy structure which had changed; cultural values and social expectations, too, had undergone fundamental shifts. Especially in those former industrial towns and in rural Poland where economic restructuring had cut the deepest, and among young Poles with limited opportunities to exercise choice in the country's transition to a market economy, migration provided them with the ability to make a change.

To some extent, we need to review our understanding of the mechanics of migration. The 'push-pull' model for evaluating international migration frames labour migration as rooted in the differential conditions of national labour markets. 'Poor' people, or at least those originating from societies whose economics are less developed than in the destination country, are pulled towards 'rich' countries because they can earn more money. Our take on this matter, influenced by the work of de Haas, is that while there is an undeniable truth to the neo-classical economic proposition, those we interviewed were moving because they had aspirations to live *better*.[30] Even if the need for an immediate injection of money was a factor, our research reveals that migration was more widely pursued as a strategy for achieving an improvement in *how* these men and women lived by changing *where* they did so.

9

Polish Migrant Integration

Introduction

At its core, the EU is based on the concept of integration. In this sense, integration across member states, both new and old, is all-encompassing – political, socio-cultural and economic. Integration, in all its forms, is facilitated by the four fundamental freedoms of the EU single market, the free movement of goods, capital, services and persons.[1] Politically and legally, the European Commission is essentially a supranational entity that adds a layer of policy and law across all member states providing a platform for integration across nation-states. The role of the EU as another layer of law and policy was viewed as a major concern by the British general public in the 2016 referendum. It is unclear how or when Britain's exit from the EU will occur. As a result, this chapter will discuss migrant integration on the assumption that the EU migrants currently residing in the UK will be able to stay in the UK indefinitely. As an institution, the European Commission created two of the greatest commitments to European integration: the Schengen Agreement and the Cohesion Policy.

The Schengen Agreement allows for free movement of individuals without the need for passports at borders, which increases migration opportunities, both for short-term and long-term migrants, as well as for economic and sociocultural integration. While not all member states of the EU are a part of the Schengen area, all new member states are expected to adopt the Schengen Agreement. The EU Cohesion Policy drives economic growth in regions throughout Europe. It provides economic support to deprived regions in both old member states, such as the convergence regions like Llanelli and Merthyr Tydfil, as well as to regions in newer member states such as Poland and Hungary. In order for macro-level integration to occur, these tenets and rights must be understood and exercised at the micro level. At this level, migration and integration are intrinsically, although not exclusively linked, as for integration to occur new cultures, norms and ways of thinking are needed. According to the International Organization for Migration, 'integration' can be considered as a process of mutual adaptation between host societies and migrants.[2] In addition to 'legal integration', there is economic, social and cultural integration.[3] Regardless of the type of integration, the process takes time. Integration is traditionally a feature of long-term migration and it is greatly enabled by shared language and bridged contacts.[4]

The concept of migrant integration has fascinated sociologists for decades in a number of different areas, including race relations, changes in social network membership over time and models of social integration.[5,6] What is common to all is that they focus on how integration that happens over time, taking into account any resistance from the general public and politicians, as well as the influence migrants have on host societies.[4,8] It should be noted at this juncture that 'integration' and 'assimilation' are not synonymous, the latter depicting how migrant populations are forced to abandon their customs and norms in favour of dominant cultures and social norms. This chapter focuses on the former, integration, and the mutual adaptation of cultures and norms alongside migrant communities, and particularly on the contemporary legal, economic, social and cultural integration of Poles into British society in one generation.

The chapter is organised around the four types of integration – legal, economic, social and cultural. Each section reviews the case-study data regarding that type of integration (where available) and highlights ways in which Poles continue to integrate with British society. The next section reviews the implications for legal integration of EU migrants. This is followed by a look at economic integration, particularly focusing on language acquisition and labour market mobility, as these issues are often vital precursors for other types of integration. The following section focuses on social integration, relying on data on social networks. Finally, we look at cultural integration, as this occurs later; here our data offer fewer insights and are therefore supported with some secondary data. We conclude by looking at the integration trajectory of Poles and the resistance of host communities.

EU Migration and Legal Integration

One key driver of integration, of all forms, across EU member states is migration. Migrants enable the transfer and inclusion of differing cultures, ideas and norms into a new society through cultural exchange. Within the EU, migration and cultural exchange of culture is facilitated through EU membership. Unlike third-country nationals entering the EU on work visas or by unauthorised means, citizens of EU member states are EU citizens and legally integrated. EU citizens are nationals of their country of birth but have the added benefit of being authorised to live and work in other EU states in the same way as national populations. Prior to the entry of Poland into the EU in 2004, Polish nationals residing in the UK were not automatically authorised to live and work in the UK and were considered third-country nationals (non-EU migrant). However, after May 1 2004, Poles were entitled, through Poland's EU membership, to live and work in the UK indefinitely.

It should be noted that under certain circumstances, there are short-term exceptions to this form of legal integration. Revisiting the example of Polish migrants/EU citizens on May 1, 2004, the Poles were granted permission to live and work in the UK from the date of enlargement, but this was not the case throughout the EU. As outlined in Chapter 1, transitional arrangements allowed existing EU member states (the UK, Ireland and Sweden chose not to exercise the right) to close their borders for seven years from the date of enlargement to curb the migratory flows. As a result of these transitional arrangements, in the immediate post-enlargement period some EU citizens had to delay their entry into labour markets in other member states.

In 2012, there were 19 million internal EU migrants and 33 million external migrants in the EU.[9] At the UK level in 2012, Poles were the second largest migrant group in the UK and the largest group of A8 migrants.[10] According to the WRS, from May 2004 to April 2011, over 1 million A8 migrants (1,133,950) entered the UK.[11] Throughout this period, 62 per cent of A8 migrants in UK were from Poland, producing the largest single inflow of migrants in UK history.[12,13] Favell argues that the demographic changes resulting from these migratory flows are the largest in Europe since the end of WW2.[14]

It is expected that anywhere from 50 to 70 per cent of Polish migrants in the UK since 2004 have stayed in the UK.[15,16] This claim is supported by the aforementioned NINo figures for 2009. Research suggests that, similarly to nomadic tribes in the Sudan or flocks of birds blown off course, these migrants are 'drifting' and have no definite plans to return to Poland or to settle in the UK (see Chapter 8). More recent research shows that some Poles return-migrate to Poland only to return to the UK once more to settle.[17] Regardless of the reason for their initial migration, these migrants have decided to stay in the UK for the long term. These groups stay in the UK for significantly longer than expected; they are legally integrated and have established communities, businesses and social networks throughout the country. While the overarching goal of the EU and of EU citizenship is European integration at the macro level, there is growing concern that while Polish migrants are staying in the UK for the long term they have little interest in integration. For example, the British Future survey conducted in December 2013 found that British workers perceive Polish migrants as 'hard-working' and 'making a contribution to Britain'; however, the same survey also reported that British workers perceived Polish migrants as 'not making an effort to integrate'.[18] In contrast, the OECD notes that countries with a high proportion of immigrants have better integration outcomes.[19] Given the uncertainty of the future integration of a sizeable Polish population in Britain, the aim of this chapter is to examine the data from the three case studies and review the ways in which Polish migrants can be integrated into British society.

Economic Integration

As EU citizens, Polish migrants are able to stay in the UK indefinitely. This contributes directly to their labour market mobility as, without visa restrictions on their time, they can acquire new skills, try new career options and be fully integrated into the British economy. Building on the IOM definition of integration, economic integration can occur when a migrant is gainfully employed in the local labour market and has the opportunity to interact with other workers, acquire language skills and get an understanding of shared workplace norms. For this economic integration to occur, as demonstrated by numerous studies around the world, migrants need to develop language skills.[20] For example, since the early nineteenth century when Cardiff was a major port city, Cardiff has been home to a local Somali population. While its members have become increasingly integrated in Welsh society over many generations, Somali migrants were unable to find employment initially because of language barriers and were largely living separately from the surrounding, increasingly diverse society. This example highlights that language skills are essential for involvement in the local labour market, which in turn embeds migrants in the wider society; it should be noted, however, that many Somalis in Cardiff still work in poorly paid employment at the bottom end of the labour market. Nevertheless, economic integration in the local labour market can work as a catalyst for socio-cultural and political integration.

While the integration of the individual migrant in local labour markets is paramount for economic integration, other factors such as geography and employment come into play as well. For example, a migrant living in a city may be more likely to integrate economically than a migrant living in a rural area because of the variety of employment opportunities available at all levels of the division of labour. In addition, a migrant working in a closed ethnic economy would be less likely to integrate than one working in the local labour market, regardless of the geographic area. By focusing on the micro and the macro factors that can influence the economic integration of migrants, it is clear that integration of any kind is a complex process and that there is no one-size-fits-all solution. To understand how migrants in the case studies are economically integrating in the Welsh labour market, we now look at labour market mobility and language acquisition in each case-study location, starting with the rural case of Llanelli.

As outlined in Chapter 4, the majority of the Poles in the Llanelli sample had their migration facilitated by recruitment agencies or were migrating because network contacts had indicated that they would be able to secure work on arrival in the town through agencies. Among those interviewed in Llanelli in 2008, just over half stated that work had been arranged through a recruitment agency before coming to Wales. In reality, the number of migrants gaining work through staffing agencies – whether before arriving in Wales or on arrival – is likely to be much higher. Recruitment agencies initially offered migrants accommodation and employment, and in this way they can be considered a surrogate social network that facilitates migration to a specific location using the same means as migrants themselves – offers of accommodation and employment. Also, in a similar way to a social network, and as a significant proportion of Poles in Llanelli were directed to the region through recruitment agencies, the agency clearly replaced some of the functions of a migrant social network by providing links to other migrants in the same position.

Poles in the sample using the recruitment agency worked at a meat-packing plant on the edge of Llanelli. The limited exposure to the local economy through the location of the plant, the hours of work and the use of the Polish language at work and in the home, reinforced the position of migrants in the meat-packing plant as the 'outsiders' at the bottom of the labour market. Indeed, across Llanelli and Merthyr there are few instances of individuals successfully making a transition beyond this 3D employment. Where migrants worked alongside locals, they often did so as agency workers recruited along with other migrant workers. New arrivals quickly learn that agency work is uncertain and that their entitlements, whether in pay or contracted hours, may be less than those of colleagues employed directly by firms.

Working almost exclusively with co-ethnics not only limits the possibility of interaction with individuals beyond the ethnic world, but also acts as a barrier to flows of information beyond the realms of this relatively enclosed population.[21] Thus, it is possible that individuals may not come to acquire information about job openings or knowledge about how to access such opportunities. In addition, migrants in this position have no incentive to acquire language skills or the desire to move beyond their current low-skilled employment. For migrants in Llanelli, the main barriers to economic integration include a closed labour market, connections to recruitment agencies and the remoteness of the rural location. If some or all of these barriers are removed, migrants could perhaps be integrated more effectively with the surrounding community; in the semi-urban case of Merthyr Tydfil some, though by no means all, of these barriers are absent.

Unlike migrants from our other cases whose selection of their migration destination was based on employment opportunities, migration to this semi-urban region was to a large extent motivated by proximity to family and friends, with approximately 65 per cent of the Merthyr sample migrating to Wales for this reason and a quarter having extended family members living with them or nearby. Around a third migrated for pre-arranged jobs, with the rest migrating with the knowledge that jobs were available. Regardless of their education level, the majority looked for and took low-skilled employment when they first arrived, primarily in the food and meat-processing sector. In the early 2000s, the majority of migrants working in Merthyr's meat-processing factories were Portuguese, but after 2004, factories and recruitment agencies servicing the area turned their attention to Poles to keep down costs and maintain control of the workforce.[22] Employment opportunities for migrant workers in Merthyr are generally limited to this sector. A small number of factory workers moved up the occupational hierarchy into language-related support services, but in general language remained an impediment to upward occupational mobility. Despite the difficulties of maintaining their position in the hierarchy of migrant labour, many Poles appeared happy with their situation and with employment that gives them a better quality of life and financial security than in Poland. Opportunities to move up the division of labour appeared to be a secondary concern, with many Poles accepting their position with a sense of resignation and an understanding that they could do little to change it.[23]

For those Poles who were unhappy with their financial situation – or increasingly, for those who could not find employment – entrepreneurship and going into business in the ethnic economy became an alternative form of employment.[24] Over recent years, competition between Polish and Portuguese entrepreneurs has had a significant impact on the town of Merthyr, both physically and culturally. Merthyr now has a range of ethnic shops, cafés and bars unimaginable a few years ago. This dramatic increase in ethnic businesses is changing the image and perception of the town, which was traditionally considered to be an area suffering from the consequences of economic decline. Asked to explain these developments in Merthyr, one interviewee answered: 'It's more multicultural if you like, which for somewhere like Merthyr Tydfil is quite unusual because the Valleys' mind-set is the norm.' Migrants in the case-study area have started an ethnic economy out of necessity and are relatively embedded in the local area in Merthyr. While they are more economically integrated into the local community through advancing English-language skills, they are still restricted in their attempts to engage in the local labour market by established economic practices.[25] In contrast to the Poles in Llanelli, this English-language advancement is a significant step to economic integration but barriers still exist in a traditionally economically depressed region (see Chapter 7). Taking into account the barriers outlined in the two case studies reviewed, migrants in the urban case should be most likely to be economically integrated with the surrounding community; they are centrally located in Cardiff, the nation's capital city, have access to a diversified labour market and have educational opportunities.

Looking at the entirety of the Cardiff sample, Poles seek low-skilled employment when initially migrating regardless of their skill, language and/or education level. Approximately half of the migrants in the sample acquired their first job at the lower end of the local labour market through contacts in their social network. After having several low-skilled positions they begin to move up the division of labour, advancing their language skills and in some cases their education level. This ascent traditionally begins after living in the UK for eighteen months and continues until they reach a position that is commensurate with their skill level. For example, several migrants originally had low-skilled jobs despite being well educated and having high English-language skills. Over time, however, and through gaining confidence in their language abilities, they started working in the UK in an industry they were educated for or trained to work in at home, including university research. Due to their high levels of education (in Poland and in Britain) and their improving language ability, many had positions that would be difficult for recent British graduates to acquire. While the pre-migration professions of the migrants in this sample is unknown, it could be argued that their ascent is largely based on their ability to acquire language skills in the UK and, in the case of several migrants in the sample, to acquire British- based educational qualifications.

The Cardiff findings support the labour market progression literature in a number of ways. The migrants are actively trying to get their 'dream' job moving up from 'any job' when initially migrating.[26] Arguably the socio-economic features of Cardiff, with its diverse range of industries, act as a pull for migrants when deciding where to live in the UK in the longer term. The city, in comparison to the other South Wales locations reviewed above, provides good employment opportunities for well-educated migrants, thus helping to facilitate migratory ascent in the local labour market.

In comparing the findings from the three cases, there are markedly different attitudes to labour market mobility and economic integration among migrants in these locations. These 'attitudes' can range from over-achievers, who are interested in climbing the division of labour, to those individuals who are content with a job of any kind and have no specific aims to progress. Those with higher levels of education and training actively pursue a career of upward mobility, as we found among those we interviewed in Cardiff. They were prepared to tolerate work not commensurate with their level of education and training, even if it was only temporary. The low-skilled nature of this work was initially attractive to migrants' as they wanted to ensure a flow of wages from the time of arrival in the UK. However, while in low-skilled employment, it was clear that these migrants were searching for better positions in the local labour market. Once migrants have better positions, it reinforces their motivation that are no longer solely economic, and encourages them to stay in the UK for longer periods. In contrast, migrants in Merthyr Tydfil and Llanelli are, broadly speaking, individuals who were struggling the most to make ends meet in Poland. In many cases, they will have been coping with more than one job to raise sufficient income to make ends meet. In Llanelli, our research showed that their chief aim is usually to remain with an employer found through an employment agency on arrival. Like their fellow nationals living in Cardiff, they are keen to pursue better prospects, but they are aware that they lack the skills to progress in the labour market. These individuals are nevertheless generally content with what their employment in Wales delivers, both in terms of financial returns and lifestyle improvements. While there are many factors involved in the decision to return-migrate, it should be highlighted that continued employment in the destination country is a significant motivation to stay despite the migrants' attitude to labour market mobility.

Finally, where migrants live and work has a bearing on their employment opportunities and on their ability to remain abroad. Each of the localities offers different employment prospects. The comparatively higher-skilled migrants living in Cardiff would not have enjoyed the same employment prospects in the smaller, less diverse local economies in Llanelli and Merthyr Tydfil. As noted above, several of the migrants in the Cardiff sample made the necessary improvements in their English skills and were then able to access employment opportunities in the local economy that British graduates were competing for. For those who had been brought to work in food-processing plants in Merthyr Tydfil and Llanelli, however, their ability to continue to live away from Poland is contingent on the ongoing demand for their labour either in the plant or in other low-skilled employment. While this remains, they keep their options open. If this work dries up, or labour is sourced from elsewhere, the lack of opportunities for mobility may signal the end of their sojourn in Wales. Generally, these migrants do not possess the social and cultural capital to make themselves less vulnerable to the vicissitudes of fluctuations in local labour markets in the long term. These location-based factors combined with the characteristics of the Cardiff sample highlight the fact that these migrants are the most economically integrated migrants across the three case studies.

Social Integration

With the backdrop of EU enlargement and the free movement of migrants from Bulgaria and Romania into the UK, the capacity for EU citizens to stay in the destination country indefinitely leads to broader questions of social integration. While there are a number of ways for migrants to integrate socially, even with EU migrants residing in other EU member states, this integration can be difficult, as evidenced by the resistance to change against Portuguese migrants living in Northern Ireland.[27] Looking at the three case studies in South Wales, Polish migrants are able to integrate economically into the local economies of their respective areas to varying degrees. However, does economic integration automatically mean that these migrants are socially integrating? If not, how do the migrants make the transition, if at all?

The economic integration of migrants reviewed in the previous section relied on their ability to find stable employment in the Welsh labour market. For the best possible chance of economic integration, migrants need to be educated and have English-language skills. The importance of this language and education combination is supported by research by the EU/OECD as well as MPI.[28,29] While these traits are important for economic integration, requirements for social integration are largely based on social capital, particularly the acquisition of bridging contacts in social networks. Unlike bonding contacts that have the same characteristics (homogeneous), bridging contacts are far more diverse (heterogeneous).

The evolution of social networks can be a unique experience that, unbeknown to migrants, is having an impact on their social and economic progression in the destination country. For example, a network that is solely composed of bonding contacts may not necessarily be positive as it can cut off its members from information about the wider community in which they live.[30,31] These types of network can lead to negative social capital with the wider community, thereby threatening social cohesion.[32] This enclosed social network can then become a hurdle for the social integration of its members within the local communities. Alternatively, an increase in bridging contacts can lead to increased social integration.[33]

The findings from each of our three case studies highlights the ability of migrants, or lack thereof, to develop their social networks over time, which can be a catalyst or a barrier for social integration. For example, migrants in our Cardiff sample added more diverse groups to their local social network, including other Poles, non-Polish migrants and British nationals (i.e. bridging contacts). This did not happen quickly and major events occurred over this period, including employment changes and language acquisition. In contrast, Poles in Llanelli were hindered by the feeling of being outsiders among a homogeneous population and the safety provided by their closed social network. As a result, the social networks of Poles in Llanelli comprised mainly bonding contacts, closed off from the local community. In Merthyr Tydfil, the experience of the workplace and tensions with other migrant groups facilitated strong Polish networks comprised of bonding contacts, which were enhanced through strong competition between entrepreneurs.

From the comparison of our three case studies the question arises whether the spatial variations of the case-study areas have more of an impact on migrants' ability to socially integrate than the composition of their social network. From the overall findings, the space in which migrants are based and the composition of their social networks are intrinsically linked, and thus support one another to a certain extent. A migrant's social network provides the opportunity or the barrier for change in terms of acquiring advanced language skills and experiencing new opportunities that are integral to social integration. If the migrant is based in a remote area, working with co-ethnic migrants, with a closed social network of bonded contacts, there is little interaction with the surrounding community, which discourages engagement and integration. However, there are many cases of migrant isolation in ethnic economies that are in the centre of large urban areas, thus making social network composition more important than migrant location. While location can provide an additional hurdle to overcome with cultural integration, often more likely in cities, the homogeneity of a social network is not mutually exclusive to a non-urban area.

The composition of the social networks that Polish migrants in the UK create during their migration period has an effect on their social integration in the long term. There is clear evidence that the social networks of post-2004 intra-EU migrants have had a bearing on the relative development of their English-language skills, interaction with the wider community and future migration patterns. However, a closed social network can greatly limit a migrant's ability to integrate in the destination country – both economically and socially. In addition, the composition of a migrant's social network is often affected by their location – rural, semi-urban or urban, while their network composition is not mutually exclusive to their location.

As with other social scientists who have investigated the longer-term intentions of migrants from states that joined the EU in 2004, in each of our case-study localities many of our participants intended to stay in the UK for the foreseeable future.[34, 35] What we have highlighted is that the evolution of the social networks of migrants' in-country has an important bearing on how they socially integrate and settle into new societies for the long term. Those migrants with greater levels of competency in English are able to forge bridging networks with new non-Polish friends and contacts in the localities into which they have moved. For those migrants with limited English-language skills, it is difficult to break out of networks which pre-date migration, or those that are built with small groups of other Polish migrants. Language barriers considerably hinder migrant/non-migrant interaction, as they limit the acquisition of bridging contacts, particularly at the early stages of migration. This point is significant, as it ties a major characteristic of economic integration to social integration.

Why does it matter if migrant networks evolve in different ways, and that some are better able to connect with members of the local population? As White has suggested, it may be that for some migrants there is a 'satisfactory' level of integration, which enables them to conduct tasks that are essential to their lives in the UK.[36] There are, however, consequences for migrants, for the local societies in which they have settled and for policy-makers responsible for the management of international migration. For individual migrants, it leaves them reliant on intermediaries to access services, which are essential for the development and well-being of all citizens, whether in healthcare, employment or education. The less able they are to extend their personal, social and professional networks, the more susceptible they are to shocks to the section of the labour market in which they are employed, often outside the major urban centres in the UK. This means that migrants will have limited opportunity to access other forms of employment in which non-English-speakers can be employed. Research has shown that the impacts also extend to migrant children, who, outside school, are dependent on their parents' social networks to access key services, which can often compound their exclusion.[37]

Based on the shared language and bridging contact components of integration, different types of integration are inextricably linked. For example, an economically integrated migrant is more likely to be culturally integrated than one that has not been economically integrated. Studies note that cities, as traditional magnets for new migrants, are more likely to provide migrants with the support they need to socially integrate.[38, 39] This is supported by the findings from our three case studies. Poles in the Cardiff sample were the most economically integrated and were also the most socially integrated. By contrast, Poles in the Llanelli sample were the least economically integrated and were also the least socially integrated. In addition, many studies highlight the need for regional and national policy to support integration measures in order for sustainable social integration to occur.[40, 41] The social integration of Poles in specific parts of the UK has recently become the subject of several policy insights, yet the influence of varying social networks has yet to be directly assessed for this migrant group.[42, 43]

Cultural Integration

According to the Migration Policy Institute, migrants become culturally integrated by sharing their culture within a host society whilst simultaneously gaining an understanding of the host society culture; sharing/understanding religious values and engaging with individuals outside the ethnic economy are all seen to be important in this context.[44] In addition, the expert panel report from an IFA conference on Migration and Cultural Integration in Europe includes language sharing and food norms in its definition of cultural integration.[45] Given the varying definitions of cultural integration, the importance of language skills and other forms of integration alongside the religious similarities of host societies and migrant groups, this section will focus on the ethnic economy (food-based) transition to the local economy.

The Polish ethnic economies created by ethnic businesses and their consumers post-2004 in many UK cities were originally anchors within the Polish migrant community, a place to find Polish food items and Polish newspapers and a locale for exchange in the Polish language. While non-Poles were not excluded from the stores, it was difficult, because of the language barrier and the community created, for a non-Polish speaker to navigate this economy. As time passed and Polish consumers have settled in the UK, they use British supermarkets more and Polish shops less. In response to the dwindling demand from migrant consumers, many of these ethnic businesses throughout the UK are repositioning themselves as Polish delicatessens and diversifying the products they offer. These actions are predominantly due to economic considerations, but these businesses are inadvertently culturally integrating within local communities and economies.

Research on Polish ethnic entrepreneurs in Birmingham in the UK highlights that while these businesses are initially created to serve the Polish community many have now started to employ non-Polish staff and target the host community.[46] Another study focuses specifically on ethnic firms' diversification into mainstream markets and notes that this has yet to happen for the Polish entrepreneurs in Glasgow.[47] However, the research from Scotland also notes that an unintentional transition has occurred from the ethnic entrepreneurs solely serving the ethnic economy to now serving both the ethnic economy and other non-co-ethnics. The latter use the shop as a speciality store in the same way a speciality delicatessen would be occasionally frequented.

There was evidence of such a transition in Merthyr over recent years, where the willingness of members of the host community to buy products from migrant shops has been a significant factor in the expansion of migrant entrepreneurship. As one Polish entrepreneur, Ania, commented: 'That's why I like it, the locals are interested in what we sell and the national foods. Most of them try different things on holidays so they are not scared of trying something new.' To allow the local consumers to better access their stores, the entrepreneurs began to hire staff from the local area. As well as making members of host communities feel more comfortable, such staffing changes are perhaps made in an effort to maintain employment numbers within a changing talent pool, with many Poles returning to Poland. There is also evidence that some Polish ethnic entrepreneurs in Cardiff are beginning to transition in a similar way. All of the ethnic entrepreneurs in the sample, when initially migrating, said that they would live in the UK for a few months to earn some money and return-migrate. However, they have all overstayed, which could arguably be attributed to their business becoming rooted in the local economy and wider community.[48] Combining this anchor with the change in demand from their primary customer base (Polish migrants) and changes in supply within the labour pool, entrepreneurs have to diversify their businesses to survive. The biggest challenge will be for ethnic food stores, as they are traditionally the last to diversify. As there are several Polish food stores in Cardiff, even if these transitions occur the variety of stores in Cardiff will perhaps make it difficult to stay in business over the long term.

Concluding Remarks

Using material from our three case-study localities from the South Wales region, this chapter focused on the legal, economic, social and cultural integration of post-2004 Poles who remained in the UK for the long term. This long-term migration was facilitated by the acquisition of EU citizenship from the date of enlargement. Beyond legal integration, we used data gathered from the three case-study locations to determine the likelihood of other types of integration by Polish migrants over time. A combination of primary and secondary data were discussed in the chapter, both as enablers or disablers of integration, from which a linear model of migrant integration was reviewed.

Based on this argument, a migrant cannot advance beyond legal integration without first achieving some level of economic integration. When social integration is being achieved, migrants can work on achieving cultural integration. As we have seen, each of these stages of integration takes time. While all the migrants benefit from legal integration, each case-study establishes a different timeline for economic, social and cultural integration. For example, Poles in the Cardiff sample appear to integrate economically much quicker than the Poles in the Llanelli sample, not least because of a diversified labour market and the desire of migrants in Cardiff to acquire advanced English-language skills to access available employment opportunities. It will be interesting to explore, through further research, whether the same migrants have achieved a higher degree of cultural integration across the South Wales region.

The increased resistance to migrants by host societies across the EU has been noticeable since early 2014. With a hostile general public and concerned politicians, the distinction between third-country nationals and EU migrants is negligible in the face of the 'us v. them' discourse that has emerged. As a result, concerned with the influx of third-country nationals, Austria suspended the Schengen Agreement in early 2016. While this action does not have the same impact on EU migrants as it does on third-country nationals, the suspension of a fundamental pillar of European integration moves closer. More specific to EU migrants, the result of the June 2016 referendum as well as the increase in immigrant-related hate crimes over the summer means that general public sentiment is drastically shifting, possibly stalling integration efforts.

10

Policy Implications

Introduction

Freedom of movement is one of the founding principles of the EU. Through this principle, UK citizens can live and work in another member state and EU citizens have a fundamental right to live and work in the UK. Since the founding of the European Economic Community through the Treaty of Rome in 1957, one of the primary aims of European cooperation has been to provide support for national European economies by developing a mobile and flexible labour force. Once in employment, individuals from one country can, if they satisfy certain conditions, access the same benefits – welfare, healthcare and education, for example – as nationals of the host country. As well as operationalizing the cooperation on which the EU is founded, freedom of movement has the potential to break down stereotypes and prejudices, thus helping to build solidarity across national boundaries and solve pressing social and economic problems more effectively through collective endeavour.

Realising the importance of this principle in European integration, all European citizens have access to the EU labour market. This is not a policy that can be enabled during a time of economic boom and disabled during a time of economic bust. It is a supranational mandate for migration within the member states of the EU. In regard to the UK, the British government in Westminster determines the overall decision about who is allowed to work in each nation within the UK. In regard to EU migrants, the UK government policies must conform to the EU freedom of movement principle and subsequent laws; however, there is growing conflict regarding this principle.

POLICY IMPLICATIONS

Given the large number of CEE migrants that entered the UK post-2004, which had an impact on the British policy toward Bulgarian and Romanian accession in 2007 and the Croatian accession in 2013, there is increasing concern about the impact of EU migrants on the UK economy. In early 2013, four EU member states, including the UK, called for legislative changes to make it harder for EU citizens to pursue free movement and claim benefits in another member state. Higher living standards and more generous welfare benefits in some countries had, it was argued, brought huge numbers of what the UK Home Secretary Theresa May called 'benefit tourists' into older member states from newer states in CEE.[1] While the impact of labour migration on places and local economies across the UK is highly contested, evidence suggests that the benefits are largely positive.[2]

In regards to migration, while the EU governs the free movement principle, the UK government determines who is allowed to work in each nation and the social policies regarding migration are governed at the national level. As a result, the nations of the UK have government oversight relating to social aspects of migration. Focusing specifically on Wales, with devolution the Welsh government has responsibility for migrants across all policy areas, including housing, welfare services, education and language provision. Policy towards migrants in Wales is thus developed in line with the Welsh government's Programme for Government and UK and European legislation.[3]

One of the most notable economic impacts is the flexibility free movement provides to reduce local and regional labour market disparities. Wales is a good case study in this sense, not least because it has experienced considerable periods of in- and out-migration over the last century.[4] Past economic performance has been directly impacted because people leaving Wales for other parts of the UK have been younger and more educated than those arriving in Wales, as well being more willing to migrate than people in other parts of the UK.[5]

Recent research also highlights that the net out-movement of young people from rural Wales is in line with the lack of local employment opportunities, with many local labour markets still dominated by low-skill and low-paid employment. Indeed, over recent decades rural Wales has had the lowest levels of average earnings across Wales overall.[6] At the same time, however, in some places the rural economy has diversified, expanded and grown, often in line with the arrival of new waves of migrant workers from CEE countries.⁷ With the brain drain of skilled Welsh to locations outside Wales, the brain gain of skilled CEE workers to Wales, who are willing to take low-skilled jobs is needed. Data from WRS indicate that since 2004 more than 10,000 CEE migrants have arrived in rural Wales, including Llanelli, most notably from Poland.⁸ The SWV, including Merthyr Tydfil, have experienced a similar influx between 2004 and 2011, with WRS data indicating that around 4,000 migrants arrived, again largely from Poland.⁹ Using the same WRS dataset, approximately 4,000 CEE migrants entered the local authority area of Cardiff between 2004 and 2011, with over 2,500 arriving from Poland during that period.¹⁰

As we have observed throughout the preceding chapters, these migratory trends have created many problems for local communities and policy-makers as well as for migrant workers across Wales. This chapter looks at each of these issues in turn, starting off with the rights of migrant workers in the workplace, before moving on to look at community cohesion and the impact of Polish migration on and in different policy areas.

The Value of EU Migrants to the UK and Welsh Economy

Despite claims to the contrary, there are many economic benefits to be derived from freedom of movement. The OECD estimates that free movement has lowered the unemployment rate across the EU by up to 6 per cent, by enabling a supply of workers to migrate to locations where there is a demand for workers.¹¹ The European Commission found that free movement from new to old member states between 2004 and 2009 increased the GDP of older states by around 1 per cent.¹² In addition, free movement has not undermined employment rates and the wages of nationals in host countries.¹³

Recent studies of migrant workers in Wales indicate that citizens from EU countries usually take lower-skilled, hard-to-fill jobs in food and agriculture, care work, catering, cleaning and the construction sector.¹⁴,¹⁵ As Crawley confirms:

> There are few (if any) signs of negative impacts of migration on the Welsh labour market, rather there is evidence that migration overall represents a sizeable economic boost for Wales. Migrants do not increase unemployment because they often work in sectors and regions with a

POLICY IMPLICATIONS

high level of hard-to-fill vacancies. There are zero or small negative effects on average wages.[16]

Political pressure to reduce or restrict the free movement of EU citizens could therefore restrict economic recovery and growth, enhance austerity and weaken or at least undermine the power and influence of the EU overall. Lord (Digby) Jones has argued that more skilled migrant workers from the EU are needed to plug the skills shortfall in some industries.[17]

The UK government intermittently attempts to get the long-term unemployed to work in dirty, dangerous and demanding jobs (the 3D's) which previous generations have been reluctant to do.[18, 19] In reality this means that EU workers from Poland and other new EU members states are often in competition for jobs with lower-skilled workers from inside and outside the EU as well as with Welsh workers.[20] Migrant worker families are therefore in similar circumstances to many other low-income families in Wales, facing difficulties with benefit entitlement and access to public funds. To compound matters, overall economic marginalisation is often obscured by a discourse of migrant workers as job takers, thus deflecting attention away from poor labour market conditions.[21] Although the working conditions and experiences of migrant workers can vary substantially in relation to individual skill levels and language ability, there is limited evidence (with the exception of the Cardiff case) of occupational mobility, and the majority of Polish workers remain in low-grade and low-paid manual employment. Nevertheless, in occupying hard-to-fill positions in local labour markets, it is clear that migrant workers play a critical role supporting the Welsh economy. Any new restriction on free movement as a result of the June 2016 vote for the UK to leave the EU or by other means will thus possibly hinder the supply of workers to business in some economic sectors, whilst simultaneously disadvantaging Welsh and UK citizens living and working in Europe.

In some places in Wales, a more positive discourse has emerged around migrant entrepreneurs as job creators and facilitators of redevelopment rather than job takers. This is particularly so in Merthyr Tydfil, which has, as opposed to small towns and rural areas, the critical mass of population to support new business ventures and initiatives.[22] Social enterprise initiatives in Merthyr have worked to encourage migrant entrepreneurship through enabling access to information and advice, while elsewhere individuals have been required to be more self-reliant in seeking out appropriate support. Migrants face substantial barriers to entrepreneurship, including language, start-up costs and legal requirements. Mobile business practices (hairdressers, beauty technicians and builders, for example) bypass some of these constraints, and are sometimes undertaken by migrants with professional and vocational skills out of necessity to supplement their meagre incomes from paid employment, if they have employment at all. Nevertheless, while EU migrants with varied qualifications and skills are needed by businesses across different economic sectors in Wales, recent migration has also brought about many challenges for Welsh communities and policy-makers, and for EU migrants themselves, outside as well as inside the workplace. The rapid influx of Polish migrants has undoubtedly had a direct impact on community cohesion to a greater or lesser extent in places and communities across Wales, as evidenced in Merthyr Tydfil, with similar results in Cardiff as well.

Given the economic advantages that migrants continue to bring to Wales, there should be initiatives in place to attract migrants with certain skillsets that are currently lacking in the Welsh labour market. For example, if there is a shortage of nurses in Wales then initiatives could be put in place to attract migrant nurses to Wales. However, there are currently no initiatives in place and the Welsh government has limited input into the UK government's initiatives to target specific migrant groups. The UK government bases many of its decisions regarding which migrants are needed throughout the UK on the advice of the Migration Advisory Committee (MAC), a subdivision of the Home Office.

The Rights of Migrant Workers in the Workplace

Over one hundred years ago in the early twentieth century, concerns were expressed over exploitation during the recruitment of Spanish workers for Merthyr's iron factories.[23] Similar processes are evident today. When a large meat-processing factory opened in Merthyr in the late 1990s, Tannock found that local people were suspicious and believed the company was coming to Merthyr 'because Wales was widely seen as a low-wage destination where employers could make more profits'.[24] Until 2004, Portuguese workers were the dominant migrant worker community in Merthyr's factories, yet almost immediately after EU enlargement some factories began to use agency-sourced workers from Poland to supplant those from Portugal.[25] In some companies, Polish workers replaced Portuguese workers because they had not yet joined a union while the Portuguese were long-term trade union members. As one local authority interviewee pointed out: 'There were ... quite a lot of Portuguese workers, and they got themselves unionised, at which point they were all got rid of and Polish workers were brought in.'

Over recent decades, the rights of migrant workers have become one of most contested public policy issues in the UK.[26,27] Immigration controls are often presented as a way of ensuring jobs for British workers whilst simultaneously protecting migrant workers from exploitation. In 2004, new European citizens were only permitted to work in the UK if they joined the WRS, a situation that allowed employment agencies to play a crucial role in the recruitment and supply of workers to factories across Wales. These workers have faced many problems and they were largely employed on poorer terms and conditions than UK workers.[28] As Anderson and Ruhs note,

> Agency workers have significantly fewer rights than those who are directly employed; they can be hired on lower hourly rates and on worse times and conditions, and they do not have rights to benefits such as overtime and sickness pay. They are also less likely to be members of a trade union.[29]

What follows from this is that employers have more control over desirable migrant workers than they do over hard-to-recruit and reluctant British workers.[30]

As factories have attempted to control their workers under difficult economic conditions, union membership has been frowned upon and the rights of workers in meat-processing factories across Wales have been undermined. A trade union representative suggested that many companies in the food and meat processing sector stay just the 'right side' of minimum legal requirements on any number of issues, a situation that makes it difficult for unions to support workers of all nationalities.[31] An inquiry into conditions of employment and working practices in meat- and poultry-processing factories across England and Wales found that this situation creates many problems for migrant workers. Agency workers in particular were found to experience multiple problems related to management coercion and physical and verbal abuse. Long hours and shift work spent almost entirely in the company of co-nationals undermine opportunities to integrate with local communities, and learning a new language can thus become extremely challenging.[32]

As the role of employment agencies in migrant recruitment has lessened as migrant support networks have become established, new challenges have emerged. During the recession, new contract 'permanent' arrangements have emerged in the sector and many workers are now employed on 'open-ended' or 'unlimited-permanent' contracts, which in reality refer to 'zero hours' contracts without any agreed allocation of working hours. Job insecurity remains a widespread problem for both agency and direct employees. The number of hours worked by migrants and the earnings received varies considerably. Workers are often sent home on arrival at the factory, after long journeys on public transport, with no information on when they are likely to work again. While these practices give employers great flexibility, the impact on migrant workers in Wales is often profound. If workers are put on limited hours at short notice they are often unable to claim benefits, even if they have recourse to public funds, because they have not been employed long enough to make a claim. This means that money often gets stretched too far, bills are unpaid, and workers turn to unscrupulous doorstep lenders.

Starting with the historical account of Spanish labourers at the beginning of this section, it would appear that labour exploitation is a trait associated with factory-based work in Wales. Given the internal-facing structure of a factory as well as the closed social network of many of the migrants working in the factory, this is a prime location for labour exploitation to occur. While this sector allows a significant amount of exploitation to occur owing to the low levels of transparency, similar to offshoring practices, exploitation of migrant labour occurs also in more external-facing areas such as the service sector.

In the case of Cardiff, the majority of the migrants were high-skilled but took any job when initially migrating. As a result, some migrants were working in bars or restaurants for the first few months of their migration period while other migrants were working as room attendants in hotels during this same period. Regardless of their position in the service sector, these migrants were regularly requested to work additional hours beyond the thirty-five-hour work week. For those migrants working in bars and restaurants, these frequent requests were the catalyst for the migrant to search out a better job. Migrants working in hotels saw the potential for moving up the career ladder within the organisation if they were willing to put in the time and, as a result, they decided to commit to their employer and continue working. Regardless of the outcome, this brief example highlights that the exploitation of migrant workers can occur in both internal-facing as well as external-facing positions. In addition, overworking of migrant employees may exist in other sectors with higher skill levels; however, in the case of Cardiff the exploitative practices were largely occurring in the service sector.

Community Cohesion

The Welsh government's Programme for Government seeks to address concerns over migration by creating 'a fair society free from discrimination, harassment and victimisation with cohesive and inclusive communities'.[33] Chapter 9 outlines several definitions of integration and cohesion; however, the Welsh government does not provide a single definition of community cohesion in the programme, but just a call for all groups to live together cohesively.

In 2009, the Welsh Assembly government launched its Community Cohesion Strategy – Getting on Together.[34] The overall focus was on how different groups and communities interact across all policy and service delivery areas. A Community Cohesion Unit was also established in the WAG to oversee joining up across departments to assist with implementation of the strategy and address issues that occur at the local level through better partnership working.[35] It is important to recognise at this juncture, however, as we have seen in preceding chapters, that as communities become more diverse, integration and exclusion can occur simultaneously. A number of factors are seen to impact the community cohesion at the local level, most notably perceived competition over resources, housing pressures, perceptions of increased competition for employment and services, demographic change and the sustainability of Welsh-speaking communities. However, evidence suggests that there is no straightforward relationship between the number of migrants in communities and overall levels of cohesion in Wales.[36] This policy is also supported by integration research from the OECD.[37] Research on attitudes to community cohesion found that the people of Wales generally have a strong sense of togetherness and feel comfortable with people from different backgrounds.[38] This is not to say that negative perceptions towards some groups and communities do not exist.[39, 40] However, our research found that this is more likely in small rural towns where the number of migrants constitutes a greater overall percentage of the population than in urban areas.

Interestingly, Robinson et al. found that Wales has higher perceived levels of community cohesion than England, a fact highlighted by some interviewees in Merthyr who had arrived in Wales from Poland and moved to England before settling in Wales.[41] Over recent years, however, as our own research confirms, this situation has started to change in line with a more general increase in poverty and deprivation. We can see this in increased competition for employment over recent years and in the changing social relations that subsequently emerge between migrant and local workers, between migrants of different nationalities and also between migrants of the same nationality.[42] While Welsh workers have often been reluctant to take jobs in the food- and meat-processing sector, competition for jobs between all workers has increased significantly over recent years as employment has become more difficult to find.

Specifically focused on the food- and meat-processing sector, Merthyr provides good insights into community cohesion in this sense. Whilst it was already embedded in established migratory pathways prior to 2004, the scale and intensity of EU migration from Poland has been unprecedented, with previously established Portuguese and Filipino migrant communities now constituting three-tenths and two-tenths the size of Merthyr's Polish population respectively.[43] Although low-paid, insecure employment in the meat-processing sector leaves many Poles as 'outsiders' on the social fringe,[44] complaints of discrimination outside the workplace in Merthyr were limited and many migrant workers appear to accept their position with a sense of resignation.[45, 46]

Merthyr has also had some useful policy developments of its own. The Multi Agency Diversity Forum (MADF), a subgroup of the Merthyr Tydfil Community Safety Partnership, has provided overarching local authority input through attempts to foster social cohesion; and MADF oversees the Migrant Workers Forum (MWF). Set up in 2007, the aim of MWF is to look at the major issues affecting migrant workers. Initially there was representation at MWF from a range of local agencies, including USDAW, the local authority, education, housing, Merthyr College and the voluntary sector. There has also been sporadic involvement by some employment agencies and by employers. Some progress has been made, yet problems remain and it is not clear how long these ways of working

POLICY IMPLICATIONS

will continue. While employers engage MWF, very often it appears that they do so only to keep abreast of what policies may impact their practices, rather than to bring about positive change.

Outside the food- and meat-processing sector, Cardiff provides good insights into community cohesion and how it varies with migrants' place in the labour market. Cardiff has a diverse population that is linked to its history as a port city. Despite this high-level of diversity, discrimination can still exist between ethnic groups as well as within ethnic groups. One of the major factors regarding discrimination is migrants' involvement in the labour market versus unemployment. It took several generations for the large Somali population in Cardiff not to be discriminated against because of a perception that they were living on benefits in the UK.[47] Once the population was contributing to the labour market, the perception of that ethnic group changed dramatically. In regard to the Poles in Cardiff, there has been no outward discrimination. When all of the migrants in the Cardiff sample originally migrated they were in low-skilled employment, often having several positions before moving up the division of labour. This transition occurred either through getting a better job in the British labour market or through ethnic entrepreneurship. In either regard, migrants were establishing roots in the community as well as advancing their English-language skills. The migrants' place in the divison of labour is used as an indicator of community cohesion instead of their time in the region, as people in service-sector jobs may still be viewed as short-term and transient regardless of the length of time they are in an area. Alternatively, a migrant who has transitioned beyond a job and into a career path is more likely to be perceived as contributing to the community in the long term, even if they have only lived in the community for a short time. As discussed below in more detail, issues around community cohesion are evident in all policy sectors and areas of service delivery.

Education

Long-term administrative responsibility for education has allowed Wales to develop a distinctive Welsh education system. Around 10 per cent of all children in primary and secondary education are educated through the medium of Welsh, which is available from nursery through to university level and is compulsory for all children until the age of sixteen.[48] Educational opportunities for migrant children are supported through the

Welsh government's Minority Ethnic Achievement Grant (MEAG), which aims to improve educational opportunities for all minority groups, particularly those who have English as an additional language. Shared equally between all twenty-two local authorities, in 2013–14, the value of MEAG stood at £10.5 million.[49]

The literature on the impact of migration on education in Wales highlights positive as well as negative impacts, but the overall picture remains unclear.[50] Many schools across Wales are undersubscribed, and immigration has helped to increase school enrolment and maintenance in some cases, notably in rural areas. As Crawley notes, 26 per cent of primary schools and 33 per cent of secondary schools in Wales have surplus places, and many would benefit significantly from an increase in migrant applications.[51] The increase in migrant teachers moving to the UK has also been beneficial and, contradicting popular discourse, there is a positive relationship between the number of pupils with English as an additional language and wider achievement levels.[52] However, education services across Wales have also experienced new and additional demands as a result of EU migration. In recent years an increasing number of pupils from migrant families have required supported learning in English as an Additional Language (EAL) and/or Welsh as an Additional Language (WAL). Whilst additional funding is provided through MELAP, it is the responsibility of schools and local education authorities to respond appropriately to gauge local demand. Our research found that this has necessitated rural schools taking on a proactive role in developing their own coping strategies.

Pupil Level Annual School Census (PLASC) data indicates that the number of pupils requiring EAL support has increased to a greater or lesser extent in places across Wales, with Merthyr now having the fifth highest proportion of EAL learners across all Welsh local authorities, with twenty-six different languages spoken. When they arrive in Wales, migrants attempt to get their children into the school with the highest number of pupils from their home country, which often means the local Catholic school. One of the most dramatic cases over recent years revolves around the increase in Polish pupils in Llanelli. Between 2005 and 2012 there was a tenfold increase in Polish EAL learners from 30 to just over 300 by 2012, with much of the increase concentrated at a number of local Roman Catholic schools.

This can create many operational and administrative difficulties. Our research found that attendance was a problem at infant and primary level in Merthyr, and in smaller towns, with pupils in this age cohort more reliant on parents for getting to and from school. In several cases, extended family had been brought to the UK to assist with childcare. Other contributory factors towards absenteeism include extended summer holidays in Poland and pupils being kept away from school to help parents with translation and language issues at medical and other appointments. Attendance issues can also be a consequence of cultural differences. When a child is unwell, for example, Polish parents may keep them away from school for longer than the recommended forty-eight hours. Even so, our research found that educational attainment among migrant pupils is generally very good, with most pupils quickly exceeding the language capabilities of their parents. Nevertheless, attainment can also be severely affected by other factors including: pre-existing levels of English-language ability; speed of language acquisition; availability of appropriate academic and pastoral support; and, importantly, the pupil's age of first entry into a UK school. The latter is particularly an issue when migrant pupils enter at secondary level, as children in Poland do not attend school full-time until age seven, and they often need to get their English very quickly to the level needed to fully access the curriculum.

Our research found that integration issues are few and far between among pupils of different nationalities at primary level. However, when pupils move up to larger school environments at secondary level tensions can emerge due to social pressures and the rapid increase in the numbers and visibility of migrant pupils. Problems between pupils can also reflect parental attitudes and socio-economic circumstances, particular around perceptions of economically active Polish families in small rural towns. In Merthyr and Llanelli, the concentration of EAL pupils in an urban environment has to some extent made it easier to respond to increasing numbers of migrant children, particularly in bringing Polish-speaking teachers, teaching assistants and parental volunteers into schools to support pupils. Since early 2013, the Merthyr local authority has been required by the Education Watchdog Estyn to improve the support provided to struggling schools. The LEA is addressing these issues and there has been an increased focus on understanding the culture of migrant pupils and overcoming bullying more generally. However, as Crawley notes, challenges remain around social integration, both at pupil and parent levels, and a lack of staff time and resource often means that the additional extra-curricular measures needed to encourage social integration remain beyond local resource capacity.[53]

Housing

Housing policy in Wales is devolved and responsibility lies with the Welsh government. Of the 1.35 million homes in Wales, around 70 per cent are owner-occupied, with the remainder in the rental sector under the auspices of local authorities, housing associations (16 per cent) and private landlords (14 per cent).[54] Although responsibility for primary legislation lies at Westminster, the government decides budgets for housing priorities and passes secondary legislation.[55] The national housing strategy was launched by WAG in April 2010. *Improving Lives and Communities – Homes in Wales* lays out the challenges Wales faces meeting its housing requirements.[56] A number of key themes stand out: most notably the extent by which demand continues to outstrip supply; the age and quality of current social stock; and the increased demand on housing and related support services. An ageing population and homelessness combine to make these issues formidable, and the private rented sector has become an increasingly important part of overall housing provision across the country.[57]

Housing was a particular problem during the initial wave of A8 migration to Wales, with employment agencies often arranging poor-quality, multi-occupation housing for new arrivals.[58, 59] While at one time many migrants lived in accommodation provided by employers, and a small number still do, most now quickly move on to private rented accommodation once settled. Overall issues with agency-linked accommodation have declined considerably in recent years as migrant communities have become more established and friends/family are able to assist with knowledge and experience accumulated over time. However, while problems initially encountered with multiple-occupancy housing have been largely resolved, increased demand means that the availability of rental accommodation of suitable size and quality for families is a major problem, particularly in rural areas. It should be noted that migrants living in the urban areas with no association with employment agencies also encountered problems seeking accommodation.

The Cardiff migrants heavily relied on their social networks for accommodation when initially migrating. When they moved into rented accommodation, it was with several roommates, regardless of gender, and in a part of the city offering student accommodation. Interestingly, a migrant's next move usually coincided with saving money or getting a better job. Whatever the reason for the move, it was traditionally to a pleasanter area, with fewer roommates or none at all. In general, finding better-quality accommodation appears to become easier the longer migrants live in Wales, as they are able to provide employer references as well as developing and drawing on stronger support networks. However, many migrants still live in poor-quality and expensive private-sector housing and accommodation.

Housing requirements have also changed in recent years in line with the demographic make-up of new European migrants and the shift from single male workers, who tended to live in multiple-occupancy houses, towards the private rental of family-sized houses, preferably close to school facilities. The increasing demand for private rental housing has created new challenges, with inflated rental prices and unscrupulous landlords noted in both Merthyr and Llanelli. In many places, migrants encountered problems finding good-quality and affordable rented accommodation because of the age of the available stock. Several respondents commented that despite problems with damp and mould they were still required to pay high rents. Although numbers across our samples were lower, Shelter Cymru found that one-third of Eastern European migrants have experienced some form of homelessness since arriving in Wales.[60]

The relationship between migration and housing is complex and there have been widespread accusations reported in the media that migrants get unfair access to social housing, yet this was not widely evident in our research. Most migrants entering the UK over recent years have had limited access to social housing and they made up less than 2 per cent of those in social housing in 2009.[61] As noted above, the issues identified in relation to housing have emerged alongside significant changes to the housing market more generally. Indeed, there is evidence that there will continue to be housing problems even with zero net migration.[62] Organisations such as Tai Pawb have emerged in Wales to promote equality in housing and to inform the general public about good practices in renting to start to break down stereotypes regarding housing allocations.

Health

As the demographic pattern of Polish migrants has changed in recent years, with the number of females and families increasing, ensuring access to safe and appropriate health services has increased in importance. As a Hywel Dda Local Health Board interviewee noted: 'we had ... women coming in about to give birth and we knew nothing about their medical history.' Several women in our samples had given birth since living in the UK, and the provision of language support for pregnant women was seen to be critical. In addition to primary and secondary care, socio-economic factors such as poor-quality housing and diet related to low incomes can also contribute to high levels of ill health among migrant families. Local health boards have made progress in ensuring access to general health services for migrants, and bi-lingual language-line schemes were highlighted as examples of good practices in this area. However, some health needs remain unmet, with reports of migrants failing to receive the required treatment owing to language barriers. The provision of specialist support for conditions including mental health is particularly problematic, with rural areas often lacking the critical mass to justify dedicated translation services.

Large numbers of migrants in our samples are registered with a local GP, which follows efforts by local authorities to encourage this practice, which is not required in Poland. For instance, the Hywel Dda LHB has worked with the PWMA in Llanelli to promote access to health services for migrant families, producing bilingual Polish–English information and a bilingual language-line that allowed initial consultations to be carried out remotely. Finding a dentist, NHS or otherwise, appears to be more problematic, and one Polish migrant we spoke with had been waiting five years for an initial appointment. The contribution of skilled Polish migrants – GPs and dentists – was recognised by local stakeholders as important both in filling skills shortages in the NHS and in engaging the wider Polish community.

Opinion varied as to the value of NHS services, with negative perceptions often resulting from misunderstandings fostered by language barriers. There were reports of incidents in Merthyr where migrants were prescribed drugs, treatment and even operations for conditions they did not fully understand. Conversely, there were reports of migrants not getting the treatment they needed because of a lack of people to translate effectively. Health boards do not generally have official translation budgets, and individual departments have to pay for these services. The resultant reliance on children or, less frequently, untrained migrant staff (e.g. hospital cleaners) to assist with translations due to limited resources is a dangerous trend, particularly when dealing with sensitive and complex medical conditions including mental health. Accessing appropriate support for the latter was commented upon by stakeholders as a serious challenge facing migrant workers, who are subjected to many pressures in their daily lives associated with living away from home which can often combine to have an adverse impact on their mental health. It was reported that some Poles return to Poland regularly to get check-ups, or use on-line counselling services in Poland via Skype.

No Recourse to Public Funds and the Rise of Migrant Support Networks

Despite 'welcome pack' initiatives by some local authorities, very few of the migrants in our samples had received any official information about living and working in Wales. Instead, formalised organisations such as the Polish Community of the Valleys Association in Merthyr and the Polish-Welsh Mutual Association in Llanelli provide free information and advice for migrants. In addition, there is a Polish House in Cardiff that is a meeting place for many Poles who migrated to the region after WW2. While it is not a formal organisation, the house does provide space for local outreach organisations, such as Race Equality First, to engage with new Polish migrants in the area. In the context of public spending cuts, the growing capacity for self-help and self-reliance within migrant communities has become increasingly important.

As we have noted, social enterprises have also started to offer support and knowledge sharing to migrants in some places. Y Bont Culture Hub in Merthyr is a good example of a social enterprise working in this way. The overall aim of Y Bont is to develop a space that will enable members from a wide range of cultural backgrounds to integrate and increase community cohesion through a mixture of art, culture and technology. It aims to empower individuals and assist organisations with a view to engendering community cohesion and participation, and developing greater tolerance and understanding in the Heads of the Valleys area. These initiatives are increasingly important. Although one of the European Commission's future priorities for migration is the opening up of new channels for migration, Martín and Venturini point out that until now the EU's approach to migration has been limited and fragmented, focusing largely on the different categories of migrant workers that are available to work in UK labour markets.[63] This is reflected in some of the issues around community cohesion we have highlighted. However, despite plans to develop and enhance freedom of movement across the EU, the UK government's 2015 Immigration Bill is likely to increase the pressures faced by migrant workers significantly, thus undermining those that the Modern Slavery Act intends to protect.[64] The Brexit vote of 2016 has significantly enhanced the uncertainty surrounding such issues.

Post-Brexit Politics: The End of Freedom of Movement?

In the post Brexit vote period the future of freedom of movement and the right of EU migrants to remain in the UK is uncertain. At the time of writing it appears that EU migrants currently living in the UK will be given leave to remain, although this may be dependent on the same rights being granted to British citizens in EU member states. In the summer of 2016 the UK government announced that if they have been in employment, studying or have been self- sufficient for at least five years, EU citizens are already entitled to stay and can apply for naturalisation/ citizenship; significantly, it is not the certificate that gives migrants residence, but the five years they have already been in the UK.

We have argued that EU migration has been beneficial for the Welsh economy and has also greatly enhanced cultural diversity in places such as Merthyr Tydfil in the Welsh Valleys. At the same time, however, it has also put great pressure on public services and threatened the sense of security of some communities in rural areas, thus generating negative perceptions of migrants in some places. Despite having received the highest levels of funding from the EU in recent decades, parts of South Wales also had the highest Leave vote in the UK: overall 52.5% of the Welsh population voted to leave the EU. Moving forward some argue that only skilled workers should be allowed to stay in the UK, yet it is clear from our work that many unskilled Welsh and British workers will not work in the jobs or sectors where EU migrants thrive. Brexit negotiations with the EU thus pose some difficult policy decisions.

Implications for Policy

Based on the review in this chapter of the social policies that impact migrants throughout their migration period, as well as the many benefits of and hurdles during migration outlined throughout this book, we finish this chapter with a number of recommendations for policy makers. It should be noted that these recommendations are relevant for EU

POLICY IMPLICATIONS

migrants who are able to remain in the UK. In addition, many of these recommendations can apply to other migrant groups in Wales, not only those migrants from CEE countries.

Recommendation 1: **Greater provision of language learning tailored to particular needs, in order to overcome persistent barriers to economic, social and cultural integration, occupational mobility and service usage**
A more flexible range of language learning options and styles (beyond ESOL) is needed to encourage participation among migrant workers with variable shift-working and care responsibilities. Many migrant workers are unable to gain employment in their trained professions because of inability to communicate in the higher-level technical language required. More specialised language sessions could assist with this next step in the labour market. There is a need for service providers to consider how costs for translation services can be more effectively shared across departments (e.g. health, education) to improve consistency of service and minimise the use of migrant children in this capacity.

Recommendation 2: **Continue to promote the integration of migrant workers with local communities and enhance community cohesion between all groups**
Cohesion initiatives need to effectively engage migrant and local populations to avoid heightening existing tensions around access to jobs and services. This issue was drawn into sharper focus by the recession and economic pressures faced by many residents regardless of nationality. Consideration needs to be given to the availability of physical spaces that allow different groups to interact. Schools can play an important function in rural communities, but this can only come about through the allocation of new funding; teaching staff are already straining to meet the growing requirement for EAL/WAL supported learning.

Recommendation 3: **Continue to support the work of specialist advice and advocacy organisations, including the expansion of satellite services to rural areas lacking in support**
The Polish Community of the Valleys Association in Merthyr and the Polish-Welsh Mutual Association (PWMA) in Llanelli provide good practice examples of organisations that offer support to new arrivals and

educate migrant workers about their legal rights; these organisations also play an important longer-term function in community cohesion.

Recommendation 4: **More effectively recognise and harness the professional and vocational skills of migrant workers**
Many migrant workers continue to be overqualified in their current employment. This is an inefficient use of the labour resources they represent, particularly when many possess skills absent from local labour markets. Working Links has provided training opportunities for some migrants to convert their vocational qualifications into a form recognised in the UK.

Employers have sought the assistance of the PWMA to fill specific vacancies. This good practice could be developed by encouraging migrants to register their skills with brokers who facilitate links with employers, including SMEs seeking to grow their business in rural areas.

Migrant women can face particular challenges in rural areas, where many of the professions in which they are qualified place a high value on the ability to speak Welsh. There is a need to raise early awareness of this requirement and encourage Welsh learning alongside English.

Recommendation 5: **Encourage entrepreneurial potential by reducing barriers to information and start-up finance**
Among the growing number of migrant entrepreneurs in Merthyr, many highlighted the positive influence of social enterprise such as the Y Bont initiative on their business success. This recognises the importance of physical spaces where migrants can seek advice, receive signposting to other appropriate forms of support and discuss experiences with others.

Business start-up costs are prohibitive for many migrants facing various forms of financial exclusion. Consideration should be given to how Welsh government schemes for new businesses take account of these issues. Credit Unions offer a valuable financial service and this model might be expanded to assist with elements of business start-up.

Recommendation 6: **Encourage sharing of knowledge, experience and good practice between schools in regards to the provision of EAL/WAL-supported learning**
In contrast to urban areas, large rural counties are less able to centralise EAL/WAL teaching resources because of the need for provision of support in dispersed schools with varying learner numbers. A greater

POLICY IMPLICATIONS

rural weighting should be given to the allocation of funding for this purpose. Schools are required to be responsive to local context, issues and demand. Nonetheless, there are some common issues across rural and non-rural areas in regard to EAL-supported learning such as assessing levels of cognitive language acquisition. Better mechanisms for the sharing of knowledge, experience and good practice between schools across Wales could be developed.

Notes

Notes to Chapter 1

1. European Commission, 'Moving to the European Union?' *http://ec.europa.eu/immigration/* (accessed 16 July 2016).
2. S. Drinkwater, J. Eade and M. Garapich, 'Poles apart? EU enlargement and the labour market outcomes of immigrants in the UK', *International Migration*, 47 (2009), 161–90.
3. BBC UK, 'Brexit: David Cameron to quit after the UK votes to leave EU', *http://www.bbc.com/news/uk-politics-36615028* (accessed 16 July 2016).
4. BBC UK, 'Theresa May vows to be "one nation" as new Prime Minister', *http://www.bbc.com/news/uk-politics-36788782* (accessed 16 July 2016).
5. Vote Leave, 'Briefing: The EU Immigration System is Immoral and Unfair', *http://www.voteleavetakecontrol.org/briefing_immigration* (accessed 16 July 2016).
6. European Commission, 'Moving to the European Union?'
7. J. Dobson, A. Latham and J. Salt, *On the Move? Labour Migration in Times of Recession*. (London: Policy Network Article, 2009).
8. European Commission, 'Free Movement – EU Nationals', *http://ec.europa.eu/social/main.jsp?catId=457&langId=en* (accessed 16 July 2016).
9. D. Guardia and K. Pichelmann, *Report on Labour Migration Patterns in Europe: Recent Trends and Future Challenges* (Brussels: European Economy Report to the European Commission, 2006), 16–25.
10. European Commission, 'Free Movement – EU Nationals'.
11. S. Booth, C. Howarth, C. and V. Scarpetta, *Tread Carefully: The Impact and Management of EU Free Movement on Immigration Policy* (London: Open Europe, 2012), p. 5.
12. R, Fevre, 'Labour migration and freedom of movement in the European

NOTES

Union: social exclusion and economic development', *International Planning Studies*, 3/1 (1998), 1–18.
13 Guardia and Pichelmann, *Report on Labour Migration Patterns in Europe*, pp. 16–25.
14 Guardia and Pichelmann, *Report on Labour Migration Patterns in Europe*, 16–25.
15 Dobson, Latham, and Salt, *On the move? Labour migration in times of recession*.
16 E. Recchi, E. Baldoni, F. Francavilla, and L. Mencarini, *Geographic and Job Mobility in the EU* (Luxembourg: European Commission Report, 2006).
17 C. Dustmann, M. Casanova, M. Fertig, I. Preston and C. M. Schmidt, *The Impact of EU Enlargement on Migration Flows* (London: UK Home Office Report, 2003).
18 UKBA, 'Visas and Immigration', *https://www.gov.uk/browse/visas-immigration* (accessed 16 July 2016).
19 E. Gillingham, *Report on Understanding A8 Migration to the UK since Accession* (London: Office of National Statistics, 2010).
20 Gillingham, *Report on Understanding A8 Migration to the UK since Accession*.
21 Office of National Statistics (ONS), 'International Migration', *http://www.ons.gov.uk/peoplepopulationandcommunity/populationandmigration/internationalmigration* (accessed 16 July 2016).
22 D. McCollum, L. Cooke, C. Chiroro, A. Platts, F. MacLeod and A. Findlay, *Report on Spatial, Sectoral and Temporal Trends in A8 Migration to the UK 2004–2011: Evidence from the Worker Registration Scheme* (Southampton: Centre for Population Change, 2012).
23 McCollum, Cooke, Chiroro, Platts, MacLeod and Findlay, *Report on Spatial, Sectoral and Temporal Trends*.
24 V. Baure, P. Densham, J. Millar and J. Salt, 'Migrants from Central and Eastern Europe: Local Geographies', *Population and Trends*, 129 (2007), 7–19.
25 C. Harris, D. Moran and J. R. Bryson, 'EU Accession Migration: National Insurance Number Allocations and the Geographies of Polish Labour Migration to the UK', *Tijdschrift voor Economische en Sociale Geografie*, 103 (2012), 209–21.
26 Harris, Densham, Millar and Salt, 'EU Accession Migration'.
27 Gillingham, *Report on Understanding A8 Migration*.
28 Office of National Statistics (ONS), 'Census, Office for National Statistics', *http://webarchive.nationalarchives.gov.uk/20160105160709* (accessed 16 July 2016).
29 D. Bailey and C. Sodano, 'Census: Maps show migration trends', *http://www.bbc.com/news/uk-20713380* (accessed 16 July 2016).

30 A. Favell, 'The new face of east–west migration in Europe', *Journal of Ethnic and Migration Studies*, 34/5 (2008), 701–16.
31 Drinkwater, Eade and Garapich, 'Poles apart?'
32 B. Anderson, M. Ruhs, B. Rogaly and S. Spencer, *Fair Enough? Central and East European Migrants in Low-Wage Employment in the UK* (York: Joseph Rowntree Foundation, 2006).
33 B. Anderson, N. Clark and V. Parutis, *New EU Members? Migrant Workers' Challenges and Opportunities to UK Trade Unions: A Polish and Lithuanian Case Study* (London: Trades Union Congress, 2007).
34 V. Parutis, 'Economic migrants or transnational middling? East European migrants' experiences of work in the UK', http://onlinelibrary.wiley.com/advanced/search/results (accessed 16 July 2016).
35 J. Knight, 'Migrant Entrepreneurship in a Shrinking Ethnic Economy: A study of Polish migrant small businesses in Cardiff, Wales', *Journal of Enterprising Communities: People and Places in the Global Economy*, 9 (2014), 114–31.
36 T. Whitehead, 'Thousands of foreign workers exploiting British jobs market', http://www.telegraph.co.uk/finance/jobs/4781831/Thousands-of-foreign-workers- (accessed 16 July 2016).
37 K. Burrell, 'Staying, returning, working and living: key themes in current academic research undertaken in the UK on migration movements from Eastern Europe', *Social Identities*, 16 (2010), 287–308.
38 S. Drinkwater and M. Garapich, 'Migration Plans and Strategies of Recent Polish migrants to England and Wales: Do they have any and how do they change?' Norface Migration Discussion Article (2013), 2013–23.
39 Drinkwater and Garapich, 'Migration Plans and Strategies'.
40 N. Pollard, M. Latorre, and L. Sriskandarajah, *Floodgates or Turnstiles? Post-EU Enlargement Migration Flows to (and from) the UK* (London: IPPR, 2008).
41 A. Thompson, P. Chambers and L. Doleczek, 'Welcome to Llaneski: Polish migration in South West Wales', *Contemporary Wales*, 23 (2010), 1–16.
42 A. White, 'Double Return Migration: Failed Returns to Poland Leading to Settlement Abroad and New Transnational Strategies', *International Migration*, 52/6 (2014), 72–84.
43 P. Trevena, D. McGhee and S. Heath, 'Location, location? A critical examination of patterns and determinants of internal mobility among post-accession Polish migrants in the UK', *Population, Space and Place*, 19 (2013), 671–87.
44 J. Lever and P. Milbourne, 'Migrant workers and migrant entrepreneurs: changing established-outsider relations across society and space?' *Space and Polity*, 18 (2014), 255–68.

NOTES

45 Bailey and Sodano, 'Census: Maps show migration trends'.
46 European Commission, 'Moving to the European Union?'
47 European Commission, 'Moving to the European Union?'
48 Vote Leave, 'Briefing: The EU Immigration System is Immoral and Unfair'.
49 British Futures, 'EU Migration from Romania and Bulgaria: What does the public think?' http://www.britishfuture.org/wp-content/uploads/2013/12/J1527_BRF_RomaniaBulgaria_16.12.13_2-1.pdf (accessed 16 July 2016).
50 Amnesty International, 'Amnesty launches urgent campaign on racism in the UK amid rise in reported hate crimes', https://www.amnesty.org.uk/press-releases/amnesty-launches-urgent-campaign-racism-uk-amid-rise-reported-hate-crime (accessed 16 July 2016).
51 ONS, 'Census, Office for National Statistics'.
52 H. Crawley, *Migration and Employment in Wales* (Cardiff: Wales Migration Partnership, 2013).
53 ONS, 'Census, Office for National Statistics'.
54 ONS, 'Census, Office for National Statistics'.
55 A. Hooper and J. Punter, *Capital Cardiff, 1975–2020: Regeneration, Competitiveness and the Urban Environment* (Cardiff: University of Wales Press, 2006).
56 H. Crawley, *Demographics and the Changing Face of Wales*, Centre for Migration Policy research. Presentation by the Swansea University School of the environment and society, 2006.
57 Crawley, *Demographics and the Changing Face of Wales*.
58 European Commission, 'Moving to the European Union?'

Notes to Chapter 2

1 B. Anderson, M. Ruhs, B. Rogaly, and S. Spencer, *Fair Enough? Central and East European Migrants in Low-Wage Employment in the UK* (York: Joseph Rowntree Foundation, 2006).
2 N. Pollard, M. Latorre and L. Sriskandarajah, *Floodgates or Turnstiles? Post-EU Enlargement Migration Flows to (and from) the UK* (London: IPPR, 2008).
3 A. Favell, 'The new face of east–west migration in Europe', *Journal of Ethnic and Migration Studies*, 34/5 (2008), 701–16.
4 A. Stenning and S. Dawley, 'Poles to Newcastle: Grounding new migrant flows in peripheral regions', *European Urban and Regional Studies*, 16/3 (2009), 273–94.
5 C. Dustmann and Y. Weiss, 'Return migration: theory and empirical evidence from the UK', *British Journal of Industrial Relations*, 45/2 (2007), 236–56.

NOTES

6 Dustmann and Weiss, 'Return migration'.
7 K. Burrell, 'Staying, returning, working and living: key themes in current academic research undertaken in the UK on migration movements from Eastern Europe', *Social Identities*, 16 (2010) 287–308.
8 Dustmann and Weiss, 'Return migration'.
9 A. White, 'Polish Migration in the UK: Local experiences and effects', presented at the AHRC Connected Communities Symposium: Understanding Local Experiences and Effects of New Migration, Sheffield, 26 September 2011.
10 Dustmann and Weiss, 'Return migration'.
11 Burrell, 'Staying, returning, working and living'.
12 B. Dayha, 'Pakistanis in Britain: Transients or Settlers?' *Race*, 14/3 (1973), 242–77.
13 P. Siu, 'The Sojourner', *American Journal of Sociology*, 58/1 (1952), 34–44
14 J. Eade, S. Drinkwater and M. Garapich, *Class and Ethnicity: Polish Migrants in London* (Guildford: University of Surrey Press, 2006).
15 B. Chiswick, Y. Lee and P. Miller, 'A Longitudinal Analysis of Immigrant Occupational Mobility: A test of the immigrant assimilation hypothesis', *International Migration Review*, 39/2 (2005), 332–53.
16 B. Burchell, 'A new way of analyzing labour market flows using work history data', *Work, Employment and Society*, 7/2 (1993), 237–58.
17 E. L. Ho, 'Migrant trajectories of "highly skilled" middling transnationals: Singaporean transmigrants in London', *Population, Space and Place*, 17/3 (2011), 116–29.
18 E. Helinksa-Hughes, M. Hughes, P. Lassalle and I. Skowron, 'The Trajectories of Polish Immigrant Businesses in Scotland and the Role of Social Capital', https://www.google.co.uk/search?q=the+trajectories+of+Polish+immigrant+businesss+in+Scotland&oq=the+trajectories+of+Polish+immigrant+businesss+in+Scotland&sourceid=chrome&ie=UTF-8 (accessed 10 July 2016).
19 Helinksa-Hughes, Hughes, Lassalle and Skowron, 'The Trajectories of Polish Immigrant Businesses in Scotland'.
20 J. Bell, 'Migration as Multiple Pathways: Narrative interviews with Polish migrants in Belfast, Northern Ireland', *Studia Sociologica*, 4/2 (2012), 106–18.
21 M Nowicka, 'Positioning strategies of Polish entrepreneurs in Germany: Transnationalising Bourdieu's notion of capital', *International Sociology*, 28/1 (2013), 29–47.
22 Nowicka, 'Positioning strategies of Polish entrepreneurs in Germany'.
23 J. Knight, J. Lever and A. Thompson, 'The Labour Market Mobility of Polish

Migrants: A comparative study of three regions in South Wales, UK', *Central and East European Migration Review* (2014), 1–18.
24 G. Becker, *The Economic Way of Looking at Life*, The Nobel Lecture, 9 December 1992.
25 R. Jennissen, *Report on Economic Theories of International Migration and the Role of Immigration Policy* (The Hagur: Dutch Ministry of Justice/Netherlands Interdisciplinary Demographic Institute, 2006).
26 Jennissen, *Report on Economic Theories*.
27 Jennissen, *Report on Economic Theories*.
28 M. J. Greenwood, 'Research on internal migration in the United States: a survey', *Journal of Economic Literature*, 8/1 (1975), 397–433.
29 L. Curry, 'Inefficiencies in the geographical operation of labour markets', *Regional Studies*, 19/3 (1985), 203–15.
30 D. S. Massey, J. Arango, G. Hugo, A. Kouaouci, A. Pellegrino and J. E. Taylor, 'Theories of international migration: a review and appraisal', *Population and Development Review*, 19/3 (1993), 431–66.
31 Dustmann and Weiss, 'Return migration'.
32 J. Nelson, *Access to Power: Politics and the Urban Poor in Developing Nations* (Princeton: Princeton University Press, 1979).
33 A. Fihel, P. Kaczmarczyk and M. Okólski, *Labour Mobility in the Enlarged European Union: International Migration from the EU8 Countries* (Warsaw: Centre of Migration Research, 2006).
34 S. Dreher, *Neoliberalism and Migration: An Inquiry into the Politics of Globalization* (Berlin: Lit Verlag, 2007).
35 H. de Haas, 'Migration Theory: Quo Vadis?' International Migration Institute Paper 100/1 (2014).
36 Dreher, *Neoliberalism and Migration*.
37 G. Borjas, *Friends or Strangers: The Impact of Immigrants on the US Economy* (New York: Basic Books, 1990).
38 L. Sjaastad, 'The costs and returns of human migration', *Journal of Political Economy*, 70/5 (1962), 80–93.
39 Borjas, *Friends or Strangers*.
40 S. Drinkwater and K. Clark, 'Pushed out or pulled in? Self-employment among ethnic minorities in England and Wales', *Labour Economics*, 7/5 (2000), 603–28.
41 Borjas, *Friends or Strangers*.
42 R. Verwiebe, 'Why do Europeans migrate to Berlin? Socio-structural differences for Italian, British, French and Polish nationals in the period

between 1980–2002', *International Migration* (2011) [Online Publication Version].
43 Verwiebe, 'Why do Europeans migrate to Berlin?'
44 M. Gilmartin and B. Migge, 'European Migrants in Ireland: Pathways to integration', *European Urban and Regional Studies*, 22/3 (2013), 1–15.
45 Gilmartin and Migge, 'European Migrants in Ireland'.
46 Gilmartin and Migge, 'European Migrants in Ireland'.
47 E. Kofman, 'Family-related migration: A critical review of European studies', *Journal of Ethnic and Migration Studies*, 30/2 (2004), 243–62.
48 Gilmartin and Migge, 'European Migrants in Ireland', 4.
49 Bell, 'Migration as Multiple Pathways'.
50 R. Putnam, 'E Pluribus Unum: diversity and community in the twenty-first century', *Scandinavian Political Studies*, 30/2 (2007), 137–74.
51 R. Fukuyama, 'Social capital and development: the coming agenda', *SAIS Review*, 22/1 (2002), 23–37.
52 Putnam, 'E Pluribus Unum'.
53 Putnam, 'E Pluribus Unum'.
54 A. White and L. Ryan, 'Polish "temporary" migration: the formation and significance of social networks', *Europe-Asia Studies*, 60/9 (2008), 1467–1502.
55 Massey, Arango, Hugo, Kouaouci, Pellegrino and Taylor, 'Theories of international migration', 448.
56 Massey, Arango, Hugo, Kouaouci, Pellegrino and Taylor, 'Theories of international migration'.
57 F. Garip and A. Asad, *Mexico–US Migration in Time*, International Migration Institute Working Paper (Oxford: IMI, 2013).
58 L. Ryan, R. Sales, M. Tilki and B. Siara, 'Social networks, social support and social capital: the experiences of recent Polish migrants in London', *Sociology*, 42/4 (2008), 672–90.
59 H. Jayaweera and B. Anderson, 'Migrant workers and vulnerable employment: a review of existing data', *https://www.compas.ox.ac.uk/project/migrant-workers-and-vulnerable-employment-a-review-of-existing-data/* (accessed 29 July 2016).
60 A. E. Green, D. W. Owen, P. Jones and J. Francis, *The Economic Impact of Migrant Workers in the West Midlands* (Birmingham: West Midlands Regional Observatory, 2007).
61 A. Thompson, P. Chambers, and L. Doleczek, 'Welcome to Llaneski: Polish migration in South West Wales', *Contemporary Wales*, 23 (2010), 1–16.

62 L. Chappell, M. Latorre, J. Rutter and J. Shah, *Migration and Rural Economies: Assessing and Addressing Risks* (London: IPPR Economics of Migration Working Paper 6, 2009).
63 K. Jones, *The Recruitment of A8 Migrant Workers into the UK*, presentation, Manchester University. 10 June 2008.
64 G. Epstein, 'Information cascades and decision to migrate', http://ftp.iza.org/dp445.pdf (accessed 29 July 2016).
65 D. McCollum, L. Cooke, C. Chiroro, A. Platts, F. MacLeod and A. Findlay, *Report on Spatial, Sectoral and Temporal Trends in A8 Migration to the UK 2004–2011: Evidence from the Worker Registration Scheme* (Southampton: Centre for Population Change, 2012).
66 D. Spencer, *Clandestine Crossings: Migrants and Coyotes on the Texas/Mexico Border* (Ithaca, NY: Cornell University Press, 1996).
67 Epstein, 'Information cascades and decision to migrate'.
68 White and Ryan, 'Polish "temporary" migration'.
69 White and Ryan, 'Polish "temporary" migration'.
70 Jennissen, *Report on Economic Theories*.
71 Putnam, 'E Pluribus Unum'.
72 L. Ryan, 'Migrants' social networks and weak ties: accessing resources and constructing relationships post-migration', *The Sociological Review*, 59/4 (2011), 707–24.
73 Ryan, 'Migrants' social networks and weak ties'.
74 Putnam, 'E Pluribus Unum'.
75 Ryan, 'Migrants' social networks and weak ties'.
76 M. Hickman, H. Crowley and N. Mai, *Immigration and Social Cohesion in the UK* (London: Joseph Rowntree Foundation, 2008).
77 V. Parutis, 'Economic migrants or transnational middling? East European migrants' experiences of work in the UK', http://onlinelibrary.wiley.com/advanced/search/results (accessed 16 July 2016).
78 Parutis, 'Economic migrants or transnational middling?'
79 B. Anderson, N. Clark, and V. Parutis, *New EU Members? Migrant Workers' Challenges and Opportunities to UK Trade Unions: A Polish and Lithuanian Case Study* (London: Trades Union Congress, 2007).
80 Anderson, Ruhs, Rogaly, and Spencer, *Fair Enough?*
81 Parutis, 'Economic migrants or transnational middling?'
82 Chiswick, Lee, and Miller, 'A Longitudinal Analysis of Immigrant Occupational Mobility'.

83 Chiswick, Lee, and Miller, 'A Longitudinal Analysis of Immigrant Occupational Mobility'.
84 Chiswick, Lee, and Miller, 'A Longitudinal Analysis of Immigrant Occupational Mobility'.
85 Chiswick, Lee, and Miller, 'A Longitudinal Analysis of Immigrant Occupational Mobility'.
86 A. Barrett and D. Duffy, 'Are Ireland's Immigrants Integrating into Its Labour Market?' *International Migration*, 42/3 (2008), 597–619.
87 Parutis, 'Economic migrants or transnational middling?'
88 Parutis, 'Economic migrants or transnational middling?'
89 Chiswick, Lee, and Miller, 'A Longitudinal Analysis of Immigrant Occupational Mobility'.
90 Knight, Lever and Thompson, 'The Labour Market Mobility of Polish Migrants'.
91 Pollard, Latorre, and Sriskandarajah, *Floodgates or Turnstiles?*
92 P. Trevena, 'Why do highly educated migrants go for low-skilled jobs? A case study of Polish graduates working in London', in B. Glorius et al. (eds), *Mobility in Transition: Migration Patterns after EU Enlargement* (Amsterdam: Amsterdam University Press, 2009).
93 S. Scott and P. Brindley, 'New geographies of migrant settlement in the UK', *Geography*, 97/1 (2012), 29–36.
94 P. Trevena, D. McGhee, and S. Heath, 'Location, location? A critical examination of patterns and determinants of internal mobility among post-accession Polish migrants in the UK', *Population, Space and Place*, 19 (2013), 671–87.
95 B. Jentsch, P. de Lima and B. MacDonald, 'Migrant Workers in Rural Scotland: Going to the Middle of Nowhere', *International Journal on Multicultural Societies*, 9/1 (2007), 35–53.
96 D. Sporton, '"They Control My Life" The Role of Local Recruitment Agencies in East European Migration to the UK', *Population, Space and Place*, 19/5 (2013), 443–58.
97 E. Bonacich and J. Modell, *The Economic Basis of Ethnic Solidarity: Small Businesses in the Japanese American Community* (Berkeley: University of California Press, 1980), p. 12.
98 I. Light and S. Gold, *Ethnic Economies* (London: Academic Press, 2000), p. 51.
99 F. Miera, 'Transnational strategies of Polish migrant entrepreneurs in trade and small business in Berlin', *Journal of Ethnic and Migration Studies*, 34/5 (2008), 753–70.
100 M. Boyd, 'Family and personal networks in international migration', *International Migration Review*, 23/3 (1989), 638–70.

101 M. Metykova, 'Suspended Normalcy: Eastern European Migrants in London and Edinburgh', paper presented at the Normalcy: Opportunity or Standard? The Confrontation of Eastern Eruopean and Western Culture in the EU Symposium, University of East London, 2007.
102 Burrell, 'Staying, returning, working and living'.
103 Burrell, 'Staying, returning, working and living'.
104 Light and Gold, *Ethnic Economies*.
105 A. Portes and R. Back, *Latin Journey: Cuban and Mexican Immigrants in the US* (Berkeley: University of California Press, 1985).
106 J. Krase, *Seeing Cities Change: Local Culture and Class* (Aldershot: Ashgate, 2012).
107 M. Castles and M. Miller, *The Age of Migration* (London: Macmillan Press, 2009).
108 Light and Gold, *Ethnic Economies*.
109 R. Waldinger and M. Lichter, *How the Other Half Works: Immigration and the Social Organization of Labor* (Berkeley: University of California Press, 2003).
110 M. Minniti, W. Bygrave and E. Autio, *Global Entrepreneurship Monitor, 2005 Executive Summary* (London: London Business School, 2006).
111 D. Smallbone and F. Welter, 'Entrepreneurship in transition economies: Necessity or opportunity driven?' *http://www.academia.edu/1024226/Entrepreneurship_in_transition_economies_necessity_or_op portunity_driven* (accessed 16 July 2016).
112 E. Masurel, P. Nikmap, M. Tastan and T. Vindigni, 'Motivations and performance conditions for ethnic entrepreneurship', *Growth and Change*, 33/2 (2002), 238–60.
113 A. Acs, P. Arenuis, M. Hay and M. Minniti, *The Global Entrepreneurship Monitor, 2004 Executive Report* (London, 2005).
114 Smallbone and Welter, 'Entrepreneurship in transition economies: Necessity or opportunity driven?'
115 Minniti, Bygrave and Autio, *Global Entrepreneurship Monitor, 2005 Executive Summary*.
116 C. Harris, 'Polish entrepreneurship in Britain contributes to economic growth' (Ph.D. thesis University of Birmingham, 2012).
117 P. Lassalle, M. Hughes and E. Helinska-Hughes, 'Re-theorising ethnic entrepreneurial strategies', *http://www.isbe.org.uk/ethnicentrepreneurialstrategies* (accessed 17 July 2016).
118 Parutis, 'Economic migrants or transnational middling? East European migrants' experiences of work in the UK'.
119 Anderson, Ruhs, Rogaly, and Spencer, *Fair Enough?*
120 M. D. R. Evans, 'Immigrant entrepreneurship: effects of ethnic market size and isolated labour pool', *American Sociological Review*, 54/6 (1989), 560–72.

NOTES

121 Putnam, 'E Pluribus Unum: diversity and community in the twenty-first century'.
122 M. Ram and A. Phizacklea, 'Being your own boss: ethnic minority entrepreneurs in comparative perspective', *Work, Employment and Society*, 10/2 (1995), 319–39.
123 Harris, 'Polish entrepreneurship in Britain contributes to economic growth'.
124 Lassalle, Hughes and Helinska-Hughes, 'Re-theorising ethnic entrepreneurial strategies'.
125 J. Cook, P. Dwyer and L. Waite, 'The Experiences of Accession 8 Migrants in England: Motivations, Work and Agency', *International Migration*, 49/2 (2011), 54–79.
126 Cook, Dwyer and Waite, 'The Experiences of Accession 8 Migrants in England: Motivations, Work and Agency'.
127 Thompson, Chambers, and Doleczek, 'Welcome to Llaneski: Polish migration in South West Wales'.
128 Thompson, Chambers, and Doleczek, 'Welcome to Llaneski: Polish migration in South West Wales'.
129 Thompson, Chambers, and Doleczek, 'Welcome to Llaneski: Polish migration in South West Wales'.
130 Thompson, Chambers, and Doleczek, 'Welcome to Llaneski: Polish migration in South West Wales'.
131 G. Engbersen, E. Snel and J. Boom, 'A Van Full of Poles. Liquid migration in Eastern and Central European countries', In R. Black et al. (eds), *A Continent Moving West? EU Enlargement and Labour Migration from Central and Eastern Europe* (Amsterdam: Amsterdam University Press, 2010), pp. 115–40.
132 G. Engbersen, I. Grabowska-Lusinska and A. Leerkes, 'The rise of liquid migration? Old and new patterns of migration after EU enlargement', presented at the Migration, Economic Change, Social Challenge Conference. London, 6–9 April 2011.
133 Z. Bauman, *Liquid Modernity* (Cambridge: Blackwell, 2000).

Notes to Chapter 3

1 M. Garapich, 'The migrant industry and civil society: Polish immigrants in the UK before and after EU enlargement', *Journal of Ethnic and Migration Studies*, 34/5 (2008), 732–52.
2 P. Trevena, D. McGhee, and S. Heath, 'Location, location? A critical examination of patterns and determinants of internal mobility among post-accession Polish migrants in the UK', *Population, Space and Place*, 19 (2013), 671–687.

NOTES

3 B. Jentsch, P. de Lima and B. MacDonald, 'Migrant Workers in Rural Scotland: Going to the Middle of Nowhere', *International Journal on Multicultural Societies*, 9/1 (2007), 35–53.

4 Office of National Statistics (ONS), 'Census, Office for National Statistics', *http://webarchive.nationalarchives.gov.uk/20160105160709* (accessed 16 July 2016).

5 ONS, 'Wales Statistics', *http://wales.gov.uk/statistics-and-research/?topic=Business+and+economy&lang=en* (accessed 19 July 2016).

6 H. Crawley, *Migration and Employment in Wales* (Cardiff: Wales Migration Partnership, 2013).

7 A. Hooper and J. Punter, *Capital Cardiff, 1975–2020: Regeneration, Competitiveness and the Urban Environment* (Cardiff: University of Wales Press, 2006).

8 H. Crawley, 'Demographics and the changing face of Wales', Centre for Migration Policy Research, presentation by the Swansea University School of the Environment and Society, 2006.

9 ONS, 'Wales Statistics'.

10 Cardiff Council, *Cardiff: Developing an International and Open City* (London: British Council, 2008).

11 Crawley, *Migration and Employment in Wales*.

12 Office of National Statistics (ONS), 'Wales Data'.

13 ONS, 'Wales Statistics'.

14 Office of National Statistics (ONS), 'Wales Data'.

15 Office of National Statistics (ONS), 'Wales Data'.

16 ONS, 'Wales Statistics'.

17 Office of National Statistics (ONS), 'Wales Data'.

18 Welsh Index of Multiple Deprivation (WIMD) 'Analysis', *http://wales.gov.uk/topics/statistics/headlines/compendia2009/welsh-index-multiple-deprivation-2012-indicator-analysis/?lang=en* (accessed 19 July 2016).

19 Crawley, 'Demographics and the changing face of Wales'.

20 Change Institute, *The Somali Muslim Community in England* (London: Department of Communities and Local Government, 2009).

21 L. Hammond, 'Somali Transnational Activism and Integration in the UK: Mutually Supporting Strategies', *Journal of Ethnic and Migration Studies*, 39/6 (2013), 1001–17.

22 Hammond, 'Somali Transnational Activism and Integration in the UK: Mutually Supporting Strategies'.

23 Welsh Refugee Council, 'Wales as a Refuge', *http://welshrefugeecouncil.org.uk/asylum-in-wales-and-wrc/* (accessed 19 July 2016).

NOTES

24 *The Guardian*, 'Somalis in Cardiff', https://www.theguardian.com/uk/2006/jan/23/britishidentity.features11 (accessed 19 July 2016).
25 Welsh Index of Multiple Deprivation (WIMD) 'Analysis'.
26 Hammond, 'Somali Transnational Activism and Integration in the UK: Mutually Supporting Strategies'.
27 Office of National Statistics (ONS), 'International Migration', http://www.ons.gov.uk/ons/taxonomy/index.html?nscl=International+Migration (accessed 16 July 2016).
28 Office of National Statistics (ONS), 'Census, Office for National Statistics'.
29 N. Vershanina and M. Meyer, 'Polish Entrepreneurs and Forms of Capital', conference paper presented at the *Institute of Small Business Entrepreneurship (ISBE)* conference, 2008 in Belfast, Northern Ireland.
30 P. Nicol, A. M. Smith, R. Dunkley, and K. Morgan, 'Valleys Regional Park Interim Progress and Evaluation Report', School of Planning and Geography, Cardiff University (2013).
31 K. Morgan, 'The challenge of polycentric planning: Cardiff as a capital city region?' Papers in Planning Research, No. 185, Cardiff School of City and Regional Planning (2005).
32 European Commission, *Employment and Social Developments in Europe 2011*, Directorate-General for Employment, Social Affairs and Inclusion, Directorate A (2011).
33 Office of National Statistics (ONS), 'Wales Data'.
34 Office of National Statistics (ONS), 'Wales Data'.
35 Office of National Statistics (ONS), 'Wales Data'.
36 Welsh Index of Multiple Deprivation (WIMD) 'Analysis'.
37 Office of National Statistics (ONS), 'Census, Office for National Statistics'.
38 Office of National Statistics (ONS), 'Census, Office for National Statistics'.
39 A. Thompson, P. Chambers and L. Doleczek, 'Welcome to Llaneski: Polish migration in South West Wales', *Contemporary Wales*, 23 (2010), 1–16.
40 S. Drinkwater, 'Economic and Demographic Change in the Llanelli Area: Recent Developments and Future Possibilities', presentation to Workers Educational Association, Llanelli, 7 June 2014.
41 Drinkwater, 'Economic and Demographic Change in the Llanelli Area'.
42 Drinkwater, 'Economic and Demographic Change in the Llanelli Area'.
43 Office of National Statistics (ONS), 'Wales Data'.
44 Office of National Statistics (ONS), 'Wales Data'.
45 Office of National Statistics (ONS), 'Census, Office for National Statistics'.
46 Office of National Statistics (ONS), 'Census, Office for National Statistics'.

47 Office of National Statistics (ONS), 'Census, Office for National Statistics'.
48 Drinkwater, 'Economic and Demographic Change in the Llanelli Area'.
49 Welsh Index of Multiple Deprivation (WIMD) 'Analysis'.
50 Welsh Index of Multiple Deprivation (WIMD) 'Analysis'.
51 M. Woods and S. Watkins, 'Central and Eastern European Migrant Workers in Rural Wales', http://www.walesruralobservatory.org.uk/sites/default/files/Migrant%20Workers%202008.pdf (accessed 19 July 2016).
52 T. Threadgold, S. Clifford, A. Arwo, V. Powell, Z. Harb, X. Jiang and J. Jewell, *Immigration and Inclusion in South Wales* (York: Joseph Rowntree Foundation, 2008).
53 R. Putnam, 'E Pluribus Unum: diversity and community in the twenty-first century', *Scandinavian Political Studies*, 30/2 (2007), 137–74.
54 D. Campbell and J. Stanley, *Experimental and Quasi-experimental Designs for Research* (Chicago: Rand McNally, 1963).
55 W. Firestone, 'Alternative arguments for generalising data as applied to ualitative research', *Educational Researcher*, 22/4 (1993), 16–23.
56 G. Payne and M. Williams, 'Generalisation in qualitative research', *Sociology*, 39/2 (2005), 295–314
57 Payne and Williams, 'Generalisation in qualitative research'.

Notes to Chapter 4

1 'BBC, Town's support for migrant Poles', http://news.bbc.co.uk/1/hi/wales/south_west/5378298.stm (accessed 3 July 2016).
2 N. Pollard, M. Latorre, and L. Sriskandarajah, *Floodgates or Turnstiles? Post-EU Enlargement Migration Flows to (and from) the UK* (London: IPPR, 2008).
3 F. Znaniecki and W. I. Thomas, *The Polish Peasant in Europe and America* (Boston: The Gorham Press, 1933).
4 J. Krase, *Seeing Cities Change: Local Culture and Class* (Aldershot: Ashgate, 2012).
5 J. Rostek and D. Uffelmann, *Contemporary Polish Migrant Culture and Literature in Germany, Ireland, and the UK* (Frankfurt am Main: Peter Lang, 2011).
6 H. de Haas, 'Migration Theory: Quo Vadis?' International Migration Institute Paper 100/1 (2014).
7 M. Belka, *How Poland's EU Membership Helped Transform its Economy* (Washington, DC: Group of 30, 2013).
8 W. W. Orlowski, 'Post-accession economic development of Poland', *Eastern Journal of European Studies*, 2/2 (2011), 7–20.

9 B. Ociepka and M. Ryniejska, 'Public Diplomacy and EU Enlargement: the Case of Poland', Netherlands Institute of International Relations 'Clingedael', Discussion Papers in Diplomacy, (August 2005), 1–18
10 M. Marody. 'Polish identity in the process of Europeanisation', in W. Spohn and A. Triandafyllidou (eds), *Europeanisation, National Identities and Migration* (London: Routledge, 2003).
11 B. Lofman, 'Consumers in Rapid Transition: The Polish Experience', in L. McAlister and M. L. Rothschild (eds), *Advances in Consumer Research*, vol. 20 (Provo, UT: Association for Consumer Research, 1993), 18–22.
12 *The Economist*, 'From communism to consumerism: Consumer lending is taking root in central Europe', http://www.economist.com/node/1612739 (accessed 3 August 2016).
13 J. Kurczewski, 'Poland's seven middle classes', *Social Research*, 61/2 (1994), 395–421.
14 M. Serazio and W. Szarek, 'The art of producing consumers: A critical textual analysis of post-communist Polish advertising', *European Journal of Cultural Studies*, 15/6 (2012), 753–68.
15 M. Buchowski, 'Redefining work in a local community in Poland: Transformation and class, culture and work', in A. Procoli (ed.), *Workers and Narratives of Survival in Europe: The Management of Precariousness at the End of the Twentieth Century* (New York: State University of New York Press, 2004).
16 T. Rakowski, *Hunters, Gatherers and Practitioners of Powerlessness: An Ethnography of the Degraded in Postsocialist Poland* (Oxford: Berghahn, 2016).
17 M. Garapich, *London's Polish Borders: Transnationalizing Class and Ethnicity among Polish Migrants in London* (Stuttgart: Ibidem, 2016).
18 World Bank, 'Unemployment: Youth total by country', http://data.worldbank.org/indicator/SL.UEM.1524.ZS (accessed 3 August 2016).
19 M. Siwko, 'Values and Aspirations of the Polish Youth in the Contemporary Europe', http://www.ce.uw.edu.pl/pliki/pw/Y_10_siwko_PLyouth.pdf (accessed 3 August 2016).
20 Chancellery of the Prime Minister, *Youth – 2011* (Warsaw: Chancellery of the Prime Minister, 2011).
21 J. Cohen and I. Sirkeci, *Cultures of Migration: The Global Nature of Contemporary Mobility* (Austin: University of Texas Press, 2011).
22 J. Cohen, *The Culture of Migration in Southern Mexico* (Austin: University of Texas Press, 2004).
23 Cohen, *The Culture of Migration in Southern Mexico*.
24 D. S. Massey, J. Arango, G. Hugo, A. Kouaouci, A. Pellegrino and J. E. Taylor,

'Theories of international migration: a review and appraisal', *Population and Development Review*, 19/3 (1993), 431–66.
25 Cohen, *The Culture of Migration in Southern Mexico*.
26 T. Elrick and E. Brinkmeier, 'Changing Patterns of Polish Labour Migration after the UK's Opening of the Labour Market? Insights from Rural Case Studies in the Opolskie and Swietokrzyskie Voivodships', in K. Burrell (ed.), *Polish Migration to the UK in the 'New' European Union after 2004* (Aldershot: Ashgate, 2009).
27 A. White, 'Social remittances and migration (sub)-cultures in contemporary Poland', *Central and Eastern European Migration Review*, 3 (2016), 1–17.
28 A. White, 'Unsettling times for a settled population? Polish perspectives on Brexit', http://www.ucl.ac.uk/european-institute/highlights/2015-16/polish-perspectives-brexit (accessed 3 August 2016).
29 White, 'Unsettling times for a settled population? Polish perspectives on Brexit'.
30 Elrick and Brinkmeier, 'Changing Patterns of Polish Labour Migration'.
31 Massey, Arango, Hugo, Kouaouci, Pellegrino and Taylor, 'Theories of international migration'.
32 Cohen, *The Culture of Migration in Southern Mexico*.
33 Massey, Arango, Hugo, Kouaouci, Pellegrino and Taylor, 'Theories of international migration'.
34 A. White, 'Polish circular migration and marginality: a livelihood strategy approach', http://www.euroemigranci.pl/dokumenty/pokonferencyjna/White.pdf (accessed 3 August 2016).
35 D. Galasinka and O. Kozłowska, 'Discourses on a "normal life" among post-accession migrants from Poland to Britain', in K. Burrell (ed.), *Polish Migration to the UK in the 'New' European Union: After 2004* (Aldershot: Ashgate, 2009), pp. 87–107.
36 D. McGhee, S. Heath and P. Trevena, 'Dignity, happiness and being able to live a "normal life" in the UK – an examination of post-accession Polish migrants' transnational autobiographical fields', *Social Identities* (2012) 1–17.
37 *The Telegraph*, 'It's the economy, glupi', http://www.telegraph.co.uk/news/uknews/1481817/Its-the-economy-glupi.html (accessed 3 August 2016).
38 *The Telegraph*, 'It's the economy, glupi'.
39 F. Barton, 'Are young Polish workers robbing their country of its future?' http://www.dailymail.co.uk/news/article-386931/Are-young-Polish-workers-robbing-country-future.html (accessed 3 August 2016).

40 Massey, Arango, Hugo, Kouaouci, Pellegrino and Taylor, 'Theories of international migration'.
41 K. Kropiwiec and R. King-Ó Riain, *Polish Migrant Workers in Ireland* (Dublin: National Consultative Committee on Racism and Interculturalism, 2006).
42 de Haas, 'Migration Theory: Quo Vadis?'
43 K. Torkington, 'Place and Lifestyle Migration: The Discursive Construction of "Glocal" Place-Identity', *Mobilities*, 7/1 (2012), 71–92.
44 R. O'Reilly and M. Benson, 'Migration and the search for a better way of life: a critical exploration of lifestyle migration', *The Sociological Review*, 57/4 (2012), 608–25.
45 Office of the Committee for European Integration, *Four Years of Poland's Membership of the EU* (Warsaw: Department of Analyses and Strategies, 2008).
46 L. Ryan, R. Sales, M. Tilki and B. Siara, 'Social networks, social support and social capital: the experiences of recent Polish migrant in London', *Sociology*, 42/4 (2008), 672–90.
47 J. Eade, S. Drinkwater and M. Garapich, *Class and Ethnicity: Polish Migrants in London* (Guildford: University of Surrey Press, 2006).
48 Pollard, Latorre, and Sriskandarajah, *Floodgates or Turnstiles?*
49 P. Trevena, 'Why do highly educated migrants go for low-skilled jobs? A case study of Polish graduates working in London', in B. Glorius et al. (eds), *Mobility in Transition: Migration Patterns after EU Enlargement* (Amsterdam: Amsterdam University Press, 2009).
50 S. Scott and P. Brindley, 'New geographies of migrant settlement in the UK', *Geography*, 97/1 (2012), 29–36.
51 P. Trevena, D. McGhee, and S. Heath, 'Location, location? A critical examination of patterns and determinants of internal mobility among post-accession Polish migrants in the UK', *Population, Space and Place*, 19 (2013), 671–87.
52 Massey, Arango, Hugo, Kouaouci, Pellegrino and Taylor, 'Theories of international migration'.
53 M. Boyd, 'Family and personal networks in international migration', *International Migration Review*, 23/3 (1989), 638–70.
54 Massey, Arango, Hugo, Kouaouci, Pellegrino and Taylor, 'Theories of international migration'.
55 S. Haug, 'Migration Networks and Migration Decision-Making', *Journal of Ethnic and Migration Studies*, 34/4 (2008) 585–605.
56 L. Ryan, 'Migrants' social networks and weak ties: accessing resources and constructing relationships post-migration', *The Sociological Review*, 59/4 (2011), 707–24.

57 F. Garip and A. Asad, *Mexico–US Migration in Time*, International Migration Institute Working Paper (Oxford: IMI 2013).
58 A. White and L. Ryan, 'Polish "temporary" migration: the formation and significance of social networks', *Europe–Asia Studies*, 60/9 (2008), 1467–1502.
59 de Haas, 'Migration Theory: Quo Vadis?'
60 J. Robinson, 'Why is Next hiring thousands of cheap Eastern European workers to staff English warehouse – in area where more than 200,000 are on the dole – before they even advertise the jobs here?' http://www.dailymail.co.uk/news/article-2852931/How-hiring-thousands-cheap-Eastern-European-workers-staff-warehouse-area-200-000-dole.html (accessed 3 August 2016).
61 BBC, 'Exploitation of workers at top hotels', http://news.bbc.co.uk/1/hi/programmes/newsnight/8171318.stm (accessed 3 August 2016).
62 F. Lawrence, 'Underpaid, easy to sack: UK's second class workforce', https://business-humanrights.org/en/underpaid-easy-to-sack-uks-second-class-workforce (accessed 3 August 2016).
63 L. Chappell, M. Latorre, J. Rutter and J. Shah, *Migration and Rural Economies: Assessing and Addressing Risks* (London: IPPR Economics of Migration Working Paper 6, 2009).
64 C. Glossop and F. Shaheen, 'Accession to Recession: A8 Migration to Bristol and Hull: Executive Summary', http://www.centreforcities.org/assets/files/Accessionper cent20to%20Recession%20.pdf (accessed 28 May 2016).
65 S. Tannock, 'Bad attitude? Migrant workers, meat processing work and the local unemployed in a peripheral region of the UK', *European Urban and Regional Studies*, 22/4 (2013), 1–15.
66 J. Lever and P. Milbourne, 'Migrant workers and migrant entrepreneurs: changing established–outsider relations across society and space?' *Space and Polity*, 18 (2014), 255–68.
67 B. Jentsch, P. de Lima and B. MacDonald, 'Migrant Workers in Rural Scotland: Going to the Middle of Nowhere', *International Journal on Multicultural Societies*, 9/1 (2007), 35–53.
68 N. Coe, J. Johns and K. Ward, 'Flexibility in action: the temporary staffing industry in the Czech Republic and Poland', *Environment and Planning A*, 40/6 (2008), 1391–1415.
69 K. Ward, N. Coe and J. Jones, 'The role of temporary staffing agencies in facilitating mobility in Central and Eastern Europe', Research Report for Vedior Staffing (2008).

70 K. Jones, 'The Role of Temporary Staffing Agencies in Facilitating A8 Migration into the UK', presentation to the School of Environment and Development at the University of Manchester, 2014.
71 J. H. Friberg, 'The Polish worker in Norway: Emerging patterns of migration, employment and incorporation after EU's eastern enlargement' (doctoral thesis, University of Oslo, 2013).
72 J. H. Friberg, 'The stages of migration. From going abroad to settling down: Post-accession Polish migrant workers in Norway', *Journal of Ethnic and Migration Studies*, 38/10 (2012), 1589–1605.
73 J. H. Friberg and L. Eldring, *Labour Migrants from Central and Eastern Europe in the Nordic Countries: Patterns of Migration, Working Conditions and Recruitment Practices* (Copenhagen: Nordic Council of Ministers, 2013).

Notes to Chapter 5

1 A. Favell, 'The new face of east–west migration in Europe', *Journal of Ethnic and Migration Studies*, 34/5 (2008), 701–16.
2 B. Anderson, M. Ruhs, B. Rogaly, and S. Spencer, *Fair Enough? Central and East European Migrants in Low-Wage Employment in the UK* (York: Joseph Rowntree Foundation, 2006).
3 Anderson, Ruhs, Rogaly, and Spencer, *Fair Enough?*
4 'Poland Central Statistics Office, 'Employment, Wages and Salaries', http://www.stat.gov.pl/gus/5840_1890_ENG_HTML.htm (accessed 19 July 2016).
5 I. Light and S. Gold, *Ethnic Economies* (London: Academic Press, 2000).
6 E. Bonacich and J. Modell, *The Economic Basis of Ethnic Solidarity: Small Businesses in the Japanese American Community* (Berkeley: University of California Press, 1980).
7 A. Portes and R. Back, *Latin Journey: Cuban and Mexican Immigrants in the US* (Berkeley: University of California Press, 1985).
8 Light and Gold, *Ethnic Economies*.
9 A. Acs, P. Arenuis, M. Hay and M. Minniti, *The Global Entrepreneurship Monitor, 2004 Executive Report* (London, 2005).
10 M. Minniti, W. Bygrave, E. Autio, *Global Entrepreneurship Monitor, 2005 Executive Summary* (London: London Business School, 2006).
11 D. Smallbone and F. Welter, 'Entrepreneurship in transition economies: Necessity or opportunity driven?' http://www.academia.edu/1024226/Entrepreneurship_in_transition_economies_necessity_or_opportunity_driven (accessed 16 July 2016).

12 C. Williams, 'The nature of entrepreneurship in the informal sector: evidence from the UK', *International Journal of Entrepreneurial Behaviour and Research*, 13 /6 (2007), 349–66.
13 P. Lassalle, M. Hughes and E. Helinska-Hughes, 'Re-theorising ethnic entrepreneurial strategies', http://www.isbe.org.uk/ethnicentrepreneurialstrategies (accessed 17 July 2016).

Notes to Chapter 6

1   P. Milbourne and K. Mason, 'Environmental injustice and post-colonial environmentalism: opencast coal mining, landscape and place', *Environment and Planning A* (forthcoming).
2   C. S. Davies, 'Abandoned Mine Shafts and Levels in the British Coalfields', *Environmental Management*, 12/4 (1988), 479–90.
3   K. Bennett, H. Beynon and R. Hudson, *Coalfields Regeneration: Dealing with the Consequences of Industrial Decline* (Bristol: The Policy Press and Joseph Rowntree Foundation, 2000).
4   P. Kenway, G. Palmer and T. MacInnes, 'Monitoring poverty and social exclusion in Wales 2009', https://www.jrf.org.uk/report/monitoring-poverty-and-social-exclusion-wales-2009 (accessed 30 August 2016).
5   V. Winckler, *Informing Debate: What is Needed to End Child Poverty in Wales?* (London: Joseph Rowntree Foundation, 2009).
6   Welsh Assembly Government, *Ambition Statement for Regeneration in Wales* (Cardiff: Welsh Government, 2010).
7   O. G. Álvarez, and S. Murray, 'From Bilbao to Merthyr: Basque Industrial Migration to Wales in the Late 19th, Early 20th Centuries', *Vasconia*, 39 (2013), 5–26.
8   H. Davies, *Fleeing Franco: How Wales Gave Shelter to Refugee Children from the Basque Country During the Spanish Civil War*, presentation in Cardiff University, 2011.
9   P. Nicol, A. M. Smith, R. Dunkley and K. Morgan, 'Valleys Regional Park Interim Progress and Evaluation Report', School of Planning and Geography, Cardiff University (2013).
10 K. Morgan, 'The challenge of polycentric planning: Cardiff as a capital city region?' Papers in Planning Research, No. 185, Cardiff School of City and Regional Planning (2005).
11 Office of National Statistics (ONS), 'Census, Office for National Statistics', http://webarchive.nationalarchives.gov.uk/20160105160709 (accessed 16 July 2016).

NOTES

12 ONS, 'Wales Statistics', http://wales.gov.uk/statistics-and-research/?topic=Business+and+economy&lang=en (accessed 19 July 2016).
13 J. Cook, P. Dwyer and L. Waite, 'The Experiences of Accession 8 Migrants in England: Motivations, Work and Agency', *International Migration*, 49/2 (2011), 54–79.
14 S. Tannock, 'Bad attitude? Migrant workers, meat processing work and the local unemployed in a peripheral region of the UK', *European Urban and Regional Studies*, 22/4 (2013), 1–15.
15 J. Lever and P. Milbourne, 'The structural invisibility of outsiders: the role of migrant labour in the meat-processing industry' (open access in *Sociology*; published online, ISSN 0038-0385, 23 December 2015).
16 Lever and Milbourne, 'The structural invisibility of outsiders'.
17 Tannock, 'Bad attitude?'
18 H. Jayaweera and B. Anderson, *Migrant Workers and Vulnerable Employment: A Review of Existing Data* (London: TUC Commission on Vulnerable Employment, 2008).
19 Lever and Milbourne, 'The structural invisibility of outsiders'.
20 J. Dobson, A. Latham and J. Salt, *On the Move? Labour Migration in Times of Recession* (London: Policy Network Paper, 2009).

Notes to Chapter 8

1 N. Pollard, M. Latorre, and L. Sriskandarajah, *Floodgates or Turnstiles? Post-EU Enlargement Migration Flows to (and from) the UK* (London: IPPR, 2008).
2 S. Drinkwater and K. Clark, 'Pushed out or pulled in? Self-employment among ethnic minorities in England and Wales', *Labour Economics*, 7/5 (2000), 603–28.
3 R. Pijpers, 'Help! The Poles Are Coming: Narrating a Contemporary Moral Panic', *Geografiska Annaler*, Series B, 88/1 (2006), 91–103.
4 M. Heinen and A. Pegels, 'EU Expansion and the Free Movement of Workers – Do continued Restrictions Make Sense for Germany?' http://www.focus-migration.de/ (accessed 12 August 2016).
5 M. Okolski and J. Salt, 'Polish Emigration to the UK after 2004: Why Did so Many Come?' *Central and Eastern European Migration Review*, http://www.ceemr.uw.edu.pl/vol-3-no-2-december-2014/articles/polish-emigration-uk-after-2004-why-did-so-many-come (accessed 12 August 2016).
6 A. Kicinger, 'Beyond the Focus on Europeanisation: Polish Migration Policy 1989–2004', *Journal of Ethnic and Migration Studies*, 35/1 (2009), 79–95.

7   J. Kurczewski, 'Poland's seven middle classes', *Social Research*, 61/2 (1994), 395–421.
8   T. Bauer and K. Zimmerman, *Assessment of Possible Migration Pressure and its Labour Market Impact Following EU Enlargement to Central and Eastern Europe* (Bonn: IZA Research Report, 2009).
9   European Parliament, 'Migration and asylum in central and Eastern Europe', http://www.europarl.europa.eu/workingpapers/libe/104/summary_en.htm (accessed 12 August 2016).
10 C. Wallace, 'Closing and opening borders: migration and mobility in East -Central Europe', *Journal of Ethnic and Migration Studies*, 28/4 (2002), 603–25.
11 J. Eade, S. Drinkwater and M. Garapich, *Class and Ethnicity: Polish Migrants in London* (Guildford: University of Surrey Press, 2006).
12 M. Okolski, 'Incomplete Migration. A new form of mobility in Central and Eastern Europe: The case of Polish and Ukranian migrants' , in J. E. Taylor and D. S. Massey (eds), *International Migration: Prospects and Policies* (Oxford: Oxford University Press, 2001), pp. 35–59.
13 A. Favell, 'The new face of east–west migration in Europe', *Journal of Ethnic and Migration Studies*, 34/5 (2008), 701–16.
14 A. Fihel, P. Kaczmarczyk and M. Okólski, *Labour Mobility in the Enlarged European Union: International Migration from the EU8 Countries* (Warsaw: Centre of Migration Research, 2006).
15 G. Engbersen, E. Snel and J. Boom, 'A Van Full of Poles: Liquid migration in Eastern and Central European countries', in R. Black et al. (eds), *A Continent Moving West? EU Enlargement and Labour Migration from Central and Eastern Europe* (Amsterdam: Amsterdam University Press, 2010), pp. 115–40.
16 Eade, Drinkwater and Garapich, *Class and Ethnicity*.
17 E. Moriarty, J. Wickham, J. Salomonska, T. Krings and A. Bobek, 'Putting Work Back in Mobilities: Migrant Careers and Aspirations', paper presented at the New Migrations, New Challenges Conference, Trinity College Dublin, 2010.
18 A. Thompson, P. Chambers and L. Doleczek, 'Welcome to Llaneski: Polish migration in South West Wales', *Contemporary Wales*, 23 (2010), 1–16.
19 Office of National Statistics (ONS), 'Census, Office for National Statistics', http://webarchive.nationalarchives.gov.uk/20160105160709 (accessed 16 July 2016).
20 Siu, 'The Sojourner'.
21 M. Castles and M. Miller, *The Age of Migration* (London: Macmillan Press, 2009).
22 A. White, 'Polish Migration in the UK: Local experiences and effects',

presented at the AHRC Connected Communities Symposium: Understanding Local Experiences and Effects of New Migration, Sheffield, 26 September 2011).
23 A. White, 'Polish circular migration and marginality: a livelihood strategy approach', http://www.euroemigranci.pl/dokumenty/pokonferencyjna/White.pdf (accessed 3 August 2016).
24 White, 'Polish circular migration and marginality: a livelihood strategy approach'.
25 L. Ryan, 'Migrants' social networks and weak ties: accessing resources and constructing relationships post-migration', *The Sociological Review*, 59/4 (2011), 707–24.
26 L. Ryan, R. Sales, M. Tilki and B. Siara, 'Social networks, social support and social capital: the experiences of recent Polish migrants in London', *Sociology*, 42/4 (2008), 672–90.
27 J. H. Friberg, 'The stages of migration. From going abroad to settling down: Post-accession Polish migrant workers in Norway', *Journal of Ethnic and Migration Studies*, 38/10 (2012), 1589–1605.
28 Engbersen, Snel and Boom, 'A Van Full of Poles: Liquid migration in Eastern and Central European countries'.
29 H. S. Becker, 'Notes on the concept of commitment', *American Journal of Sociology*, 66 (1960), 32–40.
30 H. de Haas, 'Migration Theory: Quo Vadis?' International Migration Institute Paper 100/1 (2014).

Notes to Chapter 9

1 European Parliament, 'Migration and asylum in Central and Eastern Europe', http://www.europarl.europa.eu/workingpapers (accessed 19 July 2016).
2 International Organization for Migration (IOM), 'Migration Integration', http://www.iom.int/migrant-integration (accessed 22 July 2016).
3 E. Penninx, 'Integration of migrants: Economic, social, cultural and political dimensions', in United Nations *New Demographic Regime: Population Challenges and Policy Responses* (Geneva, 2005), pp. 137–51.
4 EU Commission, *Migrant Integration: Aggregate Report* (Brussels: Directorate General Home Affairs. Qualitative Eurobarometer, 2011).
5 E. S. Bogardus, *Social Distance* (Los Angeles: Antioch Press, 1959).
6 S. N. Eisenstadt, *The Absorption of Immigrants* (Westport, CT: Greenwood Press, 1975).

NOTES

7 Eisenstadt, *The Absorption of Immigrants*.
8 Bogardus, *Social Distance*.
9 OECD, 'Indicators of Immigrant Integration 2015', http://www.oecd.org/publications/indicators-of-immigrant-integration-2015-settling-in-9789264234024-en.htm (accessed 16 July 2016).
10 Office of National Statistics (ONS), 'International Migration', http://www.ons.gov.uk/ons/taxonomy/index.html?nscl=International+Migration (accessed 16 July 2016).
11 D. McCollum, L. Cooke, C. Chiroro, A. Platts, F. MacLeod and A. Findlay, *Report on Spatial, Sectoral and Temporal Trends in A8 Migration to the UK 2004–2011: Evidence from the Worker Registration Scheme* (Southampton: Centre for Population Change, 2012).
12 McCollum, Cooke, Chiroro, Platts, MacLeod and Findlay, *Report on Spatial, Sectoral and Temporal Trends*.
13 V. Baure, P. Densham, J. Millar and J. Salt, 'Migrants from Central and Eastern Europe: Local Geographies', *Population and Trends*, 129 (2007), 7–19.
14 A. Favell, 'The new face of east–west migration in Europe', *Journal of Ethnic and Migration Studies*, 34/5 (2008), 701–16.
15 S. Drinkwater and M. Garapich, 'Migration Plans and Strategies of Recent Polish migrants to England and Wales: Do they have any and how do they change?' Norface Migration Discussion Article (2013), 2013–23.
16 N. Pollard, M. Latorre, and L. Sriskandarajah, *Floodgates or Turnstiles? Post-EU Enlargement Migration Flows to (and from) the UK* (London: IPPR, 2008).
17 A. White, 'Double Return Migration: Failed Returns to Poland Leading to Settlement Abroad and New Transnational Strategies', *International Migration*, 52/6 (2014), 72–84.
18 British Futures, 'EU Migration from Romania and Bulgaria: What does the public think?' http://www.britishfuture.org/wp-content/uploads/2013/12/J1527_BRF_RomaniaBulgaria_16.12.13_2-1.pdf (accessed 16 July 2016).
19 OECD, 'Indicators of Immigrant Integration 2015'.
20 A. Terrazas, *The Economic Integration of Immigrants in the United States: Long and Short Term Perspectives* (Washington, DC: Migration Policy Institute, 2011).
21 Z. Ciupijus, 'Mobile Central Eastern Europeans in Britain: Successful EU citizens and disadvantaged labour migrants', *Work, Employment and Society*, 25/3 (2011), 25–35.
22 S. Tannock, 'Bad attitude? Migrant workers, meat processing work and the local unemployed in a peripheral region of the UK', *European Urban and Regional Studies*, 22/4 (2013), 1–15.

23 N. Elias and J. Scotson, *The Established and the Outsiders*, in *Collected Works of Norbert Elias* (Dublin: UCD Press, 2008).
24 J. Lever and P. Milbourne, 'Migrant workers and migrant entrepreneurs: changing established–outsider relations across society and space?' *Space and Polity*, 18 (2014), 255–68.
25 J. Lever and P. Milbourne, 'The structural invisibility of outsiders: the role of migrant labour in the meat-processing industry' (open access in *Sociology*; published online, ISSN 0038-0385, 23 December 2015).
26 V. Parutis, 'Economic migrants or transnational middling? East European migrants' experiences of work in the UK', http://onlinelibrary.wiley.com/advanced/search/results (accessed 16 July 2016).
27 Migration Policy Institute (MPI), 'Integration: The role of communities, institutions and the state', http://www.migrationpolicy.org/article/integration-role-communities-institutions-and-state (accessed 20 June 2016)
28 Migration Policy Institute (MPI), 'Integration: The role of communities, institutions and the state'.
29 OECD, 'Indicators of Immigrant Integration 2015'.
30 F. Anthias and M. Cederberg, 'Using ethnic bonds in self-employment and the issue of social capital', *Journal of Ethnic and Migration Studies*, 35/6 (2009), 901–17.
31 L. Ryan, 'Migrants' social networks and weak ties: accessing resources and constructing relationships post-migration', *The Sociological Review*, 59/4 (2011), 707–24.
32 M. Hickman, H. Crowley and N. Mai, *Immigration and Social Cohesion in the UK* (London: Joseph Rowntree Foundation, 2008).
33 P. Nannestad, G. Svendsen and G. T. Svendsen, 'Bridge Over Troubled Water? Migration and Social Capital', *Journal of Ethnic and Migration Studies*, 34/4 (2008), 607–31.
34 J. H. Friberg, 'The stages of migration. From going abroad to settling down: Post-accession Polish migrant workers in Norway', *Journal of Ethnic and Migration Studies*, 38/10 (2012), 1589–1605.
35 F. Levrau, E. Piqueray, I. Goddeeris and C. Timmerman, 'Polish Immigration in Belgium since 2004: New dynamics and migration and integration', *Ethnicities*, 14/2 (2013), 303–23.
36 White, 'Double Return Migration'.
37 D. Sime and R. Fox, 'Eastern European children's family and peer relationships after migration', *Childhood* (2014).
38 T. Huddleston and D. Tjaden, *Immigrant Citizenship Survey: How Immigrants*

NOTES

Experience Integration in 15 European Cities (Brussels: King Baudouin Foundation and the Migration Policy Group, 2012).

39 B. Ray, *The Role of Cities in Immigrant Integration* (Brussels: Migration Policy Institute Europe, 2003).

40 E. Collett, *The Integration Needs of Mobile EU Citizens: Impediments and opportunities* (Brussels: Migration Policy Institute Europe, 2013).

41 Penninx, 'Integration of Migrants'.

42 Polish Scottish Heritage, 'The Experience of Polish-Scottish Integration in Scotland', *http://polishscottishheritage.co.uk/wp-content/uploads/2013/10/The-Experiance-of-Integration-Final-Report.pdf* (accessed 5 June 2016).

43 EU Commission, *Migrant Integration*.

44 Migration Policy Institute (MPI), 'Integration: The role of communities, institutions and the state'.

45 IFA, *Migration and Cultural Integration in Europe*, IFA Culture and Foreign Policy Conference Report, Brussels, December 2013.

46 C. Harris, 'Polish entrepreneurship in Britain contributes to economic rowth' (Ph.D. thesis, University of Birmingham, 2012).

47 P. Lassalle, M. Hughes and E. Helinska-Hughes, 'Re-theorising Ethnic Entrepreneurial Strategies', *http://www.isbe.org.uk/ethnicentrepreneurialstrategies* (accessed 10 May 2016).

48 M. Ram and A. Phizacklea, 'Being your own boss: ethnic minority entrepreneurs in comparative perspective', *Work, Employment and Society*, 10/2 (1995), 319–39.

Notes to Chapter 10

1 P. Dominiczak, 'Britain and Germany demand EU cracks down on "benefits tourism"', *http://www.telegraph.co.uk/news/politics/10014508/Britain-and-Germany-demand-EU-cracks-down-on-benefits-tourism.html* (accessed 29 July 2016).

2 H. Crawley, *Migration and Employment in Wales* (Cardiff: Wales Migration Partnership, 2013).

3 Welsh Assembly Government (WAG) 'Programme for Government: Equality', *http://wales.gov.uk/docs/strategies/110929chap8en.pdf* (accessed 29 July 2016).

4 P. Milbourne, 'The social and cultural impacts of English migration to rural Wales', in P. Milbourne (ed.), *Rural Wales in the Twenty-first Century: Society, Economy and Environment* (Cardiff: University of Wales Press, 2011), pp. 46–64.

NOTES

5 S. Drinkwater and D. Blackaby, 'Migration and Labour Market Differences: The Case of Wales', IZA Discussion Paper 1275 (2004).
6 Milbourne, 'The social and cultural impacts of English migration to rural Wales'.
7 Milbourne, 'The social and cultural impacts of English migration to rural Wales'.
8 J. Lever and P. Milbourne, 'Migrant workers and migrant entrepreneurs: changing established–outsider relations across society and space?' *Space and Polity*, 18 (2014), 255–68.
9 Lever and Milbourne, 'Migrant workers and migrant entrepreneurs'.
10 Office of National Statistics (ONS), 'International Migration', http://www.ons.gov.uk/ons/taxonomy/index.html?nscl=International+Migration (accessed 16 July 2016).
11 OECD, *Free Movement of Workers and Labour Market Adjustment: Recent Experiences from OECD Countries and the European Union* (Paris: OECD Publishing, 2012).
12 European Commission, *Employment and Social Developments in Europe 2011, Directorate-General for Employment* (Brussels: Social Affairs and Inclusion, 2011).
13 OECD, *Free Movement of Workers and Labour Market Adjustment Recent Experiences from OECD Countries and the European Union* (Paris: OECD Publishing, 2012).
14 L. Jones, J. Lever, S. Jones, J. Radcliffe and M. Woods, 'Migrant Workers in Rural Wales and the South Wales Valleys', presentation to the Cardiff School of Planning and Geography, December 2014.
15 M. Woods and S. Watkin, 'Central and Eastern European Migrant Workers in Rural Wales', http://www.walesruralobservatory.org.uk/sites/default/files/Migrant-%20Workers%202008.pdf (accessed 29 July 2016).
16 Crawley, *Migration and Employment in Wales*.
17 BBC, 'Skilled migrants should "plug gap", says Lord Digby Jones', http://www.bbc.co.uk/news/uk-wales-33851020 (accessed 16 July 2016).
18 S. Tannock, 'Bad attitude? Migrant workers, meat processing work and the local unemployed in a peripheral region of the UK', *European Urban and Regional Studies*, 22/4 (2013), 1–15.
19 A. Favell, 'The new face of east–west migration in Europe', *Journal of Ethnic and Migration Studies*, 34/5 (2008), 701–16.
20 Lever and Milbourne, 'Migrant workers and migrant entrepreneurs'.
21 Lever and Milbourne, 'Migrant workers and migrant entrepreneurs'.

NOTES

22   Lever and Milbourne, 'Migrant workers and migrant entrepreneurs'.
23   O. G. Álvarez and S. Murray, 'From Bilbao to Merthyr: Basque Industrial Migration to Wales in the Late 19th, Early 20th Centuries', *Vasconia*, 39 (2013), 5–26
24   Tannock, 'Bad attitude?'
25   Tannock, 'Bad attitude? '
26   Tannock, 'Bad attitude?'
27   B. Anderson and M. Ruhs, 'Migrant workers: Who needs them? A framework for analysis of staff shortages, immigration, and public policy', in M. Ruhs and B. Anderson (eds), *Who Needs Migrant Workers? Labour Shortages, Immigration, and Public Policy* (Oxford: Oxford University Press, 2010), pp. 15–52.
28   Lever and Milbourne, 'Migrant workers and migrant entrepreneurs'.
29   Anderson and Ruhs, 'Migrant workers: Who needs them?'
30   Anderson and Ruhs, 'Migrant workers: Who needs them?.
31   Lever and Milbourne, 'Migrant workers and migrant entrepreneurs'.
32   Lever and Milbourne, 'Migrant workers and migrant entrepreneurs'.
33   Welsh Assembly Government (WAG) 'Programme for Government: Equality'.
34   Welsh Assembly Government (WAG) 'Getting Along Together: A Community Cohesion Strategy for Wales', http://wales.gov.uk/docs/dsjlg/publications/commsafety/091130ccstratenv1.pdf (accessed 29 July 2016).
35   H. Crawley, *Migration and Community Cohesion in Wales* (Cardiff: Wales Migration Partnership, 2014).
36   Crawley, *Migration and Community Cohesion in Wales*.
37   OECD, 'Indicators of Immigrant Integration 2015', http://www.oecd.org/publications/indicators-of-immigrant-integration-2015-settling-in-9789264234024-en.htm (accessed 1 July 2016).
38   Drinkwater and Blackaby, 'Migration and Labour Market Differences: The Case of Wales'.
39   T. Threadgold, S. Clifford, A. Arwo, V. Powell, Z. Harb, X. Jiang and J. Jewell, *Immigration and Inclusion in South Wales* (York: Joseph Rowntree Foundation, 2008).
40   M. Woods and S. Watkins, 'Central and Eastern European Migrant Workers in Rural Wales', http://www.walesruralobservatory.org.uk/sites/default/files/Migrant%20Workers%202008.pdf (accessed 19 July 2016).
41   D. Robinson, K. Reeve, D. Platts-Fowler, S. Green, A, Walshaw, E. Batty and N. Bashir, 'An Evaluation of Getting on Together: The Community Cohesion Strategy for Wales, Cardiff', http://cdn.basw.co.uk/upload/basw_94308-3.pdf (accessed 10 January 2016).

NOTES

42 Lever and Milbourne, 'Migrant workers and migrant entrepreneurs'.
43 Office of National Statistics (ONS), 'Census, Office for National Statistics', http://webarchive.nationalarchives.gov.uk/20160105160709 (accessed 16 July 2016).
44 Lever and Milbourne, 'Migrant workers and migrant entrepreneurs'.
45 D. May, 'The interplay of three established–outsider figurations in a deprived inner-city neighbourhood', *Urban Studies*, 41/11 (2004), 2159–79.
46 N. Elias and J. Scotson, *The Established and the Outsiders*, in *Collected Works of Norbert Elias* (Dublin: UCD Press, 2008).
47 L. Hammond, 'Somali Transnational Activism and Integration in the UK: Mutually Supporting Strategies', *Journal of Ethnic and Migration Studies*, 39/6 (2013), 1001–17.
48 Statistics for Wales, 'School Census Results, 2013 Statistical Bulletin SDR 109/2013', http://dera.ioe.ac.uk/18003/1/130711-school-census-results-2013-en.pdf (accessed 1 July 2016).
49 H. Crawley, *Migration and Education in Wales* (Cardiff: Wales Migration Partnership, 2014).
50 Crawley, *Migration and Education in Wales*.
51 Crawley, *Migration and Education in Wales*.
52 Crawley, *Migration and Education in Wales*.
53 Crawley, *Migration and Education in Wales*.
54 Welsh Assembly Government (WAG) 'Programme for Government: Equality'.
55 Crawley, *Migration and Community Cohesion in Wales*.
56 Welsh Assembly Government (WAG), *Improving Lives and Communities: Homes in Wales* (Cardiff: Government Printing, 2010).
57 Welsh Assembly Government (WAG), 'Homes for Wales: A White Paper for Better Lives and Communities', http://wales.gov.uk/docs/desh/consultation/120521whitepaperen.pdf (accessed 1 July 2016).
58 D. Spencer, *Clandestine Crossings: Migrants and Coyotes on the Texas/Mexico Border* (Ithaca, NY: Cornell University Press, 1996).
59 A. Thompson, P. Chambers and L. Doleczek, 'Welcome to Llaneski: Polish migration in South West Wales', *Contemporary Wales*, 23 (2010), 1–16.
60 Shelter Cymru, *Living in Wales: The Housing and Homelessness Experiences of Central and East European Migrant Workers* (Cardiff: Shelter Cymru, 2010).
61 H. Crawley, *Migration and Housing in Wales* (Cardiff: Wales Migration Partnership, 2014).
62 Migration Observatory, 'Migrants and Housing in the UK: Experiences and Impacts', www.migrationobservatory.ox.ac.uk/sites/files/migobs/Briefing%20-%20

Migrants%20and%20Housing%20in%20the%20UK_0.pdf (accessed 1 June 2016).

63 I. Martín and A. Venturini, *A Comprehensive Labour Market Approach to EU Labour Migration Policy* (Brussels: Migration Policy Centre, 2015).

64 L. Mayblin, 'Why the UK's 2015 Immigration Bill is bad for vulnerable migrant workers', *Open Democracy*, https://www.opendemocracy.net/beyondslavery/lucy-mayblin/why-uk-s-2015-immigration-bill-is-bad-for-vulnerable-migrant-workers (accessed 31 July 31, 2016).

References

Acs, A., Arenuis, P., Hay, M. and Minniti, M., The Global Entrepreneurship Monitor, 2004 Executive Report (London, 2005).
Álvarez, O. G. and Murray, S., 'From Bilbao to Merthyr: Basque Industrial Migration to Wales in the Late 19th, Early 20th Centuries', *Vasconia* 39 (2013), 5–26.
Amnesty International, 'Amnesty launches urgent campaign on racism in the UK amid rise in reported hate crimes', *https://www.amnesty.org.uk/press-releases/amnesty-launches-urgent-campaign-racism-uk-amid-rise-reported-hate-crime* (accessed 16 July 2016).
Anderson, B., Clark, N. and Parutis, V., *New EU Members? Migrant Workers' Challenges and Opportunities to UK Trade Unions: A Polish and Lithuanian Case Study* (London: Trades Union Congress, 2007).
Anderson, B. and Ruhs, M., 'Migrant workers: Who needs them? A framework for analysis of staff shortages, immigration, and public policy', in M. Ruhs and B. Anderson (eds), *Who Needs Migrant Workers? Labour Shortages, Immigration, and Public Policy* (Oxford: Oxford University Press, 2010), pp. 15–52.
Anderson, B., Ruhs, M., Rogaly, B. and Spencer, S., *Fair Enough? Central and East European Migrants in Low-Wage Employment in the UK* (York: Joseph Rowntree Foundation, 2006).
Anthias, F. and Cederberg, M., 'Using ethnic bonds in self-employment and the issue of social capital', *Journal of Ethnic and Migration Studies*, 35/6 (2009), 901–17.
Bailey, D. and Sodano, C., 'Census: Maps show migration trends', *http://www.bbc.com/news/uk-20713380* (accessed 16 July 2016).
Barrett, A. and Duffy, D., 'Are Ireland's Immigrants Integrating into Its Labour Market?' *International Migration Review*, 42/3 (2008), 597–619.

REFERENCES

Barton, F., 'Are young Polish workers robbing their country of its future?' *http://www.dailymail.co.uk/news/article-386931/Are-young-Polish-workers-robbing-country-future.html* (accessed 3 August 2016).

Bauer, T. and Zimmerman, K., *Assessment of Possible Migration Pressure and its Labour Market Impact Following EU Enlargement to Central and Eastern Europe* (Bonn: IZA Research Report, 2009).

Bauman, Z., *Liquid Modernity* (Cambridge: Polity Press, 2000).

Baure, V., Densham, P., Millar, J. and Salt, J., 'Migrants from Central and Eastern Europe: Local Geographies', *Population and Trends*, 129 (2007), 7–19.

BBC, 'Exploitation of workers at top hotels' *http://news.bbc.co.uk/1/hi/programmes/newsnight/8171318.stm* (accessed 3 August 2016).

BBC, 'Skilled migrants should "plug gap", says Lord Digby Jones', *http://www.bbc.co.uk/news/uk-wales-33851020* (accessed 16 July 2016).

BBC, 'Town's support for migrant Poles', *http://news.bbc.co.uk/1/hi/wales/south_west/5378298.stm* (accessed 3 July 2016).

BBC UK, 'Brexit: David Cameron to quit after the UK votes to leave EU', *http://www.bbc.com/news/uk-politics-36615028* (accessed 16 July 2016).

BBC UK, 'Theresa May vows to be "one nation" as new Prime Minister', *http://www.bbc.com/news/uk-politics-36788782* (accessed 16 July 2016).

Becker, G., *The Economic Way of Looking at Life*, The Nobel Lecture, 9 December 1992.

Becker, H. S., 'Notes on the concept of commitment, *American Journal of Sociology*, 66 (1960), 32–40.

Belka, M., *How Poland's EU Membership Helped Transform its Economy* (Washington, DC: Group of 30, 2013).

Bell, J., 'Migration as Multiple Pathways: Narrative interviews with Polish migrants in

Belfast, Northern Ireland', *Studia Sociologica*, 4/2 (2012), 106–18.

Bennett, K., Beynon, H. and Hudson, R., *Coalfields Regeneration: Dealing with the Consequences of Industrial Decline* (Bristol: The Policy Press and Joseph Rowntree Foundation, 2000).

Bonacich, E. and Modell, J., *The Economic Basis of Ethnic Solidarity: Small Businesses in the Japanese American Community* (Nerkeley: University of California Press, 1980).

Booth, S., Howarth, C. and Scarpetta, V., *Tread Carefully: The Impact and Management of EU Free Movement on Immigration Policy* (London: Open Europe, 2012).

Borjas, G., *Friends or Strangers: The Impact of Immigrants on the US Economy* (New York: Basic Books, 1990).

Boyd, M., 'Family and personal networks in international migration', *International Migration Review*, 23/3 (1989), 638–70.

British Futures, 'EU Migration from Romania and Bulgaria: What does the public think?', *http://www.britishfuture.org/wp-content/uploads/2013/12/J1527_BRF_RomaniaBulgaria_16.12.13_2-1.pdf* (accessed 16 July 2016).

Buchowski, M., 'Redefining work in a local community in Poland: Transformation and class, culture and work', in A. Procoli (ed.), *Workers and Narratives of Survival in Europe: The Management of Precariousness at the End of the Twentieth Century* (New York: State University of New York Press, 2004).

Burchell, B., 'A new way of analyzing labour market flows using work history data', *Work, Employment and Society*, 7/2 (1993), 237–58.

Burrell, K., 'Staying, returning, working and living: key themes in current academic research undertaken in the UK on migration movements from Eastern Europe', *Social Identities*, 16 (2010), 287–308.

Campbell, D. and Stanley, J., *Experimental and Quasi-Experimental Designs for Research* (Chicago: Rand McNally, 1963).

Cardiff Council, *Cardiff: Developing an International and Open City* (London: British Council, 2008).

Castles, M. and Miller, M., *The Age of Migration* (London: Macmillan Press, 2009).

Change Institute, 'The Somali Muslim Community in England' (London: Department of

Communities and Local Government, 2009).

Chappell, L., Latorre, M., Rutter, J. and Shah, J., *Migration and Rural Economies: Assessing and Addressing Risks* (London: IPPR Economics of Migration Working Paper 6, 2009).

Chiswick B., Lee, Y. and Miller, P., 'A Longitudinal Analysis of Immigrant Occupational Mobility: A test of the immigrant assimilation hypothesis', *International Migration Review*, 39/2 (2005), 332–53.

Ciupijus, A., 'Mobile Central Eastern Europeans in Britain: Successful EU citizens and disadvantaged labour migrants', *Work, Employment and Society*, 25/3 (2011), 25–35.

Coe, N., Johns, J. and Ward, K., 'Flexibility in action: the temporary staffing industry in the

Czech Republic and Poland', *Environment and Planning A*, 40/6 (2008), 1391–1415.

Cohen, J., *The Culture of Migration in Southern Mexico* (Austin: University of Texas Press, 2004).

Cohen, J. and Sirkeci, I., *Cultures of Migration: The Global Nature of Contemporary Mobility* (Austin: University of Texas Press, 2011).

Collett, E., *The Integration Needs of Mobile EU Citizens: Impediments and Opportunities* (Brussels: Migration Policy Institute Europe, 2013).

Cook, J., Dwyer, P. and Waite, L., 'The Experiences of Accession 8 Migrants in England: Motivations, Work and Agency', *International Migration*, 49/2 (2011), 54–79.

Crawley, H., 'Demographics and the Changing Face of Wales', Centre for Migration Policy Research, presentation by the Swansea University School of the Environment and Society, 2006.

Crawley, H., *Migration and Employment in Wales* (Cardiff: Wales Migration Partnership, 2013).

Curry, L., 'Inefficiencies in the geographical operation of labour markets', *Regional Studies*, 19/3 (1985), 203–15.

Davies, C. S., 'Abandoned Mine Shafts and Levels in the British Coalfields', *Environmental Management*, 12/4 (1988), 479–90.

Davies, H., 'Fleeing Franco: How Wales Gave Shelter to Refugee Children from the Basque Country During the Spanish Civil War', presentation in Cardiff University, 2011.

Dayha, B., 'Pakistanis in Britain: Transients or Settlers?' *Race*, 14/3 (1973), 242–77.

de Haas, H., 'Migration Theory: Quo Vadis?' *International Migration Institute Paper*, 100/1 (2014).

Dobson, J., Latham, A. and Salt, J., *On the Move? Labour Migration in Times of Recession*. (London: Policy Network Article, 2009).

Dominiczak, P., 'Britain and Germany demand EU cracks down on "benefits tourism"', http://www.telegraph.co.uk/news/politics/10014508/Britain-and-Germany-demand-EU-cracks-down-on-benefits-tourism.html (accessed 29 July 2016).

Dreher, S., *Neoliberalism and Migration: An Inquiry into the Politics of Globalization* (Berlin: Lit Verlag, 2007).

Drinkwater, S., 'Economic and Demographic Change in the Llanelli Area: Recent Developments and Future Possibilities', presentation to Workers Education Association, Llanelli, 7 June 2014.

Drinkwater, S. and Blackaby, D, 'Migration and Labour Market Differences: The Case of Wales', IZA Discussion Paper 1275 (2004).

Drinkwater, S. and Clark, K., 'Pushed out or pulled in? self-employment among ethnic minorities in England and Wales', *Labour Economics*, 7/5 (2000), 603–28.

REFERENCES

Drinkwater, S., Eade, J. and Garapich, M., 'Poles apart? EU enlargement and the labour market outcomes of immigrants in the UK', *International Migration*, 47 (2009), 161–90.

Drinkwater, S. and Garapich, M., 'Migration Plans and Strategies of Recent Polish Migrants
to England and Wales: Do they have any and how do they change?' Norface Migration Discussion Article (2013), 2013–23.

Dustmann, C., Casanova, M., Fertig, M., Preston, I. and Schmidt, C. M., *The Impact of EU Enlargement on Migration Flows* (London: UK Home Office Report, 2003).

Dustmann, C. and Weiss, Y., 'Return migration: theory and empirical evidence from the UK', *British Journal of Industrial Relations*, 45/2 (2007), 236–56.

Eade, J., Drinkwater, S. and Garapich, M., *Class and Ethnicity: Polish Migrants in London* (Guildford: University of Surrey Press, 2006).

Elias, N. and Scotson, J., *The Established and the Outsiders*, in *Collected Works of Norbert
Elias* (Dublin: UCD Press, 2008).

Elrick, T. and Brinkmeier, E., 'Changing Patterns of Polish Labour Migration after the UK's Opening of the Labour Market? Insights from Rural Case Studies in the Opolskie and Swietokrzyskie Voivodships', in K. Burrell (ed.), *Polish Migration to the UK in the 'New' European Union after 2004* (Aldershot: Ashgate, 2009).

Engbersen, G., Grabowska-Lusinska, I. and Leerkes, A., 'The rise of liquid migration? old and new patterns of migration after EU enlargement', presented at the Migration, Economic Change, Social Challenge Conference. London, 6–9 April 2011.

Engbersen, G., Snel, E. and Boom, J., 'A Van Full of Poles: Liquid migration in Eastern and Central European countries', in R. Black et al. (eds)., *A Continent Moving West? EU
Enlargement and Labour Migration from Central and Eastern Europe* (Amsterdam: Amsterdam University Press, 2010), pp. 115–40.

Epstein, G., 'Information cascades and decision to migrate', http://ftp.iza.org/dp445.pdf (accessed 29 July 2016).

European Commission, 'Moving to the European Union?' http://ec.europa.eu/immigration/ (accessed 16 July 2016).

European Commission, *Employment and Social Developments in Europe 2011, Directorate-General for Employment*, Social Affairs and Inclusion, Directorate A (2011).

REFERENCES

European Commission, 'Free Movement – EU Nationals', http://ec.europa.eu /social/main.jsp?catId=457&langId=en (accessed 16 July 2016).

European Parliament, 'Migration and asylum in central and Eastern Europe', http://www.europarl.europa.eu/workingpapers/libe/104/summary_en.htm (accessed 12 August 2016).

Evans, M. D. R., 'Immigrant entrepreneurship: effects of ethnic market size and isolated labour pool', *American Sociological Review*, 54/6 (1989), 560–72.

Favell, A., 'The new face of east–west migration in Europe', *Journal of Ethnic and Migration Studies*, 34/5 (2008), 701–16.

Fevre, R., 'Labour migration and freedom of movement in the European Union: social exclusion and economic development', *International Planning Studies*, 3/1 (1998), 1–18.

Fihel, A., Kaczmarczyk, P. and Okólski, M., *Labour Mobility in the Enlarged European Union: International Migration from the EU8 Countries* (Warsaw: Centre of Migration Research, 2006).

Firestone, W., 'Alternative arguments for generalising data as applied to qualitative research', *Educational Researcher*, 22/4 (1993), 16–23.

Friberg, J. H., 'The Polish worker in Norway: Emerging patterns of migration, employment and incorporation after EU's eastern enlargement' (doctoral thesis, University of Oslo, 2013).

Friberg, J. H., 'The stages of migration: From going abroad to settling down: Post-accession Polish migrant workers in Norway', *Journal of Ethnic and Migration Studies*, 38/10 (2012) 1589–1605.

Friberg, J. H. and Eldring, L., *Labour Migrants from Central and Eastern Europe in the Nordic Countries: Patterns of Migration, Working Conditions and Recruitment Practices* (Copenhagen: Nordic Council of Ministers, 2013).

Fukuyama, R., 'Social capital and development: the coming agenda', *SAIS Review*, 22/1 (2002), 23–37.

Galasinka, D. and Kozłowska, O., 'Discourses on a "normal life" among post-accession migrants from Poland to Britain', in K. Burrell (ed.), *Polish Migration to the UK in the 'New' European Union: After 2004* (Aldershot: Ashgate, 2009), pp. 87–107.

Garapich, M., *London's Polish Borders: Transnationalizing Class and Ethnicity among Polish Migrants in London* (Stuttgart: Ibidem, 2016).

Garapich, M., 'The migrant industry and civil society: Polish immigrants in the UK before and after EU enlargement', *Journal of Ethnic and Migration Studies*, 34/5 (2008), 732–52.

REFERENCES

Garip, F. and Asad, A., *Mexico–US Migration in Time*, International Migration Institute Working Paper (Oxford: IMI, 2013).

Gillingham, E., *Report on Understanding A8 Migration to the UK since Accession* (London: Office for National Statistics, 2010).

Gilmartin, M. and Migge, B., 'European Migrants in Ireland: Pathways to integration', *European Urban and Regional Studies*, 22/3 (2013) 1–15.

Glossop, C. and Shaheen, F., 'Accession to Recession: A8 Migration to Bristol and Hull: Executive Summary', http://www.centreforcities.org/assets/files/Accessionper cent20to%20Recession%20.pdf (accessed 28 May 2016).

Green, A. E., Owen, D. W., Jones, P. and Francis, J., *The Economic Impact of Migrant Workers in the West Midlands* (Birmingham: West Midlands Regional Observatory, 2007).

Greenwood, M. J., 'Research on internal migration in the United States: a survey', *Journal of Economic Literature*, 8/1 (1975), 397–433.

Guardia, D. and Pichelmann, K., *Report on Labour Migration Patterns in Europe: Recent Trends and Future Challenges* (Brussels: European Economy Report to the European Commission, 2006).

Hammond, L., 'Somali Transnational Activism and Integration in the UK: Mutually Supporting Strategies', *Journal of Ethnic and Migration Studies*, 39/6 (2013), 1001–17.

Harris, C., 'Polish entrepreneurship in Britain contributes to economic growth' (Ph.D. thesis, University of Birmingham, 2012).

Harris, C., Moran, D. and Bryson, J. R., 'EU Accession Migration: National Insurance Number Allocations and the Geographies of Polish Labour Migration to the UK', *Tijdschrift voor Economische en Sociale Geografie*, 103 (2012), 209–21.

Haug, S., 'Migration Networks and Migration Decision-Making', *Journal of Ethnic and Migration Studies*, 34/4 (2008), 585–605.

Heinen, M. and Pegels, A., 'EU Expansion and the Free Movement of Workers – Do Continued Restrictions Make Sense for Germany?' http://www.focus-migration.de/(accessed 12 August 2016).

Helinksa-Hughes, E., Hughes, M., Lassalle, P. and Skowron, I., 'The Trajectories of Polish Immigrant Businesses in Scotland and the Role of Social Capital', https://www.google.co.uk/searchq=the+trajectories+of+Polish+immigrant+businesss+in+Scotland&oq=the+trajectories+of+Polish+immigrant+businesss+in+Scotland&sourceid=chrome&ie=UTF-8 (accessed 10 July 2016).

Hickman, M., Crowley, H. and Mai, N., *Immigration and Social Cohesion in the UK* (London: Joseph Rowntree Foundation, 2008).

Ho, E. L., 'Migrant trajectories of "highly skilled" middling transnationals: Singaporean transmigrants in London', *Population, Space and Place*, 17/3 (2011), 116–29.

Hooper, A. and Punter, J., *Capital Cardiff, 1975–2020: Regeneration, Competitiveness and the Urban Environment* (Cardiff: University of Wales Press, 2006).

Huddleston, T. and Tjaden, D., *Immigrant Citizenship Survey: How Immigrants Experience Integration in 15 European Cities* (Brussels: King Baudouin Foundation and the Migration Policy Group, 2012).

IFA, *Migration and Cultural Integration in Europe*, IFA Culture and Foreign Policy Conference Report, Brussels, December 2013.

Jayaweera, H. and Anderson, B., 'Migrant workers and vulnerable employment: a review of existing data', https://www.compas.ox.ac.uk/project/migrant-workers-and-vulnerable-employment-a-review-of-existing-data/ (accessed 29 July 2016).

Jennissen, R., *Report on Economic Theories of International Migration and the Role of Immigration Policy* (The Hague: Dutch Ministry of Justice/Netherlands Interdisciplinary Demographic Institute, 2006).

Jentsch, B., de Lima, P. and MacDonald, B., 'Migrant Workers in Rural Scotland: Going to the Middle of Nowhere', *International Journal on Multicultural Societies*, 9/1 (2007), 3–53.

Jones, K., *The Recruitment of A8 Migrant Workers into the UK*, presentation, Manchester University, 10 June 2008.

Jones, L., 'The Role of Temporary Staffing Agencies in Facilitating A8 Migration into the UK', presentation to the School of Environment and Development at the University of Manchester, 2014.

Jones, L., Lever, J., Jones, S., Radcliffe, J. and Woods, M., 'Migrant Workers in Rural Wales and the South Wales Valleys', presentation to the Cardiff School of Planning and Geography, December 2014.

Kenway, P., Palmer, G. and MacInnes, T., 'Monitoring poverty and social exclusion in Wales 2009', https://www.jrf.org.uk/report/monitoring-poverty-and-social-exclusion-wales-2009 (accessed 30 August 2016).

Kicinger, A., 'Beyond the focus on Europeanisation: Polish Migration Policy 1989–2004', *Journal of Ethnic and Migration Studies*, 35/1 (2009), 79–95.

Knight, J., 'Migrant Entrepreneurship in a Shrinking Ethnic Economy: A study of Polish migrant small businesses in Cardiff, Wales', *Journal of Enterprising Communities: People and Places in the Global Economy*, 9 (2014), 114–31.

Knight, J., Lever, J. and Thompson, A., 'The Labour Market Mobility of Polish

Migrants: A comparative study of three regions in South Wales, UK', *Central and East European Migration Review* (2014), 1–18.

Kofman, E., 'Family-related migration: A critical review of European studies', *Journal of Ethnic and Migration Studies*, 30/2 (2004), 243–62.

Krase, J., *Seeing Cities Change: Local Culture and Class* (Aldershot: Ashgate, 2012).

Kropiwiec, K. and King-Ó Riain, R., *Polish Migrant Workers in Ireland* (Dublin: National Consultative Committee on Racism and Interculturalism, 2006).

Kurczewski, J., 'Poland's seven middle classes', *Social Research*, 61/2 (1994), 395–421.

Lassalle, P., Hughes, M. and Helinska-Hughes, E., 'Re-theorising ethnic entrepreneurial strategies', *http://www.isbe.org.uk/ethnicentrepreneurialstrategies* (accessed 17 July 2016).

Lawrence, F., 'Underpaid, easy to sack: UK's second class workforce', *https://business-humanrights.org/en/underpaid-easy-to-sack-uks-second-class-workforce* (accessed 3 August 2016).

Lever, J. and Milbourne, P., 'Migrant workers and migrant entrepreneurs: changing established–outsider relations across society and space?' *Space and Polity*, 18 (2014), 255–68.

Lever, J. and Milbourne, P., 'The structural invisibility of outsiders: the role of migrant labour in the meat-processing industry' (open access in *Sociology*; published online, ISSN 0038-0385, 23 December 2015).

Levrau, F., Piqueray, E., Goddeeris, I. and Timmerman, C., 'Polish Immigration in Belgium since 2004: New dynamics and migration and integration', *Ethnicities*, 14/2 (2013), 303–23.

Light, I. and Gold, S., *Ethnic Economies* (London: Academic Press, 2000).

Lofman, B., 'Consumers in Rapid Transition: The Polish Experience', in L. McAlister and M.

L. Rothschild (eds), *Advances in Consumer Research*, vol. 20 (Provo, UT: Association for Consumer Research, 1993), pp. 18–22.

Luthra, R., Reich, L., Platt, L. and Salamonska, J., 'Migrant diversity, migration motivations and early integration: the case of Poles in Germany, the Netherlands, London and Dublin', ISER Working Paper Series 2014–18, Institute for Social and Economic Research (2014).

Martín, I. and Venturini, A., *A Comprehensive Labour Market Approach to EU Labour Migration Policy* (Brussels: Migration Policy Centre, 2015).

Massey, D. S., Arango, J., Hugo, G., Kouaouci, A., Pellegrino, A. and Taylor, J. E.,

'Theories of international migration: a review and appraisal', *Population and Development Review* 19/3 (1993), 431–66.

Masurel, E., Nikmap, P., Tastan, M. and Vindigni, T., 'Motivations and performance conditions for ethnic entrepreneurship', *Growth and Change*, 33/2 (2002), 238–60.

May, D., 'The interplay of three established–outsider figurations in a deprived inner-city neighbourhood', *Urban Studies*, 41/11 (2004), 2159–79.

Mayblin, L., 'Why the UK's 2015 Immigration Bill is bad for vulnerable migrant workers', *Open Democracy*, https://www.opendemocracy.net/beyondslavery/lucy-mayblin/why-uk-s-2015-immigration-bill-is-bad-for-vulnerable-migrant-workers (accessed 31 July 2016).

McCollum, D., Cooke, L., Chiroro, C., Platts, A., MacLeod, F. and Findlay, A., *Report on Spatial, Sectoral and Temporal Trends in A8 Migration to the UK 2004–2011: Evidence from the Worker Registration Scheme* (Southampton: Centre for Population Change, 2012).

McGhee, D., Heath, S. and Trevena, P., 'Dignity, happiness and being able to live a "normal life" in the UK: an examination of post-accession Polish migrants' transnational autobiographical fields', *Social Identities*, 18/6 (2012), 1–17.

Metykova, M., 'Suspended Normalcy: Eastern European Migrants in London and Edinburgh', paper presented at the Normalcy: Opportunity or Standard? The Confrontation of Eastern European and Western Culture in the EU Symposium, University of East London, 2007.

Miera, F., 'Transnational strategies of Polish migrant entrepreneurs in trade and small business in Berlin', *Journal of Ethnic and Migration Studies*, 34/5 (2008), 753–70.

Migration Observatory, 'Migrants and Housing in the UK: Experiences and Impacts', www.migrationobservatory.ox.ac.uk/sites/files/migobs/Briefing%20-%20Migrants%20and%20Housing%20in%20the%20UK_0.pdf (accessed 1 June 2016).

Migration Policy Institute (MPI), 'Integration: The role of communities, institutions and the state', http://www.migrationpolicy.org/article/integration-role-communities-institutions-and-state (accessed 20 June 2016).

Milbourne, P., 'The social and cultural impacts of English migration to rural Wales', in P. Milbourne (ed.), *Rural Wales in the Twenty-First Century: Society, Economy and Environment* (Cardiff: University of Wales Press, 2011), pp. 46–64.

Milbourne, P. and Mason, K. 'Environmental injustice and post-colonial environmentalism: opencast coal mining, landscape and place', *Environment and Planning A* (forthcoming).

Minniti, M., Bygrave, W. and Autio, E., *Global Entrepreneurship Monitor, 2005 Executive Summary* (London: London Business School, 2006).

Morgan, K., 'The challenge of polycentric planning: Cardiff as a capital city region?' Papers in Planning Research, No. 185, Cardiff School of City and Regional Planning (2005).

Moriarty, E., Wickham, J., Salomonska, J., Krings, T. and Bobek, A., 'Putting Work Back in Mobilities: Migrant Careers and Aspirations', paper presented at the New Migrations, New Challenges Conference, Trinity College Dublin, 2010.

Nannestad, P., Svendsen, G. and Svendsen, G.T., 'Bridge Over Troubled Water? Migration and Social Capital', *Journal of Ethnic and Migration Studies*, 34/4 (2008), 607–31.

Nelson, J., *Access to Power: Politics and the Urban Poor in Developing Nations* (Princeton: Princeton University Press, 1979).

Nicol, P., Smith, A. M., Dunkley, R. and Morgan, K., 'Valleys Regional Park Interim Progress and Evaluation Report', School of Planning and Geography, Cardiff University (2013).

Nowicka, M., 'Positioning strategies of Polish entrepreneurs in Germany: Transnationalising Bourdieu's notion of capital', *International Sociology*, 28/1 (2013), 29–47.

Ociepka, B. and Ryniejska, M., 'Public Diplomacy and EU Enlargement: the Case of Poland', Netherlands Institute of International Relations 'Clingendael', Discussion Papers in Diplomacy (August 2005), 1–18

OECD, *Free Movement of Workers and Labour Market Adjustment: Recent Experiences from OECD Countries and the European Union* (Paris: OECD Publishing, 2012).

OECD, 'Indicators of Immigrant Integration 2015', http://www.oecd.org/publications/indicators-of-immigrant-integration-2015-settling-in-9789264234024-en.htm (accessed 1 August 2016).

Office of National Statistics (ONS), 'International Migration', http://www.ons.gov.uk/peoplepopulationandcommunity/populationandmigration/internationalmigration (accessed 16 July 2016).

Office of National Statistics (ONS), 'Census, Office for National Statistics', http://webarchive.nationalarchives.gov.uk/20160105160709 (accessed 16 July 2016).

REFERENCES

Office of National Statistics (ONS), 'Wales Statistics', http://wales.gov.uk/statistics-and-research/?topic=Business+and+economy&lang=en (accessed 19 July 2016).

Okolski, M., 'Incomplete Migration: A new form of mobility in Central and Eastern Europe: The case of Polish and Ukranian migrants', in J. E. Taylor and D. S. Massey (eds), *International Migration: Prospects and Policies* (Oxford: Oxford University Press, 2001), pp. 35–59.

Okolski, M. and Salt, J., 'Polish Emigration to the UK after 2004; Why Did so Many Come?' *Central and Eastern European Migration Review*, http://www.ceemr.uw.edu.pl/vol-3-no-2-december-2014/articles/polish-emigration-uk-after-2004-why-did-so-many-come (accessed 12 August 2016).

O'Reilly, R. and Benson, M., 'Migration and the search for a better way of life: a critical exploration of lifestyle migration', *The Sociological Review*, 57/4 (2012), 608–25.

Orlowski, W. W., 'Post-accession economic development of Poland', *Eastern Journal of European Studies*, 2/2 (2011), 7–20.

Parutis, V., 'Economic migrants or transnational middling? East European migrants' experiences of work in the UK', http://onlinelibrary.wiley.com/advanced/search/results (accessed 16 July 2016).

Payne, G. and Williams, M., 'Generalisation in qualitative research', *Sociology*, 39/2 (2005), 295–314

E. Penninx, 'Integration of migrants: Economic, social, cultural and political dimensions', in United Nations *New Demographic Regime: Population Challenges and Policy Responses* (Geneva, 2005), pp. 137–51.

Phizacklea, A. and Ram, M.,, 'Being your own boss: ethnic minority entrepreneurs in comparative perspective', *Work, Employment and Society*, 10/2 (1995), 319–39.

Pijpers, R., 'Help! The Poles Are Coming: Narrating a Contemporary Moral Panic', *Geografiska Annaler*, Series B, 88/1 (2006), 91–103.

Poland Central Statistics Office, 'Employment, Wages and Salaries', http://www.stat.gov.pl/gus/5840_1890_ENG_HTML.htm (accessed 19 July 2016).

Polish Scottish Heritage, 'The Experience of Polish–Scottish Integration in Scotland', http://polishscottishheritage.co.uk/wp-content/uploads/2013/10/The-Experiance-of-Integration-Final-Report.pdf (accessed 5 June 2016).

Pollard, N., Latorre, M. and Sriskandarajah, L., *Floodgates or Turnstiles? Post-EU Enlargement Migration Flows to (and from) the UK* (London: IPPR, 2008).

Portes, A. and Back, R., *Latin Journey: Cuban and Mexican Immigrants in the US* (Berkeley: University of California Press, 1985).

Putnam, R., 'E Pluribus Unum: diversity and community in the twenty-first century', *Scandinavian Political Studies*, 30/2 (2007), 137–74.

Rakowski, T., *Hunters, Gatherers and Practitioners of Powerlessness: An Ethnography of the Degraded in Postsocialist Poland* (Oxford: Berghahn, 2016).

Ray, B., *The Role of Cities in Immigrant Integration* (Brussels: Migration Policy Institute Europe, 2003).

Recchi, E., Baldoni, E., Francavilla, F. and Mencarini, L., *Geographic and Job Mobility in the EU* (Luxembourg: European Commission Report, 2006).

Robinson, D., Reeve, K., Platts-Fowler, D., Green, S., Walshaw, A., Batty, E. and Bashir, N., 'An Evaluation of Getting on Together: The Community Cohesion Strategy for Wales, Cardiff', http://cdn.basw.co.uk/upload/basw_94308-3.pdf (accessed 10 January 2016).

Robinson, J., 'Why is Next hiring thousands of cheap Eastern European workers to staff English warehouse – in area where more than 200,000 are on the dole – before they even advertise the jobs here?' http://www.dailymail.co.uk/news/article-2852931/How-hiring-thousands-cheap-Eastern-European-workers-staff-warehouse-area-200-000-dole.html (accessed 3 August 2016).

Rostek, J. and Uffelmann, D., *Contemporary Polish Migrant Culture and Literature in Germany, Ireland, and the UK* (Frankfurt am Main: Peter Lang, 2011).

Ryan, L., 'Migrants' social networks and weak ties: accessing resources and constructing relationships post-migration', *The Sociological Review*, 59/4 (2011), 707–24.

Ryan, L., Sales, R., Tilki, M. and Siara, B., 'Social networks, social support and social capital: the experiences of recent Polish migrants in London', *Sociology*, 42/4 (2008), 672–90.

Scott, S. and Brindley, P., 'New geographies of migrant settlement in the UK', *Geography*, 97/1 (2012), 29–36.

Serazio, M. and Szarek, W., 'The art of producing consumers: A critical textual analysis of post-communist Polish advertising', *European Journal of Cultural Studies*, 15/6 (2012) 753–68.

Shelter Cymru, *Living in Wales: The Housing and Homelessness Experiences of Central and East European Migrant Workers* (Cardiff: Shelter Cymru, 2010).

Sime, D. and Fox, R., 'Home abroad: Eastern European children's family and peer relationships after migration', *Childhood* (2014).

Siu, P., 'The Sojourner', *American Journal of Sociology*, 58/1 (1952), 34–44.

REFERENCES

Siwko, M., 'Values and Aspirations of the Polish Youth in the Contemporary Europe', http://www.ce.uw.edu.pl/pliki/pw/Y_10_siwko_PLyouth.pdf (accessed 3 August 2016).

Sjaastad, L., 'The costs and returns of human migration', *Journal of Political Economy*, 70/5 (1962), 80–93.

Smallbone, D. and Welter, F., 'Entrepreneurship in transition economies: Necessity or opportunity driven?' http://www.academia.edu/1024226/Entrepreneurship_in_transition_economies_necessity_or_opportunity_driven (accessed 16 July 2016).

Spencer, D., *Clandestine Crossings: Migrants and Coyotes on the Texas/Mexico Border* (Ithaca, NY: Cornell University Press, 1996).

Sporton, D., '"They Control My Life": the Role of Local Recruitment Agencies in East European Migration to the UK', *Population, Space and Place*, 19/5 (2013) 443–58.

Statistics for Wales, 'School Census Results, 2013 Statistical Bulletin SDR, 109/2013', http://dera.ioe.ac.uk/18003/1/130711-school-cen,sus-results-2013-en.pdf (accessed 1 July 2016). [remove underlining and print black]

Stenning, A. and Dawley, S., 'Poles to Newcastle: Grounding new migrant flows in peripheral regions', *European Urban and Regional Studies*, 16/3 (2009), 273–94.

Tannock, S., 'Bad attitude? Migrant workers, meat processing work and the local unemployed in a peripheral region of the UK', *European Urban and Regional Studies*, 22/4 (2013), 1–15.

Terrazas, A., *The Economic Integration of Immigrants in the United States: Long and Short Term Perspectives* (Washington, DC: Migration Policy Institute, 2011).

The Daily Telegraph, 'It's the economy, glupi', http://www.telegraph.co.uk/news/uknews/1481817/Its-the-economy-glupi.html (accessed 3 August 2016).

The Economist, 'From communism to consumerism: Consumer lending is taking root in central Europe', http://www.economist.com/node/1612739 (accessed 3 August 2016).

The Financial Times, 'Polish bus drivers find UK roads paved with gold', http://www.ft.com/cms/s/1/522719a6-9a3d-11d9-a094-00000e2511c8.html#axzz-4GIORq1ND (accessed 3 August 2016).

The Guardian, 'Somalis in Cardiff', https://www.theguardian.com/uk/2006/jan/23/britishidentity.features11 (accessed 19 July 2016).

Thompson, A., Chambers, P. and Doleczek, L., 'Welcome to Llaneski: Polish migration in South West Wales', *Contemporary Wales*, 23 (2010), 1–16.

Threadgold, R., Clifford, S., Arwo, A., Powell, V., Harb, A., Jiang, X. and Jewell, J., *Immigration and Inclusion in South Wales* (York: Joseph Rowntree Foundation, 2008).

Torkington, K., 'Place and Lifestyle Migration: The Discursive Construction of "Glocal" Place-Identity', *Mobilities*, 7/1 (2012), 71–92.

Trevena, P., 'Why do highly educated migrants go for low-skilled jobs? a case study of Polish graduates working in London', in B. Glorius et al. (eds), *Mobility in Transition: Migration Patterns after EU Enlargement* (Amsterdam: Amsterdam University Press, 2009).

Trevena, P., McGhee, D. and Heath, S., 'Location, location? A critical examination of patterns and determinants of internal mobility among post-accession Polish migrants in the UK', *Population, Space and Place*, 19 (2013), 671–87.

UKBA, 'Visas and Immigration', *https://www.gov.uk/browse/visas-immigration* (accessed 16 July 2016).

Vershanina, N. and Meyer, M., 'Polish Entrepreneurs & Forms of Capital', conference paper presented at the Institute of Small Business Entrepreneurship (ISBE) Conference, Belfast, Northern Ireland, 2008.

Verwiebe, R., 'Why do Europeans migrate to Berlin? Socio-structural differences for Italian, British, French and Polish nationals in the period between 1980–2002', *International Migration* (2011) [Online Publication Version].

Vote Leave, 'Briefing: The EU Immigration System is Immoral and Unfair', *http://www.voteleavetakecontrol.org/briefing_immigration* (accessed 16 July 2016).

Waldinger, R. and Lichter, M., *How the Other Half Works: Immigration and the Social Organization of Labor* (Berkeley: University of California Press, 2003).

Wallace, C., 'Closing and opening borders: migration and mobility in East-Central Europe', *Journal of Ethnic and Migration Studies*, 28/4 (2002), 603–25.

Ward, K., Coe, N. and Jones, J., 'The role of temporary staffing agencies in facilitating mobility in Central and Eastern Europe', Research Report for Vedior Staffing (2008).

Welsh Assembly Government (WAG), *Ambition Statement for Regeneration in Wales* (Cardiff: Welsh Government, 2010).

Welsh Assembly Government (WAG) 'Getting Along Together: A Community Cohesion Strategy for Wales', *http://wales.gov.uk/docs/dsjlg/publications/commsafety/091130ccstratenv1.pdf* (accessed 29 July 2016).

REFERENCES

Welsh Assembly Government (WAG), 'Homes for Wales: A White Paper for Better Lives and Communities', *http://wales.gov.uk/docs/desh/consultation/120521whitepaperen.pdf* (accessed 1 July 2016).

Welsh Assembly Government (WAG), *Improving Lives and Communities: Homes in Wales*, (Cardiff: Government Printing, 2010).

Welsh Assembly Government (WAG) 'Programme for Government: Equality', *http://wales.gov.uk/docs/strategies/110929chap8en.pdf* (accessed 29 July 2016).

Welsh Index of Multiple Deprivation (WIMD) 'Analysis', *http://wales.gov.uk/topics/statistics/headlines/compendia2009/welsh-index-multiple-deprivation-2012-indicator-analysis/?lang=en* (accessed 19 July 2016).

Welsh Refugee Council, 'Wales as a Refuge', *http://welshrefugeecouncil.org.uk/asylum-in-wales-and-wrc/* (accessed 19 July 2016).

White, A., 'Double Return Migration: Failed Returns to Poland Leading to Settlement Abroad and New Transnational Strategies', *International Migration*, 52/6 (2014), 72–84.

White, A., 'Polish circular migration and marginality: a livelihood strategy approach', *http://www.euroemigranci.pl/dokumenty/pokonferencyjna/White.pdf* (accessed 3 August 2016).

White, A., 'Polish Migration in the UK: Local experiences and effects', presented at the AHRC Connected Communities Symposium: Understanding Local Experiences and Effects of New Migration, Sheffield, 26 September 2011.

White, A., 'Unsettling times for a settled population? Polish perspectives on Brexit', *http://www.ucl.ac.uk/european-institute/highlights/2015-16/polish-perspectives-brexit* (accessed 3 August 2016).

White, A. and Ryan, L. 'Polish "temporary" migration: the formation and significance of social networks', *Europe-Asia Studies*, 60/9 (2008), 1467–1502.

Whitehead, T., 'Thousands of foreign workers exploiting British jobs market', *http://www.telegraph.co.uk/finance/jobs/4781831/Thousands-of-foreign-workers-* (accessed 16 July 2016).

Williams, C., 'The nature of entrepreneurship in the informal sector: evidence from the UK', *International Journal of Entrepreneurial Behaviour and Research*, 13/6 (2007), 349–66.

Winckler, V., *Informing Debate: What is Needed to End Child Poverty in Wales?* (London: Joseph Rowntree Foundation, 2009).

REFERENCES

Woods, M. and Watkins, S., 'Central and Eastern European Migrant Workers in Rural Wales', *http://www.walesruralobservatory.org.uk/sites/default/files/Migrant%20Workers%202008.pdf* (accessed 19 July 2016).

World Bank, 'Unemployment: Youth total by country', *http://data.worldbank.org/indicator/SL.UEM.1524.ZS* (accessed 3 August 2016).

Znaniecki, F. and Thomas, W. I., *The Polish Peasant in Europe and America* (Boston: The Gorham Press, 1933).

Index

Accession Treaty, 8
accommodation, 16, 29–30, 79, 83, 84, 89–90, 105, 123, 125, 147, 168, 192–3
advertising, 67
agriculture, 30, 67, 70, 90, 125, 182
Amnesty International, 12
Amsterdam Treaty, 7
Anderson, Bridget, 35, 185
Annual Population Survey, 12
Asad, Asad L., 29, 81
aspirations, 77, 87, 146, 152–3, 157, 163
Austria, 8, 179

Bauman, Zygmunt, 37
Becker, Gary, 24
Belfast, 23, 28
benefit tourism, 63, 181
benefits *see* welfare benefits
Benson, Michaela, 76
Berlin, 27–8
Birmingham, 36, 177
Bonacich, Edna, 33, 92
bonding contacts, 29, 30–1, 34, 173–4
Bont, Y (culture hub), 118, 195
Borjas, George, 26–7
Boyd, Monica, 79

Bradford, 13
Brexit, 6, 12, 59, 139, 164, 179, 183, 196
bridging contacts, 30, 173–6
Brinkmeier, Emilia, 69, 70
Bristol, 13, 41, 82
British citizenship, 143, 196
British Future survey, 12, 167
Bryson, John R., 10
Buchowski, Michal, 67
Bulgaria, 3, 181
Bulgarian migrants, 11–12, 173
Burrell, Kathy, 34
Butetown, 44

Caerphilly, 117
Cameron, David, 139
Canton, 89–90, 92, 96
Cardiff
  accommodation, 89–90, 192–3
  Butetown, 44
  Canton, 89–90, 92, 96
  case-study data, 16–17, 88–106
  City Road, 89–90, 92, 96
  community cohesion, 189
  cultural integration, 177–8
  deprivation levels, 43–4
  diversity, 13, 17, 41, 189

INDEX

docklands, 13, 41
economic integration, 171–3, 176
economy, 41–4
education levels, 41
ethnic economy, 44–5, 92–7, 153, 177–8
ethnic entrepreneurship, 93–7, 153, 177–8
family relations, 102–5
human capital development, 98–100
labour market experiences, 90–2, 97–8, 146, 171–3
labour market mobility, 97–8, 171–3
location, 40, 42
migrant identity, 100–2
migration history, 13, 41, 44, 92
number of migrants, 15, 44
Polish House, Newport Road, 39, 92, 195
population, 40, 43
as Regional Competitiveness and Employment region, 14, 41
research methodology, 52–4
sample characteristics, 53, 89
sample selection, 52–3
service sector, 17, 40–1, 186–7
social characteristics, 44–5
social integration, 174, 176
social networks, 89, 90, 91–2, 94–6, 98, 100, 105, 171, 174, 192–3
Somali population, 13, 41, 44, 167–8, 189
support organisations, 39, 92
Tiger Bay, 13, 41
unemployment, 43
working conditions, 146
Castles, Stephen, 143
Catholicism, 45, 89–90, 92, 119, 190

census data, 10–11, 12–13, 44, 48, 51, 108, 143
chain migration, 22, 44, 103, 124
childcare, 90, 191
children, 77, 101, 147–8, 153, 156, 159, 176
Chiswick, Barry, 32
circular migration, 21–2, 91, 141–4
Citizens' Advice Bureau (CAB), 113–14, 118
citizenship
British, 143, 196
EU, 7, 26, 63–4, 86, 100–2, 150–1, 166–7, 178
City Road, Cardiff, 89–90, 92, 96
Clark, Ken, 27
cleaning jobs, 182
coal mining, 45, 107, 108
co-ethnic workers, 33–6, 93–7, 98
Cohen, Jeffrey, 68–9, 72
Cohesion Policy, 13–14, 164–5
commitment, 29, 147–9, 155–6, 162
communism, 134
community cohesion, 187–9, 195, 197
competition for scarce resources, 115, 132–3, 149, 187
constrict theory, 30
construction industry, 93, 97, 125, 182
consumerism, 66–7, 68
Convergence regions, 13–14, 45–7, 49, 165
Cook, Joanne, 37
cost/benefit theory, 26–7, 74, 76
cost of living, 49, 67, 72, 74, 76, 87, 91, 131, 145, 146, 151
Crawley, Heaven, 182–3, 190, 191
Croatia, 3, 181
Croatian migrants, 11–12

250

INDEX

CSA Recruitment, 123–4, 125, 128
cultural capital, 64, 100
cultural integration, 165, 176–8
'cultures of migration', 64–73
currency exchange rates, 25, 76, 90–1
Cyprus, 3
Czech Republic, 3, 66

Daily Mail, 73
Daily Telegraph, 73
data analysis methods, 53–4, 55
Davies, Hywel, 108
de Haas, Hein, 66, 76, 81, 163
de Lima, Philomena, 83
dental care, 194
deprivation, 43–4, 47–8, 52, 107
disadvantage theory, 34–5
domestic jobs, 109
double migration, 144
Drinkwater, Stephen, 27, 51
Dustmann, Christian, 25

Eade, John, 22, 142
economic inequality, 67
economic integration, 165, 167–73, 176, 178
economic motivations, 16, 24–7, 37, 63–4, 72–7, 86–7, 105, 130, 145–6, 151–3, 163
economic recession, 4, 11, 53, 91, 94, 115
education, 45, 90, 92, 96, 97, 98–100, 130, 134, 156, 159, 171, 189–91, 198–9
Elrick, Tim, 69, 70
employment agencies, 5, 11, 18, 22, 29–30, 33, 56, 70, 71, 78, 82–6, 91–2, 110–11, 121–9, 168–9, 185–6, 192

Engerbsen, Godfried, 37, 142, 144
English as an additional language (EAL) pupils, 190–1, 198–9
Estonia, 3
ethnic economy, 11, 16, 33–6, 44–5, 92–7, 98, 116–18, 153, 170, 176–8
ethnic enclave economy, 34, 92
ethnic entrepreneurship, 34–6, 93–7, 116–18, 153, 159, 170, 176–8, 183–4, 198
European Commission, 164, 182, 195
European Free Trade Association (EFTA), 7
European Territorial Cooperation regions, 14
European Union (EU)
  2004 expansion, 3, 8–10, 38, 64, 86, 140–1
  2007 expansion, 3, 11–12, 181
  2013 expansion, 3, 11–12, 181
  Accession Treaty, 8
  Amsterdam Treaty, 7
  Brexit, 6, 12, 59, 139, 164, 179, 183, 196
  citizenship, 7, 26, 63–4, 86, 100–2, 150–1, 166–7, 178
  Cohesion Policy, 13–14, 164–5
  establishment of, 6, 180
  Free Movement Directive, 7–8
  free movement of goods and capital, 7, 164
  free movement of labour, 7–10, 140–1, 164, 180–1
  and integration, 164–7
  Maastricht Treaty, 7
  migration policy, 6, 7–10, 18–19, 140–1, 164–7, 180, 195
  original aims of, 6–7
  research on integration, 173

251

INDEX

Schengen Agreement, 7, 164, 179
transition arrangements for new member states, 8–10, 11–12, 64–5, 86, 166, 181
exploitation, 82, 85, 112–13, 184–7

family relations, 80, 102–5, 131–2, 147–8
Favell, Adrian, 20, 166
Fihel, Agnieszka, 26, 142
Filipino migrants, 55, 188
financial crisis, 4, 73
focus groups, 52
food processing industry, 17, 57, 71, 82–3, 108–16, 122, 125–9, 146, 169–70, 182, 184–6, 188–9
France, 65, 140
Free Movement Directive, 7–8
French migrants, 45, 107
Friberg, Jon Horgen, 83–4, 144
Fukuyama, Francis, 28

Garip, Filiz, 29, 81
gatekeepers, 52, 55, 56, 58
generalisation of findings, 59
geographic spread of migrants, 5, 11, 12–15, 32–3, 40, 78, 82
German migrants, 12
Germany, 8, 23, 27–8, 65, 69, 140–1
Glamorgan GATES initiative, 114, 118
Glasgow, 23, 36, 177
global migration market theory, 26–7
globalisation, 25, 26–7
GP registration, 133, 194
Grabowska-Lusinska, Izabela, 142

'hamsters', 22, 141
Harris, Catherine, 10, 35

hate crimes, 12
Haug, Sonja, 79
health, 107, 134, 193–5
healthcare sector, 49, 109, 194
Heath, Sue, 33, 78–9
Helinksa-Hughes, Ewa, 23
'herd behaviour', 29–30
Hickman, Mary, 31
high-skilled jobs, 23, 25, 171, 194
Home Office, 64, 143, 184
homelessness, 192, 193
home-ownership, 77, 152–3
hospitality industry, 90, 182, 186–7
host community resistance, 178–9
housing *see* accommodation
Hull, 82
human capital, 5, 16, 17, 26–7, 32, 98–100, 130
Hungary, 3, 66, 165

identity, 100–2, 158–9
illegal migration, 21, 30
Immigration Bill, 195–6
Indian migrants, 11, 12, 13
informal economy, 34, 92
integration, 12, 18, 28, 118–19, 140, 162, 164–79, 191, 195, 197
International Organization for Migration (IOM), 165, 167
Internet cafés, 89, 92, 103
interviews, 16, 52–3, 54–5, 56–7, 58
intra-UK migration, 10, 13, 45, 48–9
Ireland, 8, 28, 64, 142, 166
Irish migrants, 4, 12, 13, 41, 45, 48, 107, 121
Italian migrants, 4, 45, 48, 107, 121

Jentsch, Birgit, 33, 83
jobseeker's allowance, 9, 107

INDEX

Jones, Digby, Lord, 183
Jones, Katharine, 29

Knight, Julie, 23
Kofman, Eleonore, 28
Kurczewski, Jacek, 66–7

Labour Force Survey data, 52
labour market
   and agencies *see* employment agencies
   agricultural work, 30, 90, 125, 182
   childcare jobs, 90
   cleaning jobs, 109, 182
   co-ethnic workers in the ethnic economy, 33–6, 93–7, 98
   construction industry, 93, 97, 125, 182
   domestic jobs, 109
   food processing industry, 17, 57, 71, 82–3, 108–16, 122, 125–9, 146, 169–70, 182, 184–6, 188–9
   healthcare sector jobs, 49, 109, 194
   high-skilled jobs, 23, 25, 171, 194
   hospitality industry jobs, 90, 182, 186–7
   impact of migrants upon, 3–4
   low-skilled jobs, 11, 17, 25, 30–2, 35, 49, 90–1, 97–8, 108–10, 125–6, 169–72, 182–3
   migrant experiences of, 5, 16, 90–2, 108–10, 114–16, 122–30, 146, 167–73
   mobility within, 4, 17, 31–3, 97–8, 110–14, 128–30, 167–73
   overtime, 127–8
   retail sector jobs, 109
   seasonal work, 21, 33, 78, 90, 97, 141
   service sector jobs, 17, 30, 186–7
   social care jobs, 49, 125, 182
   and trade union membership, 108, 111–12, 185
   3D jobs, 20, 35, 90–1, 97–8, 169, 183
   wages, 51, 91, 110, 127–8
   workers' rights, 184–7
   working conditions, 82, 112–16, 125–8, 146, 183, 184–7
   zero hours contracts, 82, 112–13, 125–6, 186
Lampeter, 54, 55
language skills, 23, 32, 44, 80–1, 84, 97–100, 115, 124, 128–30, 134, 161–2, 167–78, 197
Lassalle, Paul, 35, 36
Latvia, 3
Leave campaign, 6, 12, 196
legal integration, 165, 166–7, 178
Leicester, 13, 45
Lever, John, 23
lifestyle, 75–7, 87, 105, 133–5, 146, 151–5, 157, 162–3
liquid migration, 37–8, 142, 143–4
Lithuania, 3
Lithuanian migrants, 31
Liverpool, 13, 41
Llanelli
   accommodation, 125, 168
   behaviour in public places, 154–5
   case-study data, 17–18, 121–35
   composition of industries, 49, 51
   as Convergence region, 14, 49, 165
   cost of living, 49
   demographic shifts, 51–2
   deprivation levels, 52
   economic integration, 168–9, 172, 176

INDEX

economy, 49–51
employment agencies, 56, 83–4, 121–9, 168–9
family relations, 131–2
human capital development, 130
labour market experiences, 122–30, 146, 168–9, 172
labour market mobility, 128–30, 168–9, 172
lack of transport links, 48
location, 48, 50
migration history, 48
number of migrants, 15, 48–9
pace of life, 154–5
population, 51
research methodology, 56–7
sample characteristics, 57
social integration, 174, 176
social networks, 121–2, 123, 124–5, 132–3, 174
support organisations, 195
unemployment, 51
wages, 51, 127–8
working conditions, 125–8, 146
Llanybydder, 54, 55
London, 13, 29, 32, 41, 78, 81, 142
low-skilled jobs, 11, 17, 25, 30–2, 35, 49, 90–1, 97–8, 108–10, 125–6, 169–72, 182–3

Maastricht Treaty, 7
MacDonald, Brian, 83
McGhee, Derek, 33, 78–9
McNulty, Tony, 64
Malta, 3
mass media, 66–7
Massey, D. S., 25, 29, 69, 72, 73, 79
May, Theresa, 181

media reporting, 3, 11, 48, 63, 73, 82, 121, 124, 139
mental health, 194–5
Merthyr Tydfil
case-study data, 17, 107–20
coal mining, 45, 107, 108
community cohesion, 188–9, 195
as Convergence region, 14, 45–7, 165
cultural integration, 177
deprivation levels, 47–8, 107
economic integration, 169–70, 172
economy, 45–7
education levels, 47
education system, 190–1
employment agencies, 82–3, 110–11
ethnic economy, 116–18, 153, 170, 177
ethnic entrepreneurship, 116–18, 153, 170, 177, 183–4
health, 107, 194
labour market experiences, 108–16, 169–70, 172
labour market mobility, 110–14, 169–70, 172
location, 45, 46, 107
migration history, 45, 107–8
number of migrants, 15, 48, 108
Portuguese migrants, 17, 55, 82–3, 108–9, 111–12, 117, 118, 170, 184–5, 188
research methodology, 54–6
sample characteristics, 55–6, 108
social integration, 118–19, 174, 195
social networks, 116–19, 169–70, 174
support organisations, 113–14, 116, 118, 195
unemployment, 47, 107
wages, 107, 110
working conditions, 112–16

254

INDEX

methodology, 16, 39–40, 52–9
Metykova, Monika, 34
Mexican migrants, 29, 69, 72, 81
Meyer, Michael, 45
middling transnationalism, 31–2
migrant identity, 100–2, 158–9
migrant numbers
   census data, 10–11, 44, 48, 108, 143
   National Insurance Number data, 10, 11, 48, 54, 108, 166–7
   and public opinion, 139
   WRS data, 9–10, 14–15, 44, 48–9, 54, 64, 108, 166, 182
migrant paradox, 11, 31
Migrant Workers Forum (MWF), 188–9
Migration Advisory Committee (MAC), 184
Migration and Cultural Integration in Europe conference, 176
migration phases
   final phase, 157–61
   settling in phase, 145–9
   transitional phase, 149–57
migrant trajectories, 16, 23–4, 31–2, 145–61
migrant typologies, 16, 22–4
migration patterns, 16, 21–4, 140–5
migration policy,
   EU, 6, 7–10, 18–19, 140–1, 164–7, 180, 195
   UK, 6, 9–10, 11–12, 18–19, 64–5, 86, 180–1, 184, 195–6
   Wales, 6, 18–19, 181–99
Migration Policy Institute (MPI), 173, 176
migration theory
   economic migration, 16, 24–7

ethnic economy, 16, 33–6
integration, 165
labour market mobility, 16, 31–3
migrant trajectories, 16, 23–4, 31–2
migrant typologies, 16, 22–4
migration patterns, 16, 21–4, 140–5
motivations for migration, 24–8
motivations for staying, 36–8
non-economic migration, 16, 27–8
return migration, 16, 36–8
settlement, 16, 36–8, 143–4
social networks, 16, 28–31
migratory drift, 4, 11, 37–8, 139–63, 167
Miller, Mark, 143
Minority Ethnic Achievement Grant (MEAG), 190
Modell, John, 33, 92
Modern Slavery Act, 196
Moran, Dominique, 10
Moriarty, Elaine, 142
motivations
   economic, 24–7, 37, 63–4, 72–7, 86–7, 105, 130, 145–6, 151–3, 163
   for migration, 24–35, 63–4, 70–7, 86–7, 105, 130
   non-economic, 27–8, 37, 64, 70–4, 86–7, 103–5, 146–9, 154–63
   for staying in UK, 4, 18, 36–8, 103–5, 122, 145–61
Multi Agency Diversity Forum (MADF), 188
Munich, 23

National Health Service (NHS), 194
National Insurance Number (NINo) data, 10, 11, 48, 54, 108, 166–7
Nelson, Joan, 25–6

INDEX

neo-classical economic theory, 21, 25, 26, 163
neo-liberalism, 26–7
Netherlands, 83, 144
Nomenclature of Territorial Units for Statistics (NUTS), 41–3, 45–7, 49–51
non-economic motivations, 16, 27–8, 37, 64, 70–4, 86–7, 103–5, 146–9, 154–63
North Atlantic Treaty Organisation (NATO), 66
Northern Ireland, 23, 28, 32, 78, 82, 173; *see also* United Kingdom
Norway, 144
Nowicka, Magdalena, 23

Okolski, Marek, 142
O'Reilly, Karen, 76
Organisation for Economic Cooperation and Development (OECD), 66, 167, 173, 182, 187
outreach organisations *see* support organisations
overstaying, 4, 11, 36–8, 139–63
overtime, 127–8

pace of life, 154–5, 157, 162–3
Pakistani migrants, 13
participant observation, 52
Parutis, Violetta, 31–2, 35
Payne, Geoff, 59
planned length of stay, 3, 4, 11, 36–7, 90–1, 102, 139–40, 144–5
Poland
   accession to EU, 3, 68, 86
   advertising industry, 67
   agriculture, 67, 70
   capital of culture awards, 102
   communism, 134
   consumer culture, 66–7, 68
   cost of living, 67, 72, 87, 146, 151
   cultural change, 66–8, 102, 163
   'culture of migration', 64–73
   diversity, 102
   economic inequality, 67
   economic restructuring, 66–7, 163
   industry, 67
   mass media, 66–7
   migration history, 39, 65
   NATO membership, 66
   OECD membership, 66
   political culture, 66
   standard of living, 67, 134
   unemployment, 67, 86
Polish Community of the Valleys Association (PCVA), 114, 116, 118, 195
Polish House, Cardiff, 39, 92, 195
Polish migrants
   accommodation, 16, 29–30, 79, 83, 84, 89–90, 105, 123, 125, 147, 168, 192–3
   aspirations, 77, 87, 146, 152–3, 157, 163
   behaviour in public places, 154–5
   and British citizenship, 143, 196
   chain migration, 22, 103, 124
   children, 77, 101, 147–8, 153, 156, 159, 176
   circular migration, 22, 91, 141–4
   commitment to migration, 29, 147–9, 155–6, 162
   and community cohesion, 187–9, 195, 197
   cultural integration, 165, 176–8
   demographics, 3, 11, 193–4

INDEX

economic integration, 165, 167–73, 176, 178
education, 45, 90, 92, 96, 97, 98–100, 130, 134, 156, 159, 171, 189–91, 198–9
and employment agencies *see* employment agencies
entrepreneurship, 11, 34–6, 93–7, 116–18, 153, 159, 170, 176–8, 183–4, 198
and the ethnic economy, 11, 33–6, 44–5, 92–7, 98, 116–18, 153, 170, 176–8
exploitation of, 82, 85, 112–13, 184–7
family relations, 80, 102–5, 131–2, 147–8
geographic spread, 5, 11, 14–15, 32–3, 40, 78, 82
growing distance from life in Poland, 157–9
hate crimes committed against, 12
health, 134, 193–5
host community resistance to, 178–9
human capital development, 5, 17, 32, 98–100, 130
and identity, 100–2, 158–9
impact on UK labour market, 3–4
impact on UK migration policy, 11–12
integration, 12, 18, 28, 118–19, 140, 162, 164–79, 191, 195, 197
labour market experiences, 5, 16, 90–2, 108–16, 122–30, 146, 167–73
labour market mobility, 4, 17, 31–3, 97–8, 110–14, 128–30, 167–73
language skills, 23, 32, 80–1, 84, 97–100, 115, 124, 128–30, 134, 161–2, 167–78, 197

legal integration, 165, 166–7, 178
and migratory drift, 4, 11, 37–8, 139–63, 167
motivations for migration, 24–35, 63–4, 70–7, 86–7, 105, 130
motivations for staying in UK, 4, 18, 36–8, 103–5, 122, 145–61
numbers of, 3, 9–11, 14–15, 44, 48–9, 54, 64, 108, 139, 143, 166–7, 182
overstaying, 4, 11, 36–8, 139–63
phases of migration, 145–61
planned length of stay, 3, 4, 11, 36–7, 90–1, 102, 139–40, 143, 144–5
post-World War 2 migrants, 39, 65, 92, 195
public opinion of, 12, 65, 111, 119–20, 167, 178
relationships formed in the UK, 103–4, 156, 162
and religion, 45, 89–90, 92, 119, 190
remittance payments, 25–6, 113
representations in popular culture, 65
return migration, 10, 11, 16, 36–8, 144, 167
rights in the workplace, 184–7
in rural locations, 5, 11, 17–18, 32–3, 78, 83, 121–35, 168–9
in semi-urban locations, 5, 11, 17, 107–20, 169–70
settlement in the UK, 11, 18, 36–8, 143–4, 158–61, 167
social integration, 165, 173–6, 178, 191, 195
social networks *see* social networks
support organisations, 39, 92, 97, 113–14, 118, 195–6, 197–8
travel arrangements, 30, 83, 84–5, 123

257

INDEX

in urban locations, 5, 11, 16–17, 88–106, 171–3
value to UK and Welsh economy, 182–4
wages, 91, 110, 127–8
welfare benefits, 9, 107, 112, 114, 134, 183
working conditions, 82, 112–16, 125–8, 146, 18, 184–7
Polish restaurants, 52, 94, 95
Polish salons, 92, 95, 96, 116
Polish shops, 89, 92, 95, 96, 117, 153, 176–8
Polish-Welsh Mutual Association, 195
popular culture, 65, 66–7
Portuguese migrants, 13, 17, 41, 55, 82–3, 108–9, 111–12, 117–18, 170, 173, 184–5, 188
public opinion, 12, 65, 111, 119–20, 139, 167, 178
push/pull theory, 27, 63, 76, 163
Putnam, Robert, 28–9, 30, 58

questionnaires, 52, 55

Race Equality First, 195
Rakowski, Tomasz, 67
real-wage equilibrium, 25, 26
recruitment agencies *see* employment agencies
refugees, 44
Regional Competitiveness and Employment (RCE) regions, 13–14, 41
relationships, 103–4, 131, 156, 162
religion, 45, 89–90, 92, 119, 190
remittances, 25–6, 44, 113
rental housing, 147–8, 192–3
reputation, 147, 148, 155, 162
research limitations, 16, 57–9
research methodology, 16, 39–40, 52–9
researcher positionality, 58
retail sector, 109
return migration, 10, 11, 16, 36–8, 144, 167
Robinson, David, 188
Romania, 3, 181
Romanian migrants, 11–12, 37, 173
Ruhs, Martin, 185
rural locations, 5, 11, 13, 17–18, 32–3, 48–52, 78, 83, 121–35, 168–9, 181–2
Russian migrants, 45, 107
Ryan, Louise, 29, 30, 79, 81, 144

sample characteristics, 53, 55–6, 57, 89, 108
sample selection, 16, 52–3, 58
scarce resources, competition for, 115, 132–3, 149, 187
Schengen Agreement, 7, 164, 179
school attendance, 190–1
schools, 45, 90, 92, 96, 134, 156, 159, 189–91, 198–9
Scotland, 33, 78, 83, 177; *see also* United Kingdom
'searchers', 22–3, 141–2
seasonal work, 21, 33, 78, 90, 97, 141
self-employment, 9, 33, 35, 92, 116; *see also* ethnic entrepreneurship
semi-urban locations, 5, 11, 13, 17, 45–8, 107–20, 169–70
service sector, 17, 30, 40–1, 186–7
settlement, 11, 16, 18, 36–8, 143–4, 158–61, 167
Shelter Cymru, 193
Sirkeci, Ibrahim, 68–9

INDEX

Sjaastad, Larry, 26–7
Slough, 13
Slovakia, 3
Slovakian migrants, 15, 37
Slovenia, 3
social capital, 28–9, 31, 78, 84, 98, 173–4
social care, 49, 125, 182
social housing, 193
social integration, 165, 173–6, 178, 191, 195
social networks
  and accommodation, 79, 89, 105, 132, 147, 192–3
  in Cardiff, 89, 90, 91–2, 94–6, 98, 100, 105, 171, 174, 192–3
  and commitment to migration, 29, 147–9, 155–6, 162
  and employment agencies, 83–4
  and the ethnic economy, 33–6, 94–6, 116
  and ethnic entrepreneurship, 23, 33–6, 94–6, 116
  and finding employment, 30, 79, 123, 124–5, 132–3, 147, 171
  formation and use of, 4, 5, 16, 17, 29–31, 91–2, 105, 116, 132–3, 159, 173–6
  and integration, 165, 173–6
  and labour market mobility, 91–2, 98, 105
  in Llanelli, 121–2, 123, 124–5, 132–3, 174
  in Merthyr Tydfil, 116–19, 169–70, 174
  migration facilitated by, 11, 17–18, 29–30, 70–2, 78–82, 121, 147
  as motivation for migration, 70–2, 78–82, 124
  as motivation to stay, 147–9, 155–6, 162
  theory on, 16, 28–31
Somali migrants, 12, 13, 41, 44, 167–8, 189
Spanish migrants, 13, 41, 107–8, 184
standards of living, 67, 75–7, 87, 133–5, 151–3, 181
'stayers', 22, 23, 36, 142
'storks', 22, 23, 141
students, 9
Sui, Paul, 143
support organisations, 39, 92, 97, 113–14, 118, 195–6, 197–8
Sweden, 8, 64, 166

Tai Pawb, 193
Tannock, Stuart, 111, 184
temporal rhythms, 154–5, 157, 162–3
Thomas, Florian, 65
Thompson, Andrew, 23, 37, 143
3D (dirty, dangerous and dull) jobs, 20, 35, 90–1, 97–8, 169, 183
Tiger Bay, 13, 41
trade unions, 108, 111–12, 124, 185
transient migration, 21–2
transition arrangements, 8–10, 11–12, 64–5, 86, 166, 181
travel arrangements, 30, 83, 84–5, 123
Trevena, Paulina, 33, 78–9

unemployment, 43, 47, 51, 67, 86, 107, 182
United Kingdom (UK)
  2004 accession transition arrangements, 8–10, 64–5, 86, 166
  2007 accession transition arrangements, 11–12, 181

INDEX

2013 accession transition arrangements, 11–12, 181
Brexit, 6, 12, 59, 139, 164, 179, 183, 196
citizenship, 143
geographic spread of migrants, 32–3, 78, 82
Immigration Bill, 195–6
migration policy, 6, 9–10, 11–12, 18–19, 64–5, 86, 180–1, 184, 195–6
migration within, 10, 13, 45, 48–9
Modern Slavery Act, 196
number of migrants, 3, 9–11, 64, 139, 143, 166–7
value of migrants to the economy, 182–4
see also Northern Ireland; Scotland; Wales
United States, 29, 30, 65, 69, 72, 81
urban locations, 5, 11, 13, 16–17, 40–5, 88–106, 171–3

Verwiebe, Roland, 27–8
Vershanina, Natalia, 45

wages, 51, 91, 107, 110, 127–8
Wales
  Cohesion Policy regional classifications, 14, 41, 45–7, 49
  community cohesion policy, 187–9
  education policy, 189–91
  geographic spread of migrants, 5, 12–15, 33, 40
  health policy, 193–5
  housing policy, 192–3
  intra-UK migration, 13, 45, 48–9

migration history, 4, 12–13, 39–40
migration policy, 6, 18–19, 181–99
numbers of migrants, 14–15, 182
out-migration, 181–2
rights for migrant workers, 184–7
value of migrants to the economy, 182–4
see also Cardiff; Llanelli; Merthyr Tydfil; United Kingdom (UK)
Wallace, Claire, 141
Ward, Kevin, 83
Weiss, Yoram, 25
'welcome pack' initiatives, 195
welfare benefits, 9, 107, 112, 114, 134, 181, 183
Welsh as an additional language (WAL) pupils, 190–1, 198–9
Welsh Index of Multiple Deprivation (WIMD) Report, 43–4, 47–8, 52
Welshpool, 54, 55
White, Anne, 22, 30, 69–70, 72, 143–4, 175
Williams, Malcolm, 59
Work Registration Scheme (WRS) data, 9–10, 14–15, 44, 48–9, 54, 64, 108, 166, 182
workers' rights, 184–7
working conditions, 82, 112–16, 125–8, 146, 183, 184–7
Wrexham, 15

zero hours contracts, 82, 112–13, 125–6, 186
Znaniecki, William, 65
Zychlin, 70–1